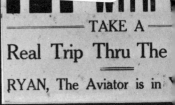

W9-BCN-395

TAKE A

Real Trip Thru The

RYAN, The Aviator is in

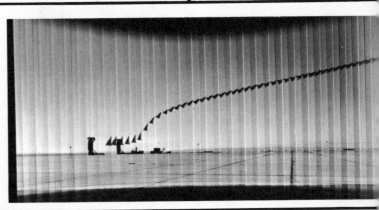

FLY WITH ME

TAKE A

Real Trip Thru The Clouds

RYAN, The Aviator is in Your City

Ryan, the Aviator

Best wishes and personal regards to George Foster.

T. Claude Ryan

William Wagner

Ryan, the Aviator

Being The Adventures & Ventures
of Pioneer Airman & Businessman
T. Claude Ryan

by **William Wagner**

in collaboration with Lee Dye

McGraw-Hill Book Company

New York St. Louis San Francisco Düsseldorf
Johannesburg Kuala Lumpur London Mexico
Montreal New Delhi Panama Rio de Janeiro
Singapore Sydney Toronto

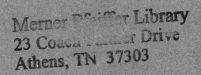

SPONSORING EDITOR Dale L. Dutton
DIRECTOR OF PRODUCTION Stephen J. Boldish
DESIGNER Naomi Auerbach
EDITING SUPERVISORS Barbara Church/Carolyn Nagy
EDITING AND PRODUCTION STAFF Gretlyn Blau,
  Teresa F. Leaden, George E. Oechsner

RYAN, THE AVIATOR

07-067670-4

1234567890 HDBP 754321

To Claude—

And to Earl, George, Bob, John, and Millard.
To Doc, Pablo, Hoppy, Al, Pete, and scores of others named and unnamed who are all part of the Ryan saga.

Foreword

Ryan, the Aviator, THE STORY OF AVIATION PIONEER T. Claude Ryan, by William Wagner, has been read with more than casual interest. I have known Claude Ryan for half a century and have long felt that the story of his remarkable career should be compiled and published. William Wagner has now accomplished that mission with skill and literary merit. This book has the twin virtues of being an entertaining biography of an air pioneer and a real contribution to aviation history.

We are now, in 1970, late in the seventh decade of the history of aviation since the first flight on December 17, 1903. Claude Ryan has been intimately and prominently connected with the last fifty years of that period.

I first heard about Claude Ryan from General H. H. (Hap) Arnold, who, while commanding Rockwell Field in San Diego, California, in 1922, sold Claude a war surplus training plane for $400, thus launching him on his aviation career. Thereafter, Arnold, the great World War II air leader, a remarkably astute judge of men, followed Ryan's career with interest and admiration.

When General Arnold made the brilliant decision in 1939 to turn the primary training of our World War II flyers over to civilian flying schools (nearly one million airmen were ultimately required), Claude Ryan was a member of the small group called upon to perform that prodigious task.

The Ryan biography is a significant contribution to aviation history because he was intimately connected with many of its most dramatic episodes, including the building of the *Spirit of St. Louis* for Lindbergh. Forty years later, the Ryan Aeronautical Company designed and produced the electronic gear which made possible the first landing on the moon. In the meantime, Ryan's company designed, developed, and built many aircraft which greatly contributed to the allied air victory. In the post-Lindbergh, post-War era, Ryan designed and produced planes which made many contributions to civil aviation. Thus, Ryan, with the engineers, scientists, and administrators he assembled and led, has made significant contributions to all principal phases in United States aviation progress. This book faithfully and accurately records the details which support this estimate.

I recommend this biography especially to Claude's contemporaries in the development of United States air power, civil and military, since it will revive many memories for them, inducing a nostalgia for United States aviation history and a renewed admiration and respect for all who made our achievement possible.

This book is recommended to all who are interested in or curious about how we got where we are today in the air world. It will also be useful for those who plan or are pursuing careers in aviation.

Any reader of this book will be rewarded for he must leave it with a wholesome sense of satisfaction. Here is the record of a man who achieved remarkable success in an aviation career without flamboyance, theatrics, legerdemain, or luck. Claude Ryan never abandoned his sound principles and copy-book maxims or compromised his integrity for the lure of quick gain or eventual profit.

This record of a remarkable aviation career is all here, told with sympathy and feeling but with accuracy and with interest and profit for its readers.

IRA C. EAKER
Lieutenant General, USAF(Ret.)

Preface

IF A MAN HAS A LIFE WORK, aviation and the Ryan Aeronautical Company truly has been mine.

For thirty-three years I had but one basic job—to tell the story of the company and its founder, T. Claude Ryan. But it was told in a hundred ways in media and on occasions too numerous to mention.

Now, at last, I have had the time and opportunity to put it all together in a single package—this book. I think the reader, whether aviation buff or layman, will find the story of Claude Ryan and his pioneering role in aviation of equal interest. And, that interest will be rewarded in both human and technical terms.

Perhaps the most fascinating part of Claude's life is how, because of a quirk of fate, he missed out on the greatest business opportunity which aviation ever presented. Yet it was probably this lost opportunity which did much to develop his character, strengthen his determination, and help mold the success he subsequently enjoyed.

In every career there are critical decision points usually centered around personalities whose influence becomes the factor which tips the scale toward success. Claude Ryan often cites the four men who had the greatest influence on him—his father; Joe Brennan, San Diego harbormaster; Gen. H. H. Arnold; and Admiral John H. Towers. The roles they and many others played in his life are what this book is all about.

Above all, Claude has been a pilot's pilot and an apostle of aviation. His greatest satisfactions have been as a pilot; in creating new aircraft concepts; in helping others know the joys of flying; and last but not least, in his family.

The book has no hero and no villains, although it is hard to be close to a man for nearly all your business career and not develop some prejudices in his favor. All of God's children are different; all are subject to human foibles. If we've touched on what might be considered the flaws of some, it is only to keep history in proper perspective.

You ask, and so do I, just how accurate is this book? Well, we've checked and cross-checked the facts and aviation lore of the day; we believe we have come as close as humanly possible, four decades after the events, in recreating precisely what did happen.

The other day two cars on the highway outside the office collided. Three of us saw, or thought we saw, how the accident happened. But we have three entirely different versions of the collision. Little wonder, then, that some people familiar with aviation in the 1920s may have different recollections of the events of those pioneering days.

I am indebted to many people for their invaluable assistance. Claude Ryan, who would rather look ahead to new challenges than relive the past as a "has been," finally consented to a series of taped interviews which has given our skeleton story some of the flesh it needed. Too, after much prodding, he has at last located many early documents and pictures which have been most useful in making this a pictorial as well as narrative history.

Others who were central figures of the day have been most generous with pictures and recollections—none more so than my publicist predecessor of 1925–1927, Tom Mathews. His humor is as priceless as the facts he provided and the reader will find him quoted at length. I am deeply in his debt.

My Dutch friend and longtime associate, Harm Jan van der Linde, has been an always reliable source of historical background. So, too, have been Ed Morrow, Frank Wiley, Dan Burnett, and Walter Locke to mention but a few early Ryan employees. Everett Cassagneres, Ryan historian of the American Aviation Historical Society, has furnished helpful transcripts of many interviews he conducted with early associates of Claude Ryan.

George Brooks and his fine staff of the Missouri Historical Society, St. Louis, have been most generous and helpful in making available original material from the Lindbergh Collection. E. W. Robischon of the Smithsonian Institution (National Air and Space Museum) has provided valuable material not previously published, as has David Hatfield of the Northrop Aviation History Library.

When it comes to pictures we have been showered with wonderful cooperation. As a result, the Ryan Aeronautical Library today has one of the most complete historical photo records concerning any early aviation organization. Special mention must be made of the great camera work of Major H. A. (Jimmie) Erickson, San Diego's famed flying photographer who covered the Lindbergh era and early Ryan S-T monoplane days. Larry Booth, historian of the Title Insurance and Trust Company has generously opened his vast store of historical photos of early San Diego to our needs for this book. Peter M. Bowers, too, has been most generous in sharing historical aviation photos.

Unfortunately, it is not always clear who actually took each photo, since the same picture often reached us from as many as three different sources, with the probability that not one of the three was himself the actual photographer. So, we have used individual photo credits only when we could be sure who was behind the lens or when the prints were obtained from a private collection.

No book like this comes into being without some encouragement from others. It was not commissioned by anyone within the Ryan organization. We wanted to avoid the often self-serving company story. Rather, it is an historical document for the record without editorial direction from any front office. No one has read it in advance to "approve" its contents. Even Claude Ryan will read it for the first time when he opens his copy.

It was Capt. E. Robert Anderson of the Copley Press, an outstanding former Navy public relations officer, who first encouraged us to write the story of Claude Ryan. And, to give another service equal credit, similar encouragement came from Lieut. Gen. Ira C. Eaker, a great aviation leader and close associate of General H. H. (Hap) Arnold, Air Force Chief of Staff during World War II.

There is no way to thank all who contributed to this work, but those who are aware of the help and encouragement they gave realize that I am eternally grateful to them.

Lastly—only because the reader should know and remember it—whatever literary merit this work has is due to my collaborator, Lee Dye, a fine young newspaperman whose name I predict will be seen as the author of many books in the years to come.

We have greatly enjoyed researching, writing, illustrating, and editing this book. We hope that you, too, will find pleasure in reading the story of "Ryan, the Aviator."

William Wagner

Contents

Foreword   vii
Preface   ix

ONE   Soliloquy   1

TWO   A Young Man Dreams   3

THREE   Short Flight to Frustration   11

FOUR   Army Cadet; Forest Patrol Pilot   23

FIVE   Come Fly With Me   37

SIX   Ryan Standards Fly the Airline   51

SEVEN   The Cloudster Airliner   65

EIGHT   The Beer Run   73

NINE   Ryan M-1 Takes Wing   79

TEN   M-1s for the Air Mail   91

ELEVEN   The Plane That Pays a Profit   101

TWELVE   Response to a Wire   109

THIRTEEN   ''Spirit''—Sixty-day Wonder   117

FOURTEEN   Epilogue   137

FIFTEEN   A New Beginning—and Tragedy   157

SIXTEEN   School Days   169

SEVENTEEN S-T, the Classic Airplane   181

EIGHTEEN   Fourteen Thousand Pilots   205

NINETEEN   The Business Matures   219

Name Index   247

Index of Ryan Planes   251

Index of Other Aircraft and Spacecraft   253

Robert Watts

CHAPTER ONE

Soliloquy

THE OLD WORLD WAR I JENNY droned tediously as T. Claude Ryan guided it over the rolling coastal hills of southern California. Ryan put the Jenny into a graceful turn, watching as the foreboding profile of Palomar Mountain, shrouded in a distant haze, slipped farther past the right side. He pulled back on the stick, and the nose of the old trainer lifted gradually. The mighty Pacific Ocean fell out of sight as the plane climbed toward the blue sky. He shoved the stick forward; the Pacific settled back into place and then loomed ahead as the plane dove toward the earth.

"It was worth every moment of it," Ryan said to himself as he eased back on the stick and thought of the long, difficult route he had trudged to get there.

Far below, several boys who had been leaping from rock to rock along the shore watched in awe as the pilot stunted for his own amusement. Ryan saw the boys, gathering with others on the beach, and guided the plane into a gentle circle.

"They don't look like they've got five bucks among them," he said to himself as he reached into a shoebox beside his seat. "But what the heck!"

He pulled a cluster of handbills out of the box and tossed them over the side of the open cockpit. The boys began a mad scramble as the handbills fluttered toward the ground. They chased one until a breeze carried it out to sea, and then they fell over each other as they changed to another target.

1

Finally, a boy leaped into the air and grabbed one of the elusive slips of paper as it fluttered down.

"I got one!" he screamed.

His companions stared in awe at the slip of paper, as though it had dropped from Heaven itself.

"Fly With Me," the handbill said. "Ryan, The Aviator is in Your City." The advertisement set the price of a flight at $2.50 or $5, depending on its length.

"Wow!" one of the boys said. "Would I ever love to do that. But five dollars. That's more money than I'll see in a month."

The others didn't hear. They stared silently as the tiny plane diminished into a speck as it flew toward Newport Beach and Santa Ana, where the pilot would toss out the rest of his handbills in hopes of finding more prosperous targets.

"I sure would like to do that," one boy said, thinking.

"Whada ya mean?" his buddy asked. "You ain't got five dollars. You've never had five dollars in your whole life. How you going to do that?"

"I don't mean fly with him! I mean fly all by myself. I mean I sure would like to do what he's doing—be an aviator."

"Man, you can't do that."

"Why?"

"You just can't," the skeptical youth answered, shrugging his shoulders as though he had just supplied the final word. "You just can't."

Far above, Ryan chuckled to himself as he thought of the boys. He cut a fine figure, sitting there in the open cockpit of the two-place trainer—slender, dark, his straight hair blowing across a determined, stubborn countenance. He wore his old Army fatigues, since they provided the most protection against the slipstream and occasionally brutal winds slashing past the cockpit. At the age of twenty-four, he had already realized his greatest dream—attaining the freedom of flight.

He had achieved his goal, but there was no way he could have known in the fall of 1922 about the profound impact he would make upon an awakening world within a few short years. There was no way he could have known that because of peculiar circumstances his role in one of man's greatest dramas would be obscured, clouded by an ironic trick of fate.

But that was yet to come, and as young Ryan guided his plane over the southern California landscape his thoughts drifted to the past. He thought of the boys he had teased a few moments earlier, now lost along the distant shoreline, and he thought of the days when he, too, had stared in awe . . . .

CHAPTER TWO

A Young Man Dreams

THE BITING COLD OF FALL had already begun to set in, plunging the small world of Parsons, Kansas, into the awkward stage between the swimming hole and the ice-skating pond. Soon the snows would come, and the great plains would snuggle beneath a white security blanket that would occasionally melt into yellowed Midwestern slush.

It was a good time to be young. A boy could charge across the snow-covered countryside as though he were the first explorer. Each step would crunch into the flawless blanket and leave its mark where no one else had trod.

The world belonged to those who struck out across the cold and sometimes forbidding snow. It was a brand new world, awaiting fresh footprints.

Claude Ryan unbuttoned his long overcoat and adjusted his vest and tie, a nuisance for a boy his age. He cocked his cap over to the right side of his head and jammed his hands deep into the pockets of his woolen trousers. For a boy of thirteen, caught in the impatient moment of youth, it was as though time had chained itself to the present.

Behind Claude lay the hamlet of Parsons, where he lived with his parents, William Marion and Ida Ziegler Ryan, and sisters Louise and Kathryn.

Claude stared down the railroad tracks to where they merged into a tiny point and faded into an endless horizon. That was the way Cal Rodgers was to come, following along the Katy Railroad from the north.

On a Kansas prairie in October, 1911, Claude Ryan, left, and friend Peter Cordry await arrival of Cal Rodgers in this photo from Ryan family album.

It had been nearly a month since Rodgers had left New York on September 17, bound for Pasadena, California, in his Wright Model EX biplane. Newspaper baron William Randolph Hearst had offered $50,000 to the first man who could fly coast-to-coast within a thirty-day deadline. It was a cinch Rodgers wasn't going to make it in time to collect. His plane had already cracked up several times, but he had vowed to keep going.

For more than two years Claude had haunted the Parsons Public Library—ever since he first ran across an article in *The American Boy* entitled "How I Fly," which described a flight in a French Bleriot monoplane. The author made such a convincing case for the monoplane that it made a lifelong impression on the youthful reader. Often, after Claude had finished delivering the *Parsons Sun* each day, he would make his way down to the library to see if there was anything new on the shelves about flying.

A lot was happening in the world of aviation in 1911. It had been eight years since the Wright brothers had made their first flight. Louis Bleriot had flown across the English Channel. Glenn H. Curtiss, who had won $10,000 for America's first continuous flight by flying from Albany to New York, had moved operations to San Diego, California, where he made the world's first seaplane flight in January, 1911. And now Rodgers was trying to fly all the way across the United States.

Everyone knew it was a dangerous game. During 1910 alone, thirty-seven aviators had met their deaths. Yet fame and fortune awaited those who could rise to the new challenge of flight.

It was probably that combination which lured Calbraith P. Rodgers, a one-time motorcycle racer, to set out for the West Coast. He hadn't specifically planned on flying over Parsons. In fact, he had probably never heard of it. Bearing south of the Missouri River, he weaved his way across Missouri to the Kansas border. Just below Kansas City he picked up the

4

Katy Railroad heading south, which followed the general route he wanted to take to avoid the forbidding mountains to the west.

The tracks provided a reliable compass for Rodgers to follow. He had to stay close to a railroad anyway, since a special five-car train, carrying his wife, mother, mechanics, and $4,000 worth of spare parts, was following him across the country.

The chosen course suited Claude fine. Since Rodgers was flying along the Katy Railroad, he would pass right over Parsons.

Claude pulled his long overcoat around him as a chill swept across the Kansas plains. He had read that Rodgers had armed himself with a big cigar and several layers of sweaters and old newspapers to protect himself from the icy winds as he guided his open plane across the continent. It wouldn't be enough, Claude felt sure.

Claude walked slowly back and forth along the tracks as the minutes crawled past. Rodgers just had to make it, at least as far as Parsons, Claude told himself as he gazed down the tracks.

Finally, a tiny speck appeared in the distance and gradually separated into two wings. Moments later Rodgers was right overhead, perched amid a weird configuration of wings and wire.

Claude watched as the plane lumbered past and finally disappeared, leaving the town of Parsons far behind. The sight electrified Claude. Unlike the stories he had read, this was for real. He had seen a man fly!

Rodgers went on to complete his flight. He landed in Pasadena on November 5, nineteen days too late to win the prize. In all, he had made sixty-nine stops, including nineteen crashes. By the time he arrived in Pasadena, his plane had been rebuilt so many times that only the rudder and a single strut of the original airframe remained. Rodgers himself completed the trip with one leg in a cast.

Ever-present cigar and newspapers under jacket helped Cal Rodgers keep warm.

Buzzing high overhead in the Vin Fiz, Rodgers is westward bound.

FROM NEW YORK TO LONG BEACH
AVIATOR RODGERS LANDING ~ 191

Smithsonian Institution

One leg in a cast from his latest crack-up, Rodgers finally reached the Pacific Ocean on December 10, 1911.

Although he arrived too late to collect the prize, the flight was far from a failure. More than 20,000 people cheered as he landed in Pasadena. He was draped with an American flag. After several weeks he flew the few remaining miles to the coastline at Long Beach.

Four months later, Rodgers crashed into the Pacific during an exhibition flight and was killed.

Back in Parsons, nothing was ever quite the same again for Tubal Claude Ryan, who in one electrifying moment had been fired by the ancient dream that man might soar on wings.

Claude was born in Parsons on January 3, 1898. His father owned and operated the Excelsior Steam Laundry on Main Street, and one of Claude's first chores was to drive the old horse-drawn laundry wagon all over town during school vacations.

Parsons was one of those small Midwestern communities that never seemed to change, and the standards which had guided generations still made sense.

It was a good place to raise a boy. During the hot, muggy days of summer, Claude and his chums usually found time for a dip in one of the swimming holes along Labette Creek. Coffee's Pond was a favorite. There Claude had learned to swim when one of the older boys towed him into deep water and then swam away laughing.

The swimming holes were muddy, but nobody needed a swimming suit, and that made a big difference.

Most things happened in Parsons right on schedule, like the spring floods that followed the winter snows. Labette Creek would overflow each year at the same time it did the year before, and the low-lying part of town would become inundated. It was hard on the folks who lived in the flooded areas, but it gave Claude and his friends a great opportunity to explore their small world in a new light. Somehow, they always managed to come up with a good raft.

6

One year Claude made a canvas-covered canoe, and he was ready for the floods the following spring. When they came, Claude paddled around town in deluxe style.

The winter snows converted summer's swimming holes into ice-skating ponds, and life went on for the young folks of Parsons. It was a good life. It was not without its occasional disagreements which sometimes left Claude bruised and battered, but it was a good life.

Although his dad owned a successful business, Claude had been taught to carry his share of the load. He was expected to buy most of his own clothes and provide his own spending money. Fortunately, there were a lot of things a boy could do in Parsons to earn a little change.

He mowed lawns, pulled weeds, cleaned the stable, cared for the horse, sold the *Saturday Evening Post* and the *Ladies Home Journal,* helped in Hubbard & Lott's bookstore during Christmas rush periods, delivered groceries, and worked for 18 cents an hour as a coppersmith's helper in the Katy Railroad shops.

His first regular job was delivering papers for the *Parsons Sun,* for which he received 75 cents a week. His route covered East Main Street, with the return on East Washington, and he kept the route for several years.

He always figured he did a pretty good job, since he got plenty of compliments. But one day the *Sun* got a new circulation manager, Mrs. Ruth Schwab, former principal of Parsons High School.

One afternoon as Claude was leaving the office to deliver his papers, Mrs. Schwab told him to stop by and see her the next day to get better acquainted. But next day Claude went to a baseball game, and somehow the appointment slipped his mind. The following day a new kid named Buford Day was on hand with a note from Mrs. Schwab.

"I'm the new boy," Buford had said. The note confirmed it.

Early in his life Claude developed an interest in mechanics which was to serve him well during the years that were to follow. When Claude was seven years old Parsons got its first automobile. The owner gave rides for 25 cents each, and Claude's mother saw that he was one of the first passengers. For that tidy sum the passengers got a trip from the old Mathewson Hotel, across the tracks to 21st Street, and out to the end of the road and back.

About a year later, O. E. Reed, a neighbor of the Ryan family, bought a one-lung Olds, one of the first cars to be owned by a Parsonian. Fortunately, Mr. Reed owned a bicycle and repair shop on Washington Avenue, which he put to good use keeping the Olds running.

Claude spent hours watching Mr. Reed taking the Olds apart and putting it back together again, which he did with a great degree of regularity. Between repair jobs it ran well, and Claude bargained his way into a lot of rides to the envy of his pals.

Later, Mr. Reed purchased the granddaddy of the Model T Ford, and Claude managed to poke his hands into those greasy parts, too. He became fascinated by the intricate workings of the horseless carriage, and there were times when he forgot all about the swimming hole.

In 1912 Claude's father saw an opportunity to move the family West when one of his employees asked if he could buy the laundry. While waiting to complete the deal, the parents arranged to send their son on a summer visit with his grandparents on their farm near Vancouver, Washington.

In that unlikely location Claude got his second injection of the aviation bug. Hangared in a tent at the Army's Vancouver barracks was the biplane of an intrepid pioneer pilot, Silas Christofferson. To Claude's delight, the

7

Claude sneaked into the tent to sit at the controls of Silas Christofferson's biplane and dream about flying.

Claude graduated from a bicycle to this Flying Merkle motorcycle for his paper route.

plane frequently took to the air as Christofferson fearlessly flew across the broad Columbia River to the southern bank in Oregon.

That fall Claude's parents came west by train to Vancouver to pick up their son; together they made the trip to Orange, California, south of Los Angeles, where Claude's father purchased an orange ranch.

Claude landed a job delivering papers for the *Orange Daily News* and the *Los Angeles Express* over a hilly 15-mile route. He covered the route for the first year by bicycle, and managed to save $150, which he used to buy his first motor vehicle—a beat-up Flying Merkle 7-hp motorcycle.

Before long, he had the finest motorcycle in town. The experience he gained by patching up his Flying Merkle, along with the hours he put in on the family's newly acquired Model T Ford, began to pay off. Claude was becoming a crack mechanic.

And aviation was not forgotten either. A biplane which frequently flew over the family orange ranch served to keep interest alive. The pilot had designed and built his own plane, as well as several others, in an abandoned church in nearby Santa Ana. His name was Glenn L. Martin.

Ray McKee, an old friend from Parsons who lived in Los Angeles, frequently spent the weekends with the Ryans, and Claude and Ray decided to try their luck at building their own car. To get the program rolling, Ray purchased a Model T chassis without a body, which Claude drove to Orange from Los Angeles sitting on a box atop the gas tank.

After school each day Claude turned his attention to the tangled mass of scrap iron like a boy who was in love for the first time. He added a special sixteen-valve head and radiator, a new rear end with a high gear ratio, a new steering wheel, and bucket seats. A local sheet-metal shop made an austere body for the car, complete with flexible exhaust pipes and a tool box on the back.

The end result was a custom-built, lightweight car which whipped over the hills of Orange County like a scared jackrabbit. Since he had done most of the work, Claude got to use the car for several months until McKee took it over for himself.

Because the new owner of the laundry back in Parsons couldn't make a go of the business, the family had to return there in 1915. Claude had his prized Flying Merkle shipped back, but the mud and the slush of the Midwest proved too much for the two-wheeler. Claude sold it and turned his attention to other things.

He was in high school, and the days seemed better than ever, perhaps because the girls looked different than they had before he left for California. Moonlight hayrides proved almost as much fun as the greasy parts of his Flying Merkle.

As the days slipped past, Claude's thoughts frequently drifted back to that autumn day of 1911, when he had stood beside the railroad tracks and watched an ill-fated Cal Rodgers fly overhead. Somehow, Claude just had to take a crack at flying.

Much had happened during the six years since Rodgers' flight. The world had been at war for three tragic years, and while the bloodbath meant death and suffering for millions, it meant something else entirely for the fledgling field of aviation. As it so often does, war brought great strides of technological progress, and no field benefited as much as aviation.

Tiny workshops around the world in which pioneers had toyed with gliders and crude aeroplanes turned overnight into huge factories. Some of those factories produced thousands of planes, evolving from the crude two-seater of 1914 to bombers, fighters, and scouts.

At first the planes were used entirely for reconnaissance, since few military leaders viewed the shaky planes as a stable platform from which

Title Insurance Collection

In one of his early biplanes, Glenn L. Martin flew the skies of southern California.

Young Claude Ryan began customizing vehicles when only sixteen and has been at it ever since.

Ryan Aeronautical Library

JOIN THE
ARMY AIR SERVICE
BE AN AMERICAN EAGLE !
CONSULT YOUR LOCAL DRAFT BOARD. READ THE ILLUSTRATED
BOOKLET AT ANY RECRUITING OFFICE, OR WRITE TO THE CHIEF
SIGNAL OFFICER OF THE ARMY, WASHINGTON, D.C.

National Air Museum

to wage war. For a time, enemy pilots waved at each other as they passed in the air. Airborne chivalry inevitably gave way to hostility, however, and on some forgotten day one flyer took a potshot with a revolver at another pilot. Armed conflict had entered a new era.

On April 6, 1917, America entered the war after unrestricted warfare by German submarines had led to the loss of American ships.

The United States was ill-prepared for aerial warfare. Less than a thousand planes had been built since the Wright brothers' first flight. The Aviation Section of the Army Signal Corps had less than 250 planes. Plans were drawn for production of 22,000 planes and 44,000 engines. Curtiss put the JN4-D Jenny into production. The British deHavilland DH-4 was selected for quantity manufacture using the American 400-hp Liberty engine.

France asked the United States for 4,500 planes and 5,000 pilots, but the request had not been anticipated and the program soon bogged down in confusion. The Allies were crying for pilots.

Claude hopped a train for Joplin, Missouri, to "join up." His heart was set on becoming a Navy flyer. The age requirement was twenty-one, and four years of college were necessary. Although he passed the physical examination, Claude was only nineteen and lacked the college requirement, and so the Navy said "no."

As the world turned its attention toward the war, Claude's dad, tired of the freezing winters and torrid summers of the Midwest, remembered the mild days of California. He found a new buyer for the laundry and was able to move back to the orange ranch.

The family piled aboard the 1915 Model T, and Claude, the only member who could drive, settled behind the wheel for a long journey. Hardly a day passed during the long trip when he did not get a chance to try out his mechanical expertise on the car, now tired from towing the camp trailer. Something was always going wrong.

But as he guided the old Ford across the plains, along the Grand Canyon, and finally to the orange groves of California, his thoughts continually drifted to the sky. Somehow, someway, he was going to learn to fly!

UPI Photo

Robert Watts

CHAPTER THREE

Short
Flight
to
Frustration

AT NINETEEN, CLAUDE RYAN WAS CONSUMED WITH THE DESIRE to become a pilot, and in the summer of 1917, it was clear that what had once seemed an impossible dream was no longer merely the fanciful pastime of foolhardy experimenters.

The airplane had carved its notch in history with an expanding role in World War I. The age of aviation had begun, and Claude wanted more than anything else to be a part of that new age.

Kansas seemed distant from the orange groves of southern California. The war, too, seemed far away, although Americans were dying alongside Europeans as the world sought to regain its sanity.

Claude was in limbo, anxious to learn to fly, but frustrated at every turn. The government was having trouble providing the pilots it desperately needed for the war, and in time it had to relax its requirements. Seizing on a new opportunity, Claude drove from Orange to San Diego to take another crack at getting into the service.

San Diego was on a wartime footing. Huge Navy ships slipped in and out of the harbor as a constant reminder of the crisis which gripped the world. Military bases sprawled all over the area, but the real action was across the bay at North Coronado Island, a 2,000-acre flat covered with jackrabbits and sagebrush, where the pioneer aviator Glenn H. Curtiss had trained the Navy's first pilot.

In those days it was known as Rockwell Field, and it was the primary

Army troops at San Diego's Camp Kearny.

flight school for the aviation branch of the Army Signal Corps, although the island was shared with the Navy. Scores of JN-4 Jennies, the open-cockpit biplanes which the Army used to train its cadets, flew in and out of the island, offering an incredible sight to a lad of nineteen with a yearning for wings.

The Army gave Claude a good reception when he arrived at Rockwell Field, and by then the educational requirements had been lowered to two years of college. He couldn't meet the college requirements, but he figured there was a chance the Army would waive it.

Unfortunately for Claude, the Army still wanted its pilots to be at least twenty-one years old by the time they graduated, so he was turned down again.

It was disappointing, but although he had been rejected he had stumbled across one thin thread of hope. The Army employed some civilian pilots as flight instructors at the handsome salary of $300 a month.

Rockwell Field on North Island, San Diego, 1918.

Four history-makers-to-be at the Martin plant, Los Angeles. From left: Lawrence "Larry" Bell, test pilot Eric Springer, Glenn L. Martin, and Donald W. Douglas. The plane: a Martin MB-1 bomber.

Martin Marietta

Fighting despair, he reasoned if he could just learn a little about flying he could get a license, since all you really had to do in those days was write to the Fédération Aéronautique Internationale and say you were qualified for an Annual Sporting License. Once he had the license, perhaps he could land a job as a civilian flight instructor at Rockwell Field. He could polish off his own skills while teaching others the fundamentals. It may not have been a realistic scheme, but to an impassioned youth of nineteen, it offered hope.

After returning to his family's orange ranch near Los Angeles, Claude began shopping around for some other way to get into aviation or to learn to fly. He had read that Glenn L. Martin, who had built some airplanes a few years earlier at Santa Ana, now had a shop somewhere on Los Angeles Street. Claude finally found the address in the telephone directory.

Young Ryan made his way to the fledgling firm in hopes of getting a job having something to do with airplanes—anything, so long as it was associated with flying. He introduced himself to Martin and asked for a job.

"Sorry," Martin said after checking with his associates, Donald W. Douglas, Larry Bell, Eric Springer, and C. A. Van Dusen. No help needed. Years later, it would be Martin of Martin Aircraft, Douglas and Springer of Douglas Aircraft, Bell of Bell Aircraft, and Van Dusen of Consolidated, but in those lean years the budget wouldn't allow for another apprentice, no matter how badly he wanted to fondle their airplanes.

Then one day as he was scanning the paper Claude ran across an advertisement. "Airplane pilots make big money," the ad said in bold print. It went on to claim that for the sum of $500, young men on their way up could receive 400 minutes of flight training. That boiled down

to $1.25 a minute, but it sounded like a bargain to Claude. He discussed it with his father, who had decided long ago to do whatever he could to help his son realize his ambition, even though Mrs. Ryan didn't see things that way. (After all, what mother would want her son to embark on a dangerous career such as that?)

The senior Ryan didn't have $500, but he went to the bank and borrowed against the next season's orange crop. The following morning father and son cranked up the Model T and rumbled into downtown Los Angeles to Seventh and Spring Streets. The flying school's office was on the seventh floor of the Union Building, which was among the more fashionable buildings in Los Angeles.

In bold letters across the door were the words: "American School of Aviation." Right next door was a placard with a lawyer's name, and so Claude reasoned that everything had to be on the up and up.

A fine-looking gentleman inside introduced himself and then went out to fetch the man in charge of the school. In a few moments a dark, wiry little fellow appeared with a folder tucked under his arm.

The folder was full of pictures of a Curtiss-type pusher and a newer plane with the engine in the nose, something like the Jenny only far less sophisticated. There was also a photo of a hangar with people standing around.

Claude was sold on the basis of the pictures alone. He didn't want to wait long enough to go down to the field at nearby Venice and inspect the school. He was ready. The elder Ryan glanced at the look of excited determination on his son's face, unfolded a wad of bills and plunked them down.

The next Monday morning Claude showed up at the flight school to begin training, but it didn't look the same as it had in the pictures. Somehow, the real thing lacked the glow of prosperity that the photos had conveyed in the plush office in downtown Los Angeles.

Twelve students were enrolled, some of whom had been there for several months and still had not learned to fly.

Claude looked around and found one of the planes. It was a shaky skeleton with the motor in the rear, standing alone in the field like a skinny, forlorn tomcat.

"It won't fly," someone said.

Claude turned and saw a young man about his age, leaning against a wooden shed with a cigarette dangling from his lips. The youth sauntered over to Claude and motioned toward the rickety pusher.

"You don't expect to try to fly one of those things do you?" he said with a sneer.

"Yeah," Claude answered.

"Oh no," the fellow said with a howl. "Another one."

The youth backed off with his hands thrust deep into his pockets and studied Claude for a long moment. He took a drag on his weed and threw out his chest like an egotistical rooster.

"You guys are all nuts," he said. "Tell you what, if you want to spend your money on something worthwhile come on down to the dancehall on the pier. Ask for Al Wilson. I'm the ticket taker and I'll show you where to put your money so it'll sing to you."

"What about the other plane?" Claude asked, brushing Wilson's invitation aside. "They're supposed to have two planes."

"You'll find parts of it all around," he said. "Somebody's always cracking that thing up."

Wilson turned and ambled down the field a few feet, and then glanced over his shoulder at Claude.

"Don't be stupid," he said. "Forget about this flying rot."

Claude turned back toward the pusher. He hated to admit it, but it was a sad looking beast. It had three wheels and a brake that apparently stopped the plane by digging into the ground like a plow. He learned later that the contraption would lift off a little, but no more than a few feet. As a result, it was used to train the students to taxi, and there was a long, flat place on the so-called flying field, worn smooth where the students had taxied the pusher back and forth.

"It's the French system," Claude was told later. "It's the best way in the world to learn to fly."

Of the 400 minutes of flight instruction, 150 minutes were to consist of running the pusher back and forth along the field.

Wilson had been right about the other plane, too. When young Ryan saw it, he was dumbfounded. It had been smashed to pieces—the wings, the fuselage, everything. And all the parts had to be rebuilt by hand, since it was the only one around.

"That's part of the training, too," Claude was told. "You get to learn how to build planes as well as fly. You help rebuild them first, and then you fly them."

It was a cinch that if Claude was going to learn to fly at the American School of Aviation, he was in for a lengthy stay. And that posed a problem. He was broke, and he didn't want to ask his dad for more money. Sensing the problem, the instructor, Joseph Mattingly, motioned toward the hangar, converted from a barn and still with a dirt floor.

"There's a mattress over there on a piece of plywood and a couple of sawhorses," Mattingly said. "You can sleep there if you want to. Bring your own bedroll. There's a little hot plate in the corner and you can cook your own meals. There's one fellow already doing that. He's a Serbian. You know, from Serbia. He can speak a little English, but he has a heavy accent."

Pioneering days at Venice, California. The Mono Eagle with builder Waldo Waterman next to fuselage. Center, holding dog, is "Wally" Timm, another early pilot-builder.

Haven't flown any yet, have been working on the machines. Both in shop, but I learn a lot that way. Took the engine out of one pusher & put it in another mostly by my—self. Fitted an axle and put it on the tractor. Am counting on flying to—morrow morning early.

As far as Claude was concerned, it was a good suggestion. He could save money and sleep in the same hangar with the airplanes. Besides, the school wouldn't have to hire a night watchman, and it was already clear to Claude that their finances were stretched pretty thin.

Claude drove the family Model T into the hangar, hauled out his blankets, and pulled the sawhorses beneath a wing of an airplane. That would be a thrill itself, to sleep right under an airplane wing. In the hangar were several planes owned by amateur flyers and self-taught, would-be professionals. One of them belonged to Charlie Gun, who had a reputation for being a lousy pilot but a real daredevil. Another was owned by Al Wilson's brother, Herb; and a man named Edwin M. Fisk was building a new plane he had designed.

It was late by the time Claude finally settled down for his first night of sleeping with an airplane, beginning a love affair that would last the rest of his life. Long about midnight he heard a rumbling and saw a figure moving across the floor.

"Who's there?"

"My name's Joseph Hoff," the man answered. "I'm your roommate." It was the Serbian.

Hoff was a tailor by trade, spruced up with a dapper mustache. Claude climbed on top of a mattress and soon lapsed into deep slumber. The next day, when the rest of the students arrived, the shop began to hum under the leadership of Frank Mumford, one of the more advanced pupils. Some of the other men, like Howard Patterson, who later became a famed motion picture pilot, were also crack mechanics—a skill they obviously needed to get along at the American School of Aviation.

The best of the mechanics was a young soldier by the name of William Hawley Bowlus. Hawley lacked the experience of some of the older men, but he was a natural mechanic, the kind of man who does some things by instinct that others can never seem to master.

Hawley was a ball of fire who had joined the Army to fly only to learn that he couldn't get into flight training for the same reasons that had stopped Claude. Somehow, he had talked the Army into giving him a six-month leave of absence so he could take flight lessons at his own expense.

More than a month of his furlough had already elapsed by the time Claude arrived at the school, and Hawley hadn't had any flight training at all. The best he had been able to manage was a few trips up and down the field in the pusher.

Hawley was well liked by all the students, but he struck up a special friendship with Claude—partly because they were both much younger than the other students and partly because they spoke the same language. Claude went back to Orange one weekend and returned with the family camp trailer. Thereafter he and Hawley lived in it—parked on the edge of the field or at the "tent villa" on the beach. Ten cents worth of fish bought near the Venice pier made a passable meal, and when money was in short supply there were soft drink bottles to be collected around the hangar and redeemed.

Hawley's presence at the school gave added impetus to the drive to get the better of the two planes in flying order. His plight became a rallying point, and before long the students were working day and night. Claude and the others were obviously going to learn a lot about the skill they would need, for in those days a pilot had to be able to rebuild every part of his airplane.

It wasn't what they had bargained for, but at least they were working around airplanes and there was the added reward nearly every day of getting out and running the pusher back and forth.

While it was far from flying, the students did get the feel of how to handle the rudder and keep on a straight course. Occasionally one of them would get the pusher to lift off for a few feet, which was a neat trick, since the thing had only 75-hp and it was quite heavy. It was powered by a Hall-Scott eight-cylinder engine with individual water jackets for cooling each cylinder. The jackets were connected by little tubes that were always coming loose and spraying water in all directions as the frail rattletrap lumbered down the field.

Somehow, whenever the worst seemed to happen, Al Wilson was on hand to witness it, taunting and chiding the students for the foolish pursuit of what he regarded as a worthless goal.

After several months of hard work the efforts of the students began to pay off as the better of the two planes—the tractor—took shape. At best, it wasn't much of a plane, but the students were eager to give it a try.

But Mattingly, the instructor, wasn't quite so anxious. He had been in a severe crash a few months earlier, and as a result he wasn't too wild about getting into another plane.

The students were furious. They had slaved to rebuild the plane only to learn that the instructor was afraid to fly. After hours of pleading, punctuated by sharp demands, the students won their argument and Mattingly agreed to give it a try.

"We'll start at dawn tomorrow," he said. "But as soon as the wind kicks up we'll have to stop. These things can be death traps in a strong wind."

The next morning, as the sun yawned over the foothills of southern California, Mattingly showed up at the field and reluctantly climbed into the plane with an eager student. The plane struggled down the field, lifted off for a few brief moments, and then settled back to the ground. At the other end of the field, Mattingly and the student jumped out of the plane, picked up the tail and carried it around, and then tried the same thing going in the opposite direction.

And so it went for about an hour. None of the students were allowed to make turns with the plane. Mattingly would have none of that. If they wanted to fly straight ahead, fine, but they had to land before they reached the other end of the field, get out, carry the tail around, and then try again.

As Claude was waiting for his turn, the plane rumbled up to the hangar and Mattingly cut the engine. He leaped out, glanced at the students and mumbled something about the wind. There was only a faint breeze in the air, but it was enough for Mattingly. School was over for the day.

The next day he didn't show up at all. Three days later he came by and took a couple of students for hops down the field, but he left as soon as the wind began to stir.

It was better than a week before Claude got his first ride, and it wasn't much to shout about. Mattingly barely lifted the plane off the ground, then plopped it back down and parked it at the end of the field.

"Too much wind," he said as a faint breeze drifted across the field. "We'll knock off for the day."

By that time most of the students were up in arms, and ready to quit, but they had already paid their fee and they didn't know of another flight school in southern California. Since it was obvious they weren't going to learn to fly under Mattingly's questionable tutelage, the students insisted the school provide an instructor who wasn't afraid of airplanes.

17

We ran up and down on the ground for about ½ hour licketty split. I forgot to say that every thing was ground work because the

little engine hasn't power enough to fly. But it's fine practice and great fun.

Up there, a man was the architect of his own destiny.

Hawley Bowlus.

The next morning a big, ruddy-faced, red-headed fellow named Bill Bailey showed up and said he was the new instructor. As it turned out, he had soloed only once or twice, but at least he wasn't afraid of airplanes. Young Ryan was his first student for the day.

Claude hopped in the front cockpit. The plane lumbered along the takeoff strip and then lifted into the air as the pilot circled up to about 1,000 feet over Venice. It was Claude's first real flight, and it was everything he had expected. The southern California coastline stretched beneath him like a long white snake as the plane groaned through the air, struggling perhaps, but as free as the lacy clouds that drifted lazily toward the desert to the east.

Up there, a man was the architect of his own destiny, free to venture where no one else had been, like a young boy in Kansas plunging across newfallen snow.

In a few minutes the plane touched down at the field again. That would be all for the day. But tomorrow would be a new day.

During the following week the new instructor concentrated on teaching the students something about flying, although it was obvious he knew little about it himself.

Early one morning Hawley and the instructor climbed into the plane at the crack of dawn and roared down the strip. Claude, clad only in his pajamas, watched from the camp trailer he and Hawley shared as his buddy took off toward the ocean. The plane sputtered a little as it barely cleared a row of houses along the beach and roared out over the water.

Then it went into a bank, slipped off on a wing and crashed into the sea. Claude jumped into his dad's Model T and raced to the beach. When he got there he could see Hawley and the instructor sitting on the seawall, dripping wet like a couple of half-drowned rats. Off beyond the seawall he could see a splintered wing, but the plane itself did not appear to be damaged too severely.

Al Wilson in an early pusher biplane. He was ready to solo Ryan but Claude spoiled everything.

Ryan Aeronautical Library

Meanwhile, people from nearby homes had rushed to the scene and had somehow managed to get a line on the plane. They meant well, but as they hauled the plane through the crashing breakers it thrashed back and forth like a captured buzzard. By the time they got it to the beach it looked like a pile of kindling.

It had taken three or four months to put the plane in working condition, and only a week to crack it up. But the students gathered up the pieces and went back to work. Meanwhile Claude lined up part-time work helping as an apprentice mechanic on the new plane Fisk was building in the hangar.

It took two months to put the school's tractor biplane back in order, and then on its first flight the pilot stalled on takeoff and it cracked up again.

Although the crackup was not nearly as bad as the time before, it meant the end of the line for Hawley. His furlough was up, and it was time for him to dig out his uniform again.

The students were able to patch up the plane, but the instructor had given up and moved on to more promising fields. The students finally had a plane that could fly, but nobody to teach them how.

Meanwhile, Al Wilson's draft board had been breathing down his neck, and the obnoxious kid from the dance hall had taken another look at aviation. After all, anything would beat dragging a carbine around Europe.

One day he packed up and went to Riverside, where a fellow named Swede Meierhofer had started a flight school. Two weeks later Al had soloed and returned to Venice. He went to the owners of the American School of Aviation and asked them to sign him on as an instructor.

"We can't pay you," the owners told him.

"That's okay," Wilson said. "I'll teach your students for free if I can

Anne E. Whitacre

Claude Ryan.

19

of them seemed suited for orange groves. They were high rigs that would break the low branches of the trees, not to mention the neck of the rider.

The only thing to do was build one themselves. Besides, it would keep Claude's mind off the mailbox. So, Claude put his mechanical training to good use by designing a low tractor on a Ford chassis. He had special wheels cast to give the rig a low profile, and before long there was a tractor in the Ryan garage, possibly the first orchard tractor around.

Finally, on November 8, 1918, the letter came. He was to leave on the eleventh for Berkeley, California, to begin ground school. At last, bona fide flight training was within his grasp. The day before he was to leave a neighbor invited Claude to go fishing at Laguna Beach. It was something to do, and it would keep him from clawing the walls, so Claude agreed to go. That night, after returning from the fishing trip, there was excitement in the air. People were saying the war was about to end.

The next morning, just before leaving, Claude called the Army and learned that the armistice had been signed. World War I had just ended.

"What about my orders?" Claude asked.

"Forget it," the man said.

Los Angeles Times

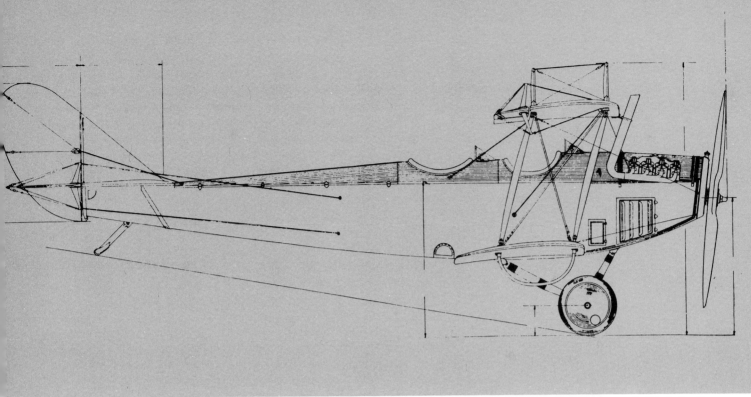

JN4-D (Service Handbook—Curtiss Aeroplane and
Motor Corp., 1918).

CHAPTER FOUR

Army Cadet; Forest Patrol Pilot

IT MATTERED LITTLE that he had nearly made it. The fact remained that world peace had robbed Claude Ryan of a personal victory. He had not wanted the war to continue, of course, but it had offered the best opportunity for him to learn to fly. And then, just as he stood on the threshold of success, the war had ended.

He managed to pull together the shattered remains of his dream. There was work to be done around the ranch helping his father, and when the tractor wasn't being used on the Ryan ranch, Claude cultivated the neighboring orchards to keep himself busy. Where he used to get $2 a day as a ranch hand, he now rated 90 cents per hour with his tractor.

But his thoughts still centered on aviation, and so he enrolled in Oregon State College at Corvallis in September, 1919, to study mechanical engineering, the nearest course in those days to aeronautical engineering. Claude also landed a part-time job working as the janitor in the YMCA library, which afforded him ample opportunity to keep abreast of developments in aviation by scanning the periodicals.

Some of the less pleasant facts about the air war were beginning to get attention. American pilots had performed brilliantly in combat—with French planes. General Billy Mitchell, the Army's great advocate of air power, returned to complain that though millions of dollars had been appropriated, not a single American plane had seen combat.

The air power message must have been getting through, for the following

23

spring, while glancing through an aviation magazine, Claude learned that the government planned to resume aviation cadet training and would accept about seventy applicants per class.

Claude immediately sent off an application, but by the end of the spring semester he had heard nothing. He went home for the summer vacation, expecting some sort of response by the time he reached Orange, but still nothing came. As always Claude kept busy, working in the packing plant at Villa Park, loading oranges in freight cars. Toward the end of the summer, he wrote the Army to ask what had happened to his application.

In a couple of days a special delivery letter arrived for Claude, stating that the Army had mailed an acceptance letter to him at Corvallis, which he apparently never received. He would have been in the opening group, but by the time the situation was finally straightened out, it was too late.

Although he had missed the first class, Claude was told to report to the balloon school at Arcadia, near Los Angeles, if he was still interested. The testing at the balloon school was not as extensive as Claude had taken two years earlier in Los Angeles, but it did involve more personal examination before a board of officers.

"The technique," Claude recalled later, "was to fire questions to see not just what you knew, but how you handled yourself under stress. I guess they thought they had me when they asked me to name the bodies of water you would travel if you went by sea from St. Petersburg (now Leningrad) to Vladivostok. I'd always been interested in geography, so I named them off without hesitation, much to their surprise, I think."

So in the summer of 1920, Tubal C. Ryan—the Army insisted on first name and middle initial—was accepted by the Army and ordered to report for flight training that fall at March Field near Riverside, California. Primary flight training took about six months, with sixty hours of flight time, including formation and night flying. The students alternated between ground school and time in the cockpit, spending one day in ground school, the next in the air.

Claude was impressed by the contrast between the precision of March Field, with its clean hangars and rows of beautifully maintained airplanes,

Hisso Jennies on the flight line, March Field, 1920.

Cadet Ryan is all smiles after his first solo in the JN6-H Jenny.

and the casual routine and sloppy equipment of the school at Venice.

It wasn't long before Ryan found out why the planes were so neat—it was part of the cadet discipline to work on the airplanes every afternoon, keeping them polished. The wartime JN4-D Jennies with OX-5 engines had been replaced by new 150-hp Hispano-Suiza Jennies, and cadets and instructors alike were enthusiastic about the fine equipment at their disposal.

Ground school . . . marching . . . calisthenics . . . training in engines . . . navigation . . . armament . . . and target practice, including hunting for jackrabbits right on the base. And flying! What more could one ask?

The new Jennies were a dream, and the instructors were the best. Army regulations required ten hours dual instruction before solo. Previous experience didn't count.

After Claude completed seven hours dual flight time, he and his instructor, Lieut. John Benton, landed at an out-of-the-way auxiliary field.

Claude watched with surprise as the instructor climbed out of the cockpit and jumped to the ground. He backed off a few paces and then shouted over the buzz of the engine:

"Ryan, you're as ready as you'll ever be!"

Enough said.

Before the instructor had a chance to change his mind, the Jenny lumbered down the field. At the other end of the graded dirt runway, the plane whipped around into the wind and Claude checked his instruments.

"This is it," he said to himself as he revved up the engine. The craft roared down the field and past the instructor, who stood with his hands on his hips, watching his student lift above the earth, alone, for the first time.

At a cross-country field.

25

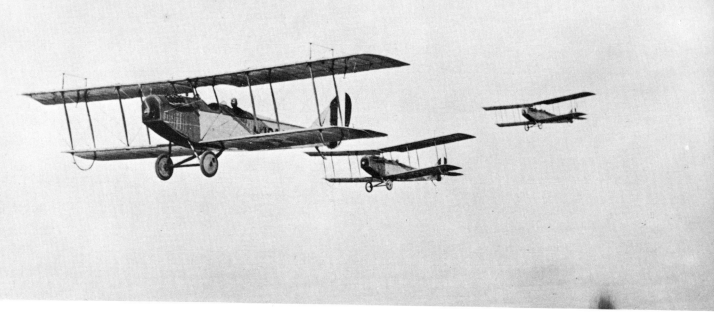

Formation flying with "... that propeller right over your shoulder ... a new and thrilling sensation."

The Jenny climbed smoothly over the southern California landscape, and for a moment Claude was standing beside the railroad tracks outside Parsons, waiting for Cal Rodgers to fly overhead. . . .

All those years he had yearned and all those hours he had waited—all that work, all that planning, all that dreaming—and it had all been worth it. The rolling hills flattened far below. The roads, sprinkled with a few cars, wormed across the landscape—confining, restricting, limiting. But it seemed to Claude that mere roads would never restrict him again.

As the biplane thundered across the landscape, Claude savored every vibration. For the moment, the Jenny was more than a mechanical vehicle. It was an extension of the pilot, a wedding between man and machine unequaled anywhere else in the wide range of human experience.

Years later, when asked to recall his feelings at that moment, Claude would shake his head slowly and confess that words were inadequate. But one thing was clear that day. Claude Ryan had entered a new era of his life, and nothing would ever be the same again.

Perhaps in years to come, he thought, others can be helped to enjoy the sight of clouds, of sunrise, of sunsets seen while soaring above the cities and farms, rivers, roads, and endless rails below. Unfettered by earthbound means of transportation, man can travel at will—where he will and when he will.

After the unauthorized early solo, Claude's instructor confined the next three flying hours to dual instruction in acrobatics, although normally this did not start until five solo hours had been completed. Along with dual and solo acrobatics came cross-country navigational flights.

During this training cadets used planes equipped with a compass, something the other trainers lacked. Pilots prepared their maps with consideration for drift due to winds aloft. At today's jet speeds, winds are a minor matter, but in those days they made a lot of difference, sometimes requiring the cadet to "crab" almost 45 degrees to make his course.

Seven or eight planes would leave at five-minute intervals, all scheduled to make five or six landings at fields perhaps 20 miles apart.

"At the farthest airport, instructor and cadets would gather for a formation flight back to March Field. When, the first time, you saw that old propeller back there right over your shoulder, going around real close to your wing, it was a new and thrilling sensation," Claude recalled.

Near graduation day, there were hedge-hopping steeplechase flights, with each cadet following the tail of the plane ahead just far enough to avoid the prop wash. Pilots never knew where the instructor was going to lead or land, and they never got more than a hundred feet off the ground. There were night flights, too, each cadet being required to make ten night landings aided by portable runway lights.

Training in simulated forced landings was an important part of the course. Not all such landings were simulated. "I had six forced landings," Claude recalled, "during the first sixty hours. That gave me a very useful skill for which, later on, I had a real need."

The final test involved a precision dead-stick landing following 3½ turns in a spin, coming out in the opposite direction from which the spin was entered at 3,000 feet altitude.

T. Claude Ryan

Studying the maps.

"You hadn't had much chance to practice dead-stick landings," Claude said, "so when the test came, you never heard such silence in all your life. With the engine stopped, all you could hear was the whistle of wind through the wires."

The student ahead of Claude overshot the mark, hit the fence, washed out the plane, but he walked away unhurt except for his pride. He quit flight training on the spot.

Claude was luckier. Overanxious to do a good job, he entered his spin from a nearly inverted position, came out of it where he should have, and made a perfect landing right on the mark. The instructor was impressed.

"Ryan," he said, "where did you ever learn to go into a spin from an inverted position?"

It had been accidental, but the instructor thought it was very clever.

It was about this time that a truck arrived from Los Angeles carrying the fuselage and wings of a huge biplane. In a few days it was assembled; then on February 24, 1921, Donald Douglas' first plane, the *Cloudster*, made its initial flight with test pilot Eric Springer at the controls. Though Claude never saw the *Cloudster* at March Field, the plane was destined to have a significant place in his career.

Claude was popular with his fellow cadets, but he knew the fact that he had the only car on the base had a great deal to do with it. Many cadets had relatives—girl cousins—in the area, which provided a constant and changing source of blind dates for Claude and his friends, who shared the only wheels available.

San Diego AeroSpace Museum

Donald Douglas brought his first plane, the *Cloudster*, to March Field for its trial flights.

All during the six-month program they had been eliminating cadets and at the completion of primary training only thirty-five of the seventy cadets who started under the commanding officer, Major Barton K. Yount, had qualified. Those remaining were rated for advanced training, which would send them on to special schools for observation flying, pursuit, or bombing. On graduation from primary training in the spring, only three were rated for the coveted pursuit pilot training, and Claude was one of them.

Claude gave much of the credit for his piloting skill to one of his instructors, Lieut. Y. A. "Little" Pitts. (There was also a Lieut. "Big" Pitts—no relation.) Pitts gave the novice, but skillful, young pilot a great deal of insight into the fine points of piloting technique.

Cadet Ryan and his campaign-hatted compatriots.

There had been a delay in sending pilots on to Kelly Field and other advanced training bases because budgeted funds for transportation had been used up. Meanwhile, Claude and the other pilots rated for pursuit training were able to keep their hand in by flying the SE-5 and Spad pursuit planes, then at March Field.

One day a request came through for volunteers for a special forest patrol service the Army had set up in California and Oregon two years earlier under the guidance of Major Henry H. (Hap) Arnold of Rockwell Field, San Diego. The pilots would fly de Havilland DH-4 biplanes over the rugged mountains of the Sierra range. It was hazardous duty, since there were few clearings in the area, thus making emergency landings a tricky business. They would report to Mather Field, near Sacramento, and the duty would be classed as observation training, rather than pursuit or bombing.

Claude was anxious to get some real flying under his belt, so he volunteered for the duty. Despite the oft-repeated warning of the hazards of flying constantly over rugged mountains in single-engine airplanes without parachutes, every cadet volunteered, though not all were able to go.

And the problem of transportation was still there. Replenishment funds for the travel budget had not been received. Claude got permission to drive to Sacramento in his own car and left in May with three of his closest buddies in the reliable Model T. Since none could afford hotels, the men took their blankets and camped along the road. Arriving before the others, they arranged to board in a private home instead of at the barracks.

For several months the group flew out of Mather as part of the Ninth Aero Squadron, getting advanced training in the big DH's. Then at the start of the fire season in summer of 1921, teams of pilot and observer were sent to operating bases; Claude was assigned to the detachment under Lieut. John Morgan at Corning, just south of Red Bluff.

During his patrols, Claude flew northwest out of Corning along the west side of the snowcapped Marble Mountains to the Oregon border, then east to Yreka and Montague where he stopped for lunch. After refueling, the return trip was over Mt. Eddy just west of 14,400-foot Mt. Shasta, then over the forests on the east side of the coastal range and back to Corning.

"We had an average of four or five fires to report on nearly every patrol," Ryan recalled. "Very seldom did we draw a blank. When we located a fire, my observer would tap out the map coordinates over a radio wireless key.

March Field

March 24 19 21

Classified as a ___ PURSUIT PILOT

APPROVED ___

B. K. YOUNT

Major Air Service Commanding

The Model-T provided reliable transportation to Claude's new forest patrol assignment.

"There were some accidents, and the patrol lost several airplanes and pilots we shoudn't have. The planes were well maintained; the fault didn't lie there. I never had any trouble, despite the number '13' painted on the fuselage, but I did do a few unnecessary things because the flights were getting pretty routine.

"Nothing exciting had happened all season, so I decided to stop in at the emergency field the Forest Service had scraped off in a deep canyon at Orleans. The field looked a little doubtful, but since I was curious about whether you could land there okay or not, I sort of faked a forced landing.

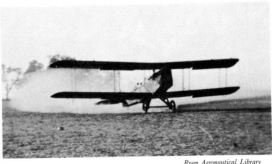

Ryan Aeronautical Library

Taking off from Corning in number "13."

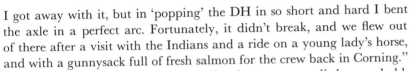

et,   d-24
    Cadet Ryan and Observer Wheisel,
    flying plane No. 13, landed at Orleans ai
    on the Montague route this afternoon,   to
    because of the fact that their motor   O
    developed a slight trouble which they
    desired to remedy before starting on
    their homeward journey.

I got away with it, but in 'popping' the DH in so short and hard I bent the axle in a perfect arc. Fortunately, it didn't break, and we flew out of there after a visit with the Indians and a ride on a young lady's horse, and with a gunnysack full of fresh salmon for the crew back in Corning."

Toward the end of the season the pilots began to get a little more bold, frequently yielding to the temptation to earn the unlimited gratitude of the young damsels of Corning. Most of the girls were crazy about the idea of flying, and although it was strictly against Army regulations, some of the pilots rendezvoused with their girl friends at obscure airfields and took them up for a brief spin.

Claude had met a pretty little girl by the name of Celia, and he was not above using his flying machine to bolster his image. Celia lived on

Claude catches Mt. Lassen in the camera lens as he cruises along on forest patrol.

T. Claude Ryan

At Orleans emergency field the natives turned out in force.

T. Claude Ryan

. . . "a forced landing . . . and a gunnysack of fresh salmon. . . ." That's Claude astride the prop.

a farm about four miles outside Corning, and for some strange reason Claude's DH biplane frequently found itself orbiting the farm as he returned from forest patrol. One day, in a wild fling of romanticism, Claude attached a box of candy to a small parachute, normally used to drop night flares, and tossed it overboard as he flew over the farm. Celia, who had dashed outside when she heard the plane, opened her arms and caught the candy. It was a tender moment, Celia standing on the ground with a parachute draped over her head, and Claude warmed by the romance of his own soul.

Young love blossomed, and it was only a matter of time before Celia began begging for a ride in Claude's plane. One day Claude arranged for Celia to meet him at a long, smooth field along the Sacramento River when he flew in from patrol. It would be an ideal spot for a late afternoon flight. When Claude arrived, he could see Celia below, waiting, and within minutes his plane touched down on the grassy field. Claude's observer, Sgt. Hal Wheisel, jumped out of the plane and wrapped Celia's tiny frame in his bulky flight coat. She looked like a teddy bear, lost inside the heavy gear, but she was game and the de Havilland soon soared again, flying in the interest of young love. All went fine until Claude returned to the field a few minutes after taking off. He had planned to stay in the air no longer than ten minutes so he could get back to the base on time. But when he flew back to the field it was covered with grazing sheep.

There was Sgt. Wheisel, far below, yelling at the disinterested critters, but they just kept on grazing. Claude circled until he grew desperate, and then made a series of low passes over the field to scare the sheep away. In time, they grew tired of the whole thing and wandered off, and Claude got the plane down. He returned to the base just in time.

Shortly after that Claude's group was transferred, and he didn't see much more of Celia.

With the coming of the rains and the end of the fire season in late September, the Corning detachment returned with the others to Mather Field where Claude was commissioned in November as a second lieutenant with pursuit pilot rating. Back at base the routine duties were broken only by an occasional incident such as the aerial pursuit of escaped prisoners.

30

Ryan Aeronautical Library

Number "13" on the side of his de Havilland biplane was never a jinx for Claude. Note weight under figure 3 which reeled out radio antenna.

In January, 1922, Claude left the Army (somehow they gave him a second commission) and went on the inactive reserve with hopes of getting a flying job as a civilian. In those days about the only men who flew for a living worked as pilots for the airmail service. Since the U.S. Post Office used de Havillands, Claude figured he had a good chance.

He put in an application, and in a few days received a polite letter stating that while he seemed well qualified, there were hundreds of equally qualified applicants on the waiting list. His name would be added, but it was clear he would be well advised not to hold his breath.

Since there were far more pilots than jobs, Claude began shopping around for something else. He figured the automotive business was going places, so he paid a call on an old family friend, George Pepperdine, who had owned the first automobile supply business in Claude's hometown of Parsons, just three doors down from the Ryan laundry. Mr. Pepperdine had moved West himself, and lived in Los Angeles as the founder and owner of the Western Auto Supply Co.

Claude got a job filling mail orders for automobile parts and began training as a branch manager. But he learned it would take several years to reach that goal, and the best he could hope for in salary would be about $200 a month.

The automobile business suddenly lost a lot of glamour, and Claude moved on in May. He went to Santa Ana and bought a laundry route, which, from his knowledge of the business gained from his father, he knew could be profitable. He didn't have to pay much for the route, since it was in a new area with few customers, but he had to buy a truck.

He began the route—which went to Newport Beach—early in the summer, and within a few months he had built it into a prosperous business. Since he kept 30 percent commission, in time he was making more money than the vice president of the auto supply company he had just left, but Claude soon grew weary of dirty sheets.

iful bungalow there. . . . g a beau-
Plane No. 13, with a man doing stunts on its right wing, entertaining the people in town today. One of the spectators was heard to remark he'd "be durned if he'd ride on any flyin' machine with that number, let alone stunts on its wings."
Woodson has installed a ee horse power

Flying DHs was good training for prospective airmail pilots.

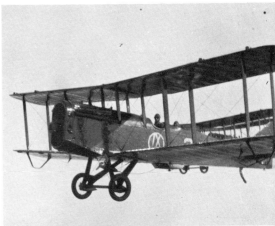

T. Claude Ryan

While Claude Ryan was working on his hopped-up car, Millard Boyd, at sixteen, was ready to fly his first plane.

Every time he gazed at the blue sky over southern California, he thought of the familiar buzz of his old DH-4, and he longed again to take to the air. Too, at a nearby airport, he'd again met a young engineer and pilot, Millard Boyd, who as a schoolboy had built and flown his own plane in 1915. Finally, he could fight it no longer. If young Millard Boyd could do it, he could too.

He sold the laundry route at a handsome profit—enough to buy a used Ford, with $100 left over. He packed up his few possessions and made his way down the coast to San Diego to do some flying on his Army reserve commission at Rockwell Field.

As he arrived in San Diego, the germ of a brazen idea began to grow in the mind of the young aviator. Why not buy a plane and become a barnstormer?

It was true he had little money, but he believed in flying as he believed in nothing else. He knew he was a good pilot. He was young, and he had his foot in the door of what he was sure would become a great industry. But if aviation was to succeed, it would do so because of young men who would ignore the perils and throw themselves into the task because they could not turn away.

Claude was such a man, and no place seemed more appropriate to start than in San Diego. The area was rich in aviation lore, even in those early days. The climate was mild year-around, and there would be little to hinder operations.

It was a beautiful community, nestled along the shore of the Pacific, and it embraced one of the finest harbors in the world.

Major Hap Arnold, father of the aerial forest patrol, was the skipper of Rockwell Field, which was just a short ferry ride from downtown San

Diego. Perhaps Arnold could help. The field had a number of old planes left over from the war, some of which reportedly were in fair condition. If Claude could just get his hands on one and then find a flight strip to set up shop, he would be ready for business. It was a long shot, but it was a chance.

He had already logged a few hours at Rockwell Field and had rented a room at the YMCA when he took time out for a shave and a haircut in a barbershop near the waterfront. Claude settled into the chair and the barber smeared a little lather on his face.

"You look windburned," the barber said. "What do you do, ride a motorcycle?"

"No," Claude answered, bursting with pride, "I'm a pilot."

The barber chuckled to himself.

"Well," he finally drawled, "I hope you've got a better eye for business than Jim Hennessey had."

"Who's Hennessey?" Claude asked.

"He was our last pilot. Doing real good until the law caught up with him. Charged with smuggling, they say, and the Feds clipped his wings. He won't be doing any flying for awhile. Nobody's taken over his old spot yet. Might be a chance for a young fellow like you . . . ."

"Where's his spot?" Claude asked.

"Down by the waterfront. You can't miss it. It's just off Broadway across the road from the railroad depot."

Moments later Claude slipped out of the chair and headed for the waterfront.

Hennessey's field wasn't the best in the world, Claude soon found out. It was near San Diego's main piers and ran parallel to the waterfront. But as Claude stepped off the field, he figured he could get a Jenny in

Major H. H. Arnold, Commanding Officer, Rockwell Field. "Hap" Arnold went on to become the Commanding General and great leader of all U.S. Air Forces in World War II.

and out without taking down too many smokestacks and electric wires. It would do.

The property was under the control of the Harbor Department, and soon Claude was seated before J. W. Brennan, the Harbor Master. Joe Brennan, a ruddy-faced Irishman with a twinkle in his eye, listened to Claude's plight.

"It'll cost you $50 a month," Brennan said.

"Wow! I don't even expect to take in that much!" Claude answered.

Brennan rubbed his chin for a moment and eyed the young flyer across the desk.

"Tell you what," he said. "We like young fellows coming into town and starting up new businesses. Suppose you try it for awhile, and then we'll take another look at the rental."

Claude thought for a moment and watched the man seated on the other side of the desk.

"Sounds good," he said, "but I don't know about that $50. I don't expect to do that much business in a whole month."

Brennan slammed his fist down on the desk and rose to his feet.

"Hell!" he shouted. "Get out there and make a success! Then we'll worry about paying the lease!"

Claude leaped to his feet, grabbed Brennan's outstretched hand, pumped it vigorously for a moment, and then dashed out the door. Soon he was across the bay in the office of Major Arnold.

"Hell, Ryan, get out there and make a success."
—Joe Brennan.

The first Jenny . . . and a piano box for an office.

"I want to buy one of the old Jennies," Claude told Arnold. "You know, one of the surplus Jennies you've got crated in the warehouse."

"It might be possible," Arnold said. "You wire Washington a bid of $400 and we'll see what happens."

The price sounded too good to be true, but Claude wired a $400 bid on a JN4-D and it was promptly accepted. He sold his Model T Ford for $300 and withdrew his savings from the bank, which amounted to $150. That gave him a grand total of $450.

He returned to Rockwell Field and laid down the $400 for the Jenny. Then he paid a couple of mechanics $25 to help him assemble the plane and put it in flying order. That left him with a meager $25 for operating expenses. Somewhere he rounded up an old piano box and converted it into an office and tool shed. At night, the Jenny could be tied down next to the YMCA handball court. He borrowed a grader and leveled the field a little, and slowly everything began to fall in place.

Ready to make his availability known to a waiting world, the San Diego *Union* cooperated with a news story in which Claude announced his "combined aerial taxi service, flight training school, and daily excursion service."

It may not have been an astonishing beginning, but for a young man of twenty-four in September of 1922, it was enough.

FORMER ARMY FLIER STARTS FIELD HERE

The Ryan Flying Co. is the newest commercial activity to come to this city.

T. C. Ryan, former army aviator and forestry patrol who is managing the company, has secured a lease on a field at the foot of Broadway, just north of the service athletic field. According to Ryan, the purpose of the new enterprise is to provide air taxi service to any part of the state, aerial sightseeing trips, courses in flight training, aerial advertising stunts and aerial photography service.

The first plane in the new service is a new Curtiss JN-4 type. This is the kind of plane that is used entirely for training purposes, it is explained, and is considered the safest type for commercial activities.

FLY WITH ME

TAKE A

Real Trip Thru The Clouds

RYAN, The Aviator is in Your City

CHAPTER FIVE

Come Fly With Me

THE EARLY DAYS WERE LEAN, but Claude was willing to do almost anything to stay in the aviation business.

His first barnstorming was out of his hometown, Orange. Claude flew the Jenny up to Santa Ana the first day to look over possible landing strips among the orange groves between his dad's ranch, at Villa Park, and Orange. He settled on a 10-acre site, with the usual power poles at one end of the strip, and made arrangements with the owner to use it for a few days.

There, and later at other communities in southern California, he cranked up the Jenny, flew over the nearby towns, and tossed leaflets over the side of the plane.

For the price of $2.50 or $5, depending on how long they wanted to stay aloft, passengers could circle their city. He got an occasional taker, but for the most part it was not a profitable venture, and he soon returned to San Diego. Flying was proving to be a meager livelihood—cold cereal, hamburgers, a 10-cent bowl of chili, and a bare room at the San Diego YMCA, to which he walked each evening after a disappointing day at the airport on the waterfront.

Homesickness came with the Christmas holiday season, and Claude took off for the family orange ranch. Typically, the Jenny conked out and Claude landed next to the highway. After repairing the plane, he visited a nearby lunch counter only to discover when he went to pay that he

37

Not makin' money, but happy to be in the aviation business at last.

was short of cash. Ryan finally talked his way out of the jam by leaving his watch as security.

During one of his low spells, Claude received an offer through a pilot friend, Jess Hart, from the mayor of Tijuana, Baja California. The mayor had purchased four war surplus Jennies and had planned a barnstorming trip down the west coast of Mexico in hopes of drumming up a little publicity for his city while making some extra money for himself. Nobody had ever tried it before, the mayor reasoned, so it was bound to be a success.

The mayor had already rounded up three pilots when he asked Claude to become the fourth. He would pay $35 a week, plus expenses. It sounded like a worthy endeavor to Claude, and he agreed. Three planes left San Diego and flew to Calexico where they picked up the fourth plane. The second day they flew to Tucson, and then on to Nogales, Arizona, where they landed at an airport in the hills at an elevation of around 4,000 feet, pretty high for the Jennies. They spent three days in Nogales while the mayor wrestled with the paperwork for the permit to take the planes into Mexico.

It became obvious at Nogales that the trip would not be without problems. The high altitude was almost too much for the Jennies, and when they finally left for Mexico, they barely got off the ground. In Mexico, despite the poor performance, the boondoggle was a tremendous success. Every time the pilots landed near one of the communities in the Mexican highlands, more passengers were on hand, anxious to take a flight.

It wasn't too bad during the mornings, but as each day wore on, the temperature rose, the air became lighter, and it grew increasingly difficult to fly. During one flight, Claude got caught in a downdraft and the small plane simply didn't have the power to pull out. He landed in a cornfield with the throttle wide open.

After that close call Claude suggested curtailing operations for the day, but the other pilots didn't want to call it quits.

To make matters worse, the mayor asked Claude to take up the Mexican Army major in charge of that district. Since the officer represented the supreme authority in that area, Claude found it hard to refuse. Unfortunately, the major's physique displayed the results of ample fortification from starchy Mexican foods; he could barely wedge his heavy frame into the plane.

Claude reluctantly climbed into the cockpit and started the engine. The old Jenny churned and groaned down the strip and somehow made it into the air. But it wasn't long before the plane was trapped in a downdraft and was plunging toward the bleak hills below.

Claude aimed the craft along a line of railroad tracks and tried to pull up, but the Jenny just kept sinking lower and lower. He sheared off both wings on telegraph poles, and the Jenny's fuselage skidded into a ravine and across the carpet of tall grass, minus wings, with Claude and the major still aboard. It finally came to a stop, nose up, with parts scattered across the ravine.

Claude leaped out and jammed his finger into a hole in the gas tank, fearful that leakage on the hot exhaust pipe could explode into a blazing inferno. He managed to stop the leak, and then began looking for the major.

The major was still strapped in his seat, uninjured, gazing straight ahead—through smashed goggles—over his ponderous belly. The major didn't speak English, and by the time he was finally extricated from the plane, he couldn't even speak Spanish. He just stared at the tangled wreckage, shaking his head.

If the episode had been terrifying for the major, it had been a great success as far as attracting sightseers in the area was concerned. Several truckloads of people suddenly appeared, including a number of "ladies of the evening" who delighted in casting aspersions on the affair.

The mayor of Tijuana realized that the crash would never have happened if the flights had been cut off earlier in the day as Claude had suggested, and so he paid Claude the balance of the week's work and provided him with transportation to San Diego.

Back in San Diego, Claude found that a carnival had come to town, and soon it proved a boon to his struggling enterprise. One fellow with the carnival was pretty well heeled, and he loved to fly. Every day he hired Claude to take him up. He took pictures from the air, and then returned

EROPLANE IS DEMOLISHED IN FALL OTRO LADO

While flying with passengers across the line yesterday evening, one of the three Curtis aeroplanes which are now in the city, on their way down the west coast, fell into a noze dive on account of treacherous air currents, due to the shape of the hills, and was demolished in the landing.

Pilot T. C. Ryan, and the passenger, a major in the Nogales, Sonora garrison miraculously escaped with only a few minor bruises, but three telegraph poles and a hundred yards of telegraph wire of the Southern Pacific de Mexico were torn down.

The aviators give pilot Ryan a great deal of credit for doing so well as he did in making such a landing, after hitting the air pockets and the currents which forced the plane downward, and give him the credit for saving his own and his passenger's life.

The plane was so badly wrecked that it is being dismantled, although much of the material can be salvaged. The engine was not injured at all, although both wings, the propellor and the landing gear were demolished.

The aviators of the party state that the altitude of Nogales is a little bit high for this type of planes, as they were not designed for taking off at more than 2,000 feet elevation, and this together with the treacherous air currents, caused by the hills surrounding Nogales, Sonora; was the cause of the accident.

Ryan Aeronautical Library

The Spanish "Otro Lado" translates as "Other Side" or across-the-border.

Ryan Aeronautical Library

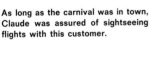

As long as the carnival was in town, Claude was assured of sightseeing flights with this customer.

San Diego waterfront, 1922, with Claude's flight strip marked at left.

to the carnival to talk with his friends about the sensational flight over San Diego.

"When we move along, you come to San Bernardino too," he argued. "It would be great for the carnival to have you along. Your plane would attract people to us, and we would attract people to you. How can you lose with a deal like that?"

Claude agreed that it sounded better than anything he had going at the time. In a couple of days the carnival moved on to San Bernardino, and Claude made the trip north in his Jenny. His friend from the carnival was supposed to have found a suitable landing strip, but as is so often the case when a nonaviator picks out an operating area, the strip he had "discovered" was far from satisfactory: it was surrounded by trees and fences and power lines. But Claude figured he could make do, and he aimed the Jenny at a bedsheet his friend had stretched out on the ground to mark a suitable landing spot.

Once safely on the ground, Claude knew he would never get the Jenny over the fence at the end of the strip with the added weight of a passenger. He could make it alone, but not with someone else in the plane with him. Then he hit upon an idea.

The first passenger arrived and climbed into the Jenny. Claude cranked up the engine, taxied to the far end of the strip and turned around. He roared down the strip at full throttle, aiming right at the fence.

After he picked up enough speed, he let the Jenny lift off a little. Then he slammed it down on the strip and bounced over the fence. The plane settled a little on the other side of the fence, but it stayed in the air. It worked, and Claude followed the same procedure with every passenger. Since most of them knew virtually nothing about aviation, there was nothing unusual about the takeoff so far as they were concerned.

Toward the end of the first day, hot desert winds blew into San Bernardino and the operation really became tricky. The second day the air was hot, and the old Jenny just didn't want to do its stuff. Claude gave up the idea as a bad deal, went back to Orange for one night, and then returned to San Diego.

Business was anything but good. He applied for a loan from the local bank to buy some badly needed equipment, but was told in no uncertain terms that although he was a fine young fellow, nobody really expected him to live very long, maybe not even long enough to pay off a note. But Claude struck up a friendship with a teller at the bank who also lived at the "Y"; he shared Claude's youthful confidence, and the new friend volunteered to endorse his note. He got the loan, bought the equipment, and was able to repay the note, but there were times when his finances ran so low he wished the equipment were food.

At another point, Claude accepted a fee of $35 to fly an OX-5 Jenny from San Diego to Santa Ana for an owner who had purchased it second-hand. After he took off, he discovered that particles of rust inside the gasoline tank kept clogging the fuel line. During the ninety-minute flight to Santa Ana he made seven forced landings in bean fields, alfalfa patches, and anywhere he could find a flat stretch to set the plane down. Each time he stopped he had to clean the carburetor in order to get the engine running again. It was a wild trip, but it added a few more dollars to the kitty.

A short time later Claude made his second excursion south of the border. A man by the name of Ed T. Aiken showed up at the waterfront airstrip driving a pickup truck. He told Claude that several months earlier an American pilot had been nabbed across the border. The pilot turned out to be Jim Hennessey, the man who had operated out of the San Diego waterfront location before Claude arrived on the scene.

Mexican authorities did not look lightly on Hennessey's activities, Aiken related. They put a guard aboard the plane and ordered the pilot to fly to the Mexican border town of Tecate, where they relieved him of his plane

Flying passengers in the Jenny from Dutch Flats.

before offering him the hospitality of a Mexican jail. The plane sat there for several months before the Mexican government decided to do anything about it. Finally, authorities decided to patch it up and fly it back to Mexico City, but by that time the plane had deteriorated substantially.

Aiken, who owned a store and garage in the community of Campo just north of the border, was awarded the contract for putting the plane back in order. However, as he later admitted, he knew little about planes, a fact that he had not bothered to convey to local authorities in Tecate. He and his automobile mechanic made the repairs he thought were necessary, put a coat of paint on the weathered fuselage, and then faced the fact that his contract called for a demonstration flight.

That was what brought Aiken to San Diego to see Claude Ryan.

"I would like to arrange for you to come down there and make that flight," Aiken told the young pilot.

"Is there a field or any place there I can use?" Claude asked.

"Oh, there're some fields around that you can use, I'm sure. I'll pay your way and you can go on the train. It only takes about an hour to get there. You go down through Tijuana on the San Diego & Arizona Eastern. I'll meet you at the depot. You can fly the plane and then catch the afternoon train home. How much would you want to do that?"

"If the airplane is in good flying condition, and if it's just a simple matter of making one flight, it would only take the day. So you pay my expenses, and $35 ought to do it."

"You've got a deal."

A few days later, Claude made the trip from San Diego to Tecate. The plane, a strange hybrid composed of different parts from several planes, was sitting beside the tracks. It was coated with a heavy gray paint, like that used for a barn, obviously applied by a man who had faith that paint does indeed cover a multitude of sins.

"Did you check the engine?" Claude asked his host.

"Oh yes. It runs fine."

"Let's start it up."

Claude climbed into the cockpit and Aiken swung the prop. It started, but while it was idling the thermometer went up to 212 degrees and the radiator started boiling over.

"You've got problems here," Claude shouted from the cockpit. "It's only idling and it's boiling over. I can't fly it like this."

"Couldn't you fly it just a little, just one little flight," Aiken pleaded. (All his contract called for was one flight, just to demonstrate that the plane could get off the ground.) But Claude shut down the engine and climbed out of the cockpit.

"Not like that," he said.

"Okay, you catch the afternoon train back to San Diego, and I'll call you when I get it fixed."

Claude returned to San Diego, and a few days later Aiken was on the phone.

"Everything is dandy now," he said. "Will you come back? I'll pay the fare and extra expenses."

Claude agreed, and a couple of days later he was sitting in the cockpit of the old relic again. The engine didn't heat up while idling, but as soon as Claude opened the throttle, the engine began to boil again.

"I still can't fly it," Claude said as he climbed down. "It's not airworthy."

Aiken nearly sobbed.

"I've got my life's savings in this thing," he said. "Surely you could just get it off the ground enough so the Mexican people would say

No. 631 $2.50
Flight Certificate

This Is to Certify That:

Mary Sherrett

has seen San Diego from the air on a WONDER AIR FLIGHT over the City and surroundings.

RYAN FLYING COMPANY
Where the Long Line of Planes Is
SAN DIEGO, CALIFORNIA

July 18th, 1924   Flown by Pilot T. C. Ryan

Ever the salesman, Claude didn't hesitate to bill himself as "Reserve Military Aviator" to gain sightseeing passengers' confidence.

it was in the air. That's all I ask. Just get it up and down again."

Claude's better judgment told him not to do it, but there was a note of desperation in Aiken's voice.

"Well," he finally said, relenting, "is there some kind of a decent field around here?"

"You bet," Aiken shouted.

They tied the plane to the rear of a car and towed it through town, collecting a gathering of curious townfolk as they rolled through the dusty streets of the village. There wasn't anything that resembled an airstrip in the area, but finally Claude and Aiken settled on a field on the outskirts of town. The grade was fairly steep, and there was a big ravine at the far end, but it was the best field available.

By the time the plane was positioned at the top of the hill, the engine had cooled down, and Claude gave Aiken his instructions. He would take off as soon as the engine started in hopes that he could get the plane up and down before all the water boiled out of the radiator.

He got the plane up without any serious problems, made a quick turn and in the right position for approach to landing. Just then the engine stopped cold. Claude was lucky. He glided onto the field and rolled to a stop, just a few feet from the edge of the ravine.

The Mexicans cheered and hailed Claude as a hero. Aiken threw his arms around him and almost cried. But Claude realized the danger he had been in, and felt more like a fool than a hero. Aiken paid him his $35 and then drove him back to San Diego, chattering all the way.

The Mexican government accepted the plane, and about a

month later Claude noticed a small item in the San Diego newspaper. "Mexican Airplane Crashes," the headline said.

It seemed that a famous French aviator employed by the Mexican government had crashed an airplane near Tecate on a ferry flight to Mexico City. The pilot had escaped injury, but the plane was demolished.

Claude chalked the incident up to experience, and then decided to concentrate his activities north of the border.

Claude figured the more people saw of his operation, the better his chances were of nabbing a few more customers. Unfortunately, there was very little traffic past his waterfront landing strip, thus reducing the chances of an occasional sightseeing passenger. Whenever there was a ballgame at the recreation field at the end of the strip, Claude would taxi his Jenny to the edge of the field, and then perch atop the biplane and watch the game. He saved the price of a ticket, and at the same time he advertised his business.

As a sideline, Claude was always on the lookout for planes that he could rebuild and sell at a profit. In those days if you had a good flying Jenny you could sell it for $500 and replace it for $400 with one still in its crate from Army surplus. Sometimes a student pilot like Preston Kirk would buy a Jenny and have Claude assemble it for him. After the plane was assembled, Ryan would teach the student to fly in his new plane. In return, Claude got the use of the plane to train other students or carry passengers.

Early Ryan flying students. From left, Merle Parker, Preston Kirk, Claude Ryan, Lee Lawson.

Young Ryan was at Rockwell Field almost every day because, although he initially took off with flight students from the small waterfront airstrip, he flew across the bay to the large Army field—then primarily a repair depot—to give landing and takeoff practice.

There were other attractions at Rockwell, not the least of which was Major Arnold's own SE-5 pursuit, the only one on the field. Ryan knew that no one else was permitted to fly it but being a civilian, and a bit more creative, Claude approached Arnold.

"Major, I'd sure like to fly your SE-5. You know, I've got a pursuit rating."

Taken aback, Arnold set his jaw, studied Claude for a moment, then just the hint of a smile crossed his face.

"Alright, Ryan!"

Brief though such exchanges were, there developed a decades long bond between Arnold and Ryan which later was to become critical to Claude's and the company's future.

One day while nosing around Rockwell Field, he ran across an old Curtiss F flying boat, which he figured he could fix up and use to fly sightseers from the Hotel Del Coronado, near Rockwell Field, one of the favorite tourist attractions in the area.

He queried Major Arnold, who admitted he hadn't even known the craft was there, but agreed to see if it could be put up for sale. In a few days the word came back that it could be sold, but that offers must be by sealed bid, with 10 percent deposit.

Claude was sure not many people would know about the flying boat's availability, and he decided to make a token bid. He figured he could afford to pay $75, and so he went to the bank and got a cashier's check for $7.50.

On his way across the bay Claude reached into his coat for the check, but it wasn't there. He searched every pocket, but he had somehow managed to mislay the check. Since the bid had to be in by 10 A.M., he wouldn't have time to catch the next ferry back to San Diego and get another check.

He fished through his pockets and came up with $6.90 in cash. When he reached Rockwell Field he put the cash in an envelope and submitted his bid, $69.

At 10:02 A.M., the executive officer turned to Claude.

"Ryan, you win the Brown Derby."

No one else had bid on the plane, and Claude had won by default. Claude then went to Arnold and asked permission to leave the flying boat at Rockwell Field.

Arnold glared across his walnut desk at Ryan, and then burst out, "Damn it, Ryan, the only reason we sold you that thing was to get rid of it, and now you want to leave it here."

After a few moments of discussion, Arnold relented and told Claude he could leave it there for no more than two weeks. That night, a pioneer flying boat pilot from San Francisco who had heard about the Curtiss too late to bid contacted Claude and asked him to sell it.

"I know exactly what you paid for it, so make your price realistic," the pilot said.

"Okay," Claude said, "you can have it for $250."

The pilot exploded, claiming the price was far too high. He slammed down the phone, but called back a couple of days later.

"All right," he said. "You win."

Free space for other planes at Dutch Flats was a come-on which soon established Ryan Field as the center of San Diego commercial aviation.

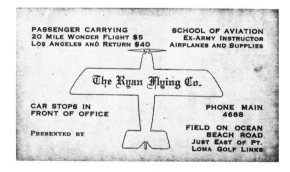

PASSENGER CARRYING
20 MILE WONDER FLIGHT $5
LOS ANGELES AND RETURN $40

SCHOOL OF AVIATION
EX-ARMY INSTRUCTOR
AIRPLANES AND SUPPLIES

The Ryan Flying Co.

CAR STOPS IN
FRONT OF OFFICE

PHONE MAIN
4688

PRESENTED BY

FIELD ON OCEAN
BEACH ROAD
JUST EAST OF PT.
LOMA GOLF LINKS

So on a $6.90 cash investment Ryan sold the flying boat for $181 net profit, and he didn't even have to move it.

But for the most part, business wasn't that good for the young aviator. He could pick up a buck here and a buck there, but at times the future looked bleak indeed. Then things took another turn.

Additional power poles had been installed for a new pier along the waterfront. In order to operate from the field, Claude had to make a low, flat turn on takeoff, then dip under the wires before continuing out over the bay. Some of the city fathers objected, stating it was extremely hazardous, but Claude put on a demonstration flight and convinced them they were wrong.

Shortly thereafter, however, Claude found a new location on a salt flat adjacent to the Marine Corps Recruit Depot in an area called Dutch Flats.

He moved his operation there in the spring of 1923 at a $15 per month rental fee. Soon he needed a hangar and office, which a building inspector designed free in return for the chance to make a parachute jump.

The men building the small new shop at Dutch Flats for Claude didn't have enough money to finish the floor properly, and so they left some floor joists out at one end of the building. They drove nails in the exterior wall where the joists should have been, and laid the floor before the building inspector showed up. "We were always very careful," one of the helpers explained, "not to store any engines on the floor at that end of the building."

The new location proved a boon to business, partly because it was in a more convenient area and partly because the "free parking" Claude offered local pilots soon made his field San Diego's aviation headquarters. In time, Claude decided to hire a fulltime mechanic, his first employee. Until then a number of nonpaid helpers like "Dapper Dan" Burnett had worked on maintenance jobs in exchange for flying time. Claude immediately thought of Hawley Bowlus, whom he had not seen since those incredible days at the American School of Aviation.

Claude drove to Los Angeles and inquired around. Finally, he learned

46

that Hawley was living in San Fernando, where he worked as a tractor mechanic for the local Ford dealer. Claude went to the dealer and was told Hawley was out answering an emergency call from someone whose tractor had broken down. Claude found him in the field, up to his ears in tractor parts.

Hawley yanked his cap off his head and threw it to the ground.

"I'll be darned," he said. "If it isn't Claude Ryan."

Claude sat down beside his friend. The two swapped a few stories about the past, and then turned toward the future.

"I've got a little flying operation down in San Diego," Claude said. "How would you like to come down and work for me?"

"Oh boy, that sure sounds great," Hawley said. "But you know, I'm married now, and my wife is expecting a baby. I've got to have a minimum of $35 a week. Could you pay that much?"

"Yeah, I think I can. When can you go to work?"

"How about next Monday?"

Claude had hired his first employee. Bowlus' bride, Inez, came in to help as a part-time secretary, and for a while Claude boarded at the Bowlus home near the Portuguese fishing colony on Pt. Loma. Next on the scene after Hawley was John van der Linde, a Dutchman from the Netherlands East Indies, who was destined to be another stalwart in the Ryan company.

Ryan didn't make a killing on every airplane deal or on his flying service and student training, but he did stay in business. And to have a "fun" airplane, Claude had Hawley clip the top wing of a Jenny, remove the cabane struts, and get a Millerized OX-5 engine for it. Later, for stunt shows put on every Sunday at Dutch Flats to attract crowds for passenger flights, Claude got a Thomas-Morse Scout and installed a 110-hp French rotary engine which made it more suitable for acrobatic work.

The main income of the business came from sightseeing flights. San Diego was becoming a southern California tourist center. Tour buses frequently brought well-heeled folks down from Los Angeles, and Claude got to know a few bus drivers with whom he could work out a deal. If they stopped by his flying field on Dutch Flats and helped convince some of their passengers to take a flight, Claude would pay them well. He offered them $1 on each fifteen-minute $5 flight, which was a handsome proposition.

The tourists brought in a steady income, but Claude was convinced that if the business was to survive, he would have to offer more than sightseeing flights. So he snatched up every opportunity to try something new, and he rarely passed up a chance to buy an airplane cheap, patch it up, and sell it to someone else for a modest profit.

One day a dapper young fellow showed up with an older man who looked like he had just come off the oil fields.

"My name's Lloyd O'Donnell," the younger man told Claude. "And this is old John," he said with a motion toward his companion, apparently a mechanic.

"I want to buy a plane," O'Donnell said. "Can you fix me up?"

"I've got one Jenny, but it's still in the crate," Claude said. "It's a real beauty—the wings have clear dope, you can even see every rib. But you'll have to pay a premium for it."

"Can you have it ready by this afternoon?"

"I think so."

"Then I'll take it."

O'Donnell disappeared and Claude set to work on the Jenny, trying to put it into flying order within a few hours. That afternoon O'Donnell returned with a check and said he was ready to pick up his airplane.

Ryan Aeronautical Library

Claude's exhibition of aerobatic flying in the TM Scout brought out the crowds every Sunday.

The jovial Dutchman from the East Indies, John van der Linde, was one of Ryan's earliest employees and longest associates.

Ryan Aeronautical Library

A "clear dope" Jenny like this one brought a premium price in 1923.

Walter Averett

Aero Digest

Lloyd O'Donnell whose escapades still made good yarns for "hangar flying."

"I was just getting ready to safety all the wires and turnbuckles with copper wire," Claude said.

"I haven't got time for that," O'Donnell said. "Just let it go and I'll safety them when I get up to Long Beach."

O'Donnell handed Claude the check, climbed into the Jenny with old John, and took off. Several days later he was back in San Diego and stopped off to see Claude.

"We had a real exciting trip," O'Donnell said. "Those doggone turnbuckles started loosening up from vibration, and I had to send old John out on the wings to tighten them up."

Claude eyed the young flyer and backed off.

"Say, Lloyd, just how much flying time have you had?"

O'Donnell glanced at his shoes and answered, "Well, before I came down to see you, I hadn't soloed, but I was almost ready. My instructor said I was qualified."

"You mean you made your first solo flight in that plane with a passenger, and then you let the guy do wing-walking on the way home?" Claude asked.

"Yeah," O'Donnell said. "Guess it sounds kind of funny, doesn't it?"

Somewhat later O'Donnell and his friend showed up again. This time they were looking for a seaplane. Claude knew of a twin-pontoon Boeing over at North Island which he agreed to assemble and, somewhat reluctantly, test-fly for O'Donnell. After working on the plane all day, one of Claude's mechanics, Martin Jensen, taxied the plane across San Diego Bay at dusk. The next morning Claude made his debut as a seaplane pilot. Years later, he recalled this account:

"I taxied out with all the boldness in the world, not worrying about a thing. I figured I could fly anything with wings. The plane was logy with the extra weight of the pontoons, and in the first turn it wanted to keep on rolling, requiring far more wheel and rudder than I was used to. But I got it around okay and made a surprisingly good landing.

"I'd completed my contract except for taxiing back to the beach. A strong breeze had come up, and then I found out the hard way what I didn't know about handling seaplanes in a crosswind. Every hundred feet or so it would weathercock into the wind because it had no water rudders, but finally I got her safely onto the beach."

The next day, just when O'Donnell was ready to take off, his wife drove up. With tears running down her cheeks, she pleaded, "Don't fly that thing. You'll kill yourself." But Lloyd would not be put off.

Half an hour after O'Donnell and his mechanic took off for Long Beach, the phone rang in the hangar at Dutch Flats.

"Claude, this is Lloyd. I'm out here in La Jolla. The engine quit on us and we landed beyond the breakers. Coming into shore the plane broke apart, but John and I swam in and we're okay."

Everything must have been okay between Lloyd and Gladys O'Donnell, too, because years later his wife became a famous race pilot in her own right, and a power in California politics.

And so it went during the first days of the Ryan Flying Co., a dollar here and a dollar there, but always building, learning, and building some more.

The Boeing Company

"I found out the hard way what I didn't know about seaplanes." Boeing 1918 model C Navy seaplane trainer.

Tom Mathews

Claude flying the Ryan Standard for publicity pictures. The "passengers" are his two sisters.

CHAPTER SIX

Ryan Standards Fly the Airline

THE YEAR WAS 1924, and Claude Ryan had emerged as a dashing young man about town with an ability to take advantage of every business opportunity. His days were filled with flying, building, and flying some more, and what spare time he had was filled with pursuits suitable for a young bachelor of twenty-six who radiated an aura of adventure.

Word of Claude's enterprise spread throughout southern California, and the business, though small, grew steadily. His financial arrangement with the bus drivers paid off so well that they showed up with more tourists than the small company could accommodate with the two-place Jennies, thus allowing Hawley Bowlus to exercise his mechanical genius to the fullest potential in rebuilding surplus planes.

Ryan latched onto several Standard J-1 biplanes. The Standard was a World War I trainer built of wood and fabric and powered by a four-cylinder 100-hp Hall-Scott engine. It was larger than the Jenny, and it had a two-passenger front cockpit. Ryan wanted to convert the open, front cockpit into a cabin capable of carrying four passengers, a seemingly impossible idea that appealed immediately to Hawley.

There were few precedents to follow, and the conversion depended on Hawley's ingenuity. The difficulties served more as a challenge than an impediment. Hawley devised his own system of engineering, labeled "fingertip aerodynamics" by his colleagues. Here is an example of how

51

Having an understanding with Major Arnold that part of revenue would go to Army Relief fund, Claude carried passengers at Rockwell Field in Standard biplane before it was changed to airline use.

Ryan Aeronautical Library

the system worked, as recalled later by Frank W. Wiley, one of Ryan's early pilots:

"We rode in the cabin and put one hand out each window until our fingertips reached the slipstream. That's the way we determined how wide we could make the cabin."

The Standards took on new dimensions that scarcely resembled the trainers originally developed in New Jersey with the aid of Japanese financing. Sometimes the outcome was pleasing, but puzzling. After the fuselage had been widened about 6 inches, the pilots were surprised to learn that the plane flew faster than before. Nobody knew why, but nobody complained, either.

The passenger compartment was equipped with a hinged cover and open side windows. The fuel tank was removed from the fuselage to enlarge the cabin and replaced by an airfoil-shaped tank mounted on top of the

Pilot Boyd Monteith and a mechanic are ready to close the hinged cabin cover as two passengers board a Ryan Standard for the ninety-minute flight to Los Angeles.

Walter Averett

center section over the upper wing. The pilot rode in an open cockpit, aft of the passenger cabin. In addition, the plane was modified to take a 150-hp Hispano-Suiza engine instead of the Hall-Scott, which had an unfriendly reputation of catching on fire. The airplane could easily carry four passengers and pilot, with baggage tied on the lower wing next to the fuselage. Passengers in the breezy "open" cabin wore light helmets but no goggles.

With three Ryan Standards in operation—each making two or three flights for every visiting bus, at $5 per passenger—tourist excursions provided the Ryan Flying Co. with a sound source of revenue, and before long the firm was operating at a respectable profit.

From the moment tourists boarded the big sightseeing buses in Los Angeles, the drivers—some of whom knew nothing of Claude's expertise as an aviator—extolled his virtues. The drivers tossed in an extra plug for Claude every chance they got, so that by the time the passengers reached San Diego, one of the things they were most interested in was the fantastic aviator whose phenomenal exploits had been so vividly portrayed.

When the buses arrived at Dutch Flats, Claude himself went aboard to make a pitch for aviation, dressed in flight jacket, helmet, and goggles. He was not the sort of fellow who normally sought the spotlight, and generally he shied away from public appearances, but when he had a chance to talk about flying he cut loose with everything he had. It was something he believed in, and he rarely missed a chance to convert others to the passion which had become his whole life.

With business expanding, Claude took on young Tom Mathews, a young chap with a gift for gab, as publicity man and general ramrod. The pay was $10.50 a week and flying lessons. Tom's particular assignment was to help Claude convince the "one foot on the ground" sightseers.

However, Mathews contends, "It was Claude's unique and engaging personality that would talk the passengers out of the buses and into an airplane. He had an honest-to-goodness belief that if he could talk anyone into his first flight, he would change that person's life for the better. Claude talked thousands of people into their first ride and flew a lot of them himself. I, too, acquired a sort of evangelical dedication that started the tourists reaching for their traveler's checks.

"We had as many as fourteen buses on the field at the same time and carried as many as 120 passengers in a ninety-minute period. With the

Sightseeing buses arrived from Los Angeles with more passengers ready to be converted into aviation enthusiasts.

revenue potential $80 per hour per plane, it wasn't unusual for me to walk around with $2,000 in my hip pocket Sunday night after the day's flights."

The new planes proved such a boon to the sightseeing business that in time the fledgling Ryan operation took at least 10,000 persons on their first flight. The passengers were more comfortable in the Ryan Standards, and most important of all, the planes carried a much larger payload. Frequent charter flights—"Los Angeles and Return, Same Day, $40"—expanded the company's reputation and bankroll. As a result, Ryan began shopping around for other ways to use his growing assets.

Ryan helped introduce the first air service to western Mexico when he sold one of the Ryan Standards to businessmen in the small town of Navojoa, Sonora. The plane was flown to the community in seven hours and was duly christened "El Condor del Rio Mayo," which means "The Condor of the River Mayo." The river empties into the Gulf of California at Navojoa.

Not long after, Lloyd O'Donnell—the man who made his passenger go out on the wings of the Jenny to tighten the turnbuckles on his first solo flight, and later cracked the seaplane up in the surf—reappeared.

This time O'Donnell had a new deal.

"Say, I've had a little trouble," he lamented to Ryan, who had little reason to doubt his word. "I'm in a bit of a bind on a situation. I've got a Hisso-Standard and I know you are looking for these Standards and I'd like to have a Jenny. A Jenny's not worth nearly as much as a Standard, but there's one difficulty about this plane.

"I landed in a farmer's field about 4 miles from Santa Ana. It was a forced landing and the farmer is holding the plane because he says I frightened his horses. They jumped through a barbed-wire fence and were injured, and he has a lawsuit against me, tying up the Standard. There's a sheriff's deputy there day and night, making sure I don't come and crank it up and take it away.

"Now, I'll trade you this Standard for a secondhand Jenny worth not half as much, but you have to take it where it is, as is, and you have to take the civil lawsuit, too."

Ryan wasn't too wild about buying a lawsuit, but he was mightily anxious to get his hands on the Standard, and he decided to take a look. He went to Santa Ana and looked up the farmer, and sure enough the sheriff's deputy was on the job, badge and all.

Ryan sized up the farmer as a nice guy who had just wanted to squeeze a few bucks out of O'Donnell. Ryan found out he could get the airplane released by putting up a bond, which he acquired for about $10. After making temporary engine repairs in the field, Ryan took off for San Diego in his newest Standard.

Ryan was alone, since he didn't want to trust the plane with its unreliable engine to anyone else. He got as far as San Onofre, about 45 miles up the coast from San Diego, and the engine quit cold. He picked out an alfalfa field and set the plane down.

The engine was really sick, and Ryan knew he could not fly the plane the rest of the way. He hitched a ride to San Diego and made a deal with a couple of fellows who were playing around with airplanes and engines. He agreed to sell them the engine for $75 if they would go up to San Onofre, take the wings off the Standard, and tow the plane back to San Diego.

Eventually, the Standard was put in good flying order. In the meantime the lawsuit had come up in Santa Ana, but by then Ryan had filed a brief and a counterlawsuit.

Agnes Allen Robinson

Four helmeted passengers pose in front of the Standard as pilot George Allen swings aboard.

Ryan Aeronautical Library

Claude had a girl friend, Robin, who used to pick him up at the field after hours in her shiny blue Packard. Instead of flying as they often did, they drove to Santa Ana in the car. When Claude reached the courthouse, he spotted the farmer sitting on the steps and went up and sat down beside him.

"You know," Ryan told the farmer, "this is pretty silly. You're suing me and you're not mad at me, and I'm suing you and I'm not mad at you, and the lawyers will get most of the money anyway."

Ryan eyed the farmer for a moment and then said:

"Why don't we call the whole thing off?"

"That's a good idea," the farmer said. So they went to the judge and told him to forget the whole thing.

Not only had Claude secured himself another Standard, but the episode had sharpened his image in Robin's eyes. The young lady, who was beautiful and wealthy, began seeing more and more of Claude, to the envy of his friends and the consternation of her mother.

Robin's mother thought her daughter could do better than tie up with a "hairbrained aviator," and she got a little worried that the affair might go too far. Besides, she already had a dentist picked out for Robin back East.

"I'm sending you back to Rochester," Robin's mother informed her daughter one day.

The news added new fire to the romance between Robin and Claude, but Robin had decided it would be all or nothing. Shortly before she was scheduled to leave, they took a little ride on a country road, out where they could be alone. Eventually, the conversation got around to matrimony.

"Have you ever had a fellow propose to you?" Claude asked.

"Oh yes, I've had several fellows propose to me."

"Well, I've never proposed to a girl and I'm not about to. You couldn't get me to propose to you if you tried because I don't want to get married, not for a long time yet, to you or anybody."

"Oh come on, just to have the experience, why don't you propose to me? I promise I won't take you up."

"I'm not taking any chances like that."

Claude's friends thought he was nuts. Robin had everything a man could want, and he had passed her up. In spite of his decision, however, Claude knew he would miss her. Robin had a great sense of humor, and they had had many good times together.

A couple of days later, her mother put Robin on the train. The train pulled out of the depot and headed south. The route took it down to the Mexican border, and then east.

Moments after leaving San Diego, Robin glanced out her window, and there was that "hairbrained aviator," hedgehopping alongside the train in his Jenny. Every now and then he zipped up a few feet to clear the telegraph wires, but most of the time he kept his plane opposite Robin's window.

Robert Watts

Just as in the early movies, Claude flew formation with the departing train, all in the interest of romance.

When the obstacles became too formidable on Robin's side of the train, Claude hopped over to the other side for awhile, and then back again. Meanwhile, Robin had gone to the open observation car for a final farewell wave. All the passengers aboard the train followed his maneuvers, running from one side to the other, curious about that strange fellow in the flying machine.

Life wasn't nearly as exciting for Robin after she reached Rochester, and for several months she wrote Claude, even after she got married. Finally, a letter arrived that began something like this:

"You wouldn't recognize me now. I'm getting quite matronly looking."

Claude didn't answer it.

And it was back to business for the airborne romeo.

56

B. Franklin Mahoney arrived on the scene in 1924 and early the next spring became a partner in Ryan Flying Co.

One productive sideline—training pilots—had been in operation since the earliest days on the flight strip on the waterfront. Young men who wanted to get into aviation on the ground floor continued to present themselves to the Ryan Flying Co. Some paid for their training by working in the shop. Others were better heeled. One such man was B. Franklin Mahoney, who arrived at Dutch Flats one day in a nifty sports car.

Mahoney was a bold and brazen—but likable—chap of twenty-three, with a lot of imagination and more money than judgment. He had grown up without learning how to work and had inherited a comfortable pile of money from his father, a prosperous merchant in Wilkes-Barre, Pennsylvania. The young Mahoney moved to San Diego with his widowed mother, Mrs. Jennie Mahoney, and there he met and married Helen Post, the daughter of a prominent San Diego family.

All was not peaches and cream between Mahoney and his wife, however, so the young sportsman began spending more and more time at the airport—after he signed up with Claude for flight training—and less and less time at home. He was fascinated by the planes, and he associated with Claude and the other pilots as much as possible. As a result, the two men struck up a friendship which was to have a profound effect upon Ryan and the history of aviation.

The newcomer wanted more than anything to get into aviation, and, if possible, become a part of Ryan's organization. He admired the mystique and the courage of the pilots, and Ryan himself had taught him to fly. But that was not enough. Several months later, while the two men were having dinner together, Mahoney advanced a bold idea. Since Ryan was already making numerous charter flights to Los Angeles, why not start a regular airline?

The idea had some merit. Ryan learned that the government was anxious to unload still more Standards, since the trainers had been replaced by newer Jennies. If he could buy more planes, and rebuild them like the others he was using in his sightseeing operation, and if he could find a field in Los Angeles, and if he could round up enough passengers. . . .

Still, such a venture would require him to spread his assets so thin that if the airline didn't carry its share of the load, his whole company might fold.

That was just what Mahoney hoped he would say.

"Let's go ahead," Mahoney urged. "We'll set it up as a partnership. You supply the planes and the pilots and all the equipment. I'll underwrite the airline operation. Any time you don't make ends meet, I'll put in whatever you need. We can split the airline profits, if there are any."

Ryan was not anxious to enter a partnership on any grounds, but it would give him a chance to expand without the risk of going it alone. He knew little about Mahoney, except that he owned property in downtown San Diego and had worked a while as a bond salesman. Claude was first inclined to say no, but he knew that the airline, even if it was not profitable, would earn publicity for the company's charter and sightseeing flights, for pilot training, and for airplane sales and service.

Even allowing for Mahoney's flamboyance and frequent bad judgment, it was a fair offer. Ryan had little to lose, and much to gain.

"And so we made a deal," Claude explained years later. "Five weeks after we started the airline, I sold him a half interest but didn't receive any cash. Mahoney just added his funds to our operation, doubling the capital the company would otherwise have had. The $7,500 he put in just about matched the cost of the planes I had at the time."

Thus began a strange partnership, and, unknown to Ryan, the first rays of a deep shadow crossed his path.

What kind of men were the partners? One who knew and worked with both was publicist Tom Mathews. "Mahoney supplied the money and

Los Angeles-San Diego Air Line

FIELDS:

LOS ANGELES, 99TH & WESTERN AVE.
TRORNWALL 6901

SAN DIEGO, ADJOINING P. T. LOMA GOLF LINKS
MAIN 4688

T. CLAUDE RYAN

The six-place Ryan Standard "Palomar" became the flagship of the fleet.

Glass plate negative/Walter Averett

enthusiasm for expansion," he wrote, "the makings and incentive for parties, and the stubborn amiability that got impossible things accomplished. His mother, a grand dame in the comfortable manner, gave the operation a certain touch of class.

"Claude went along with this—he had a good sense of humor, enjoyed the parties, and got along with everybody—but generally he was all business. He always explored every possible way to get something done without spending money before he would jump into the spending of it. I never considered Claude tight or frugal, just careful with money—a very good attribute."

Ryan bid on the disassembled Standards, which were stored in Texas, and bought them for several hundred dollars apiece. The planes were shipped to San Diego, and it was obvious why Ryan had been able to buy them for such a low price. "They had no engines and were really just a batch of parts," Ryan recalled.

But in spite of the condition, Hawley set out to put the Standards in order. Others working on the Standards included former Army pilots C. R. (Dick) Bowman and O. R. McNeel, Burnett, van der Linde, and Martin Jensen, who later became a famous pilot. Still others joined the ranks as the airline progressed.

All the planes were outfitted for airline or charter use. The third plane in the group was widened more than the others, and the larger 180-hp Hisso engine was installed. There was a side-by-side rear cockpit, allowing for either a second pilot or a mechanic, whichever seemed more urgent at the moment. This six-place version used two upper wings instead of the usual large upper and a smaller lower wing. It was the flagship of the line for awhile, and was christened with due ceremony as the *Palomar,* a name borrowed from the Spanish-style apartment house where Ryan and Mahoney shared quarters.

"The Standards at sea level would carry any load that could be put in them or tied on them," Wiley recalled. "They were very forgiving, but it took a husky pilot to move the controls. You could work yourself to death trying to make them fly level, but if you ignored their attitude, they would eventually level up because of their inherent stability."

Ryan had hired a few more employees in preparation for the establishment of the airline, including pilots George Allen, Boyd (Monty) Monteith, a fellow army cadet from March Field, and Charles Widmer.

A Ryan terminal was established on a small field at Western Avenue and 99th Street in Los Angeles. Mahoney moved there, bought a home, and oversaw the operation for a time. At both ends of the airline Ryan operated pilot training schools, flying service, airplane brokerage, and charter trips.

One of the men, hired later to run the show at the Los Angeles end of the line, was J. B. Alexander, an experienced automobile salesman. His first assignment was to get a lease on a parcel of open land nearer downtown Los Angeles than the site they were using. When he succeeded, the field was moved to Angeles Mesa Drive, now Crenshaw Boulevard, in the Baldwin Hills area.

One of the mechanics at the Los Angeles terminal was Douglas Corrigan. Years later he achieved fame as "Wrong Way" Corrigan for his flight to Ireland in a nine-year-old plane he fitted out in his spare time at the Ryan shops in San Diego.

Ryan calculated that he could make a round trip between San Diego and Los Angeles for about $22.50 and break even, so the airline fare was set at that figure. Thus it took only one passenger to stay in the black.

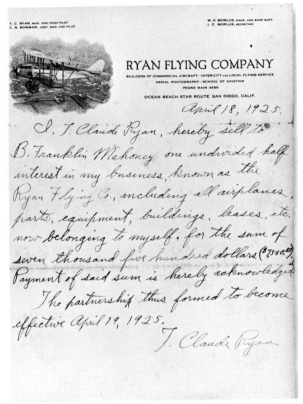

"His mother, Mrs. Jennie Mahoney, gave the operation a certain touch of class."

59

A Ryan Standard and Mahoney's TM Scout at the
Los Angeles terminal, 1925.

Frank Wiley/Montana Aeronautics Commission

One-way fare was set at $14.50 and the price included "motor car transportation" to hotels.

Daily flights were set up to leave Los Angeles at 10:00 A.M. and arrive in San Diego at 11:30 A.M.; and leave San Diego at 4:00 P.M. and arrive in Los Angeles at 5:30 P.M. The airline listed speed, safety, and comfort as its primary assets.

Finally, on March 1, 1925, Ryan, who had seen his first airplane just fourteen years earlier, made aviation history as the nation's first year-around regularly scheduled passenger airline made its debut.

Hollywood celebrities, including movie director Robert Vignola and actress Vera Reynolds, helped launch the operation. They were passengers aboard the plane Claude was piloting, one of the three planes on the inaugural flight out of Los Angeles. Scores of onlookers gathered at Dutch Flats to witness the first arrival of a Ryan Airlines, Inc., scheduled flight.

For year-around weather, the route was one of the best in the country. Even so, the fog and occasional rains could be a problem. The windshield of the open cockpit had no wipers, of course, and that made flying in bad weather a problem. The solution was fairly simple, Claude recalled. "When it rained I'd just stand up in the cockpit and look over the windshield. At 80 mph and 100 feet altitude we could get along okay. As soon as we got over the ocean near Huntington Beach when flying south we had it made. We knew there weren't any power lines to worry about over the water!"

Christened the "Los Angeles–San Diego Air Line," the operation immodestly referred to air transportation as "the most perfect form of travel known to man."

A great step forward it may have been, but perfect it wasn't.

The first forced landing came soon thereafter. As told by Wiley:

"I was riding with Charlie Widmer in the *Palomar*. We were going to Los Angeles from San Diego without passengers, both of us riding in the side-by-side rear cockpit. The coastal fog extended inland to the mountains and we were flying on top. Near Oceanside, the unpredictable French Hisso quit, and with understandable misgivings Charlie glided down into the fog, which was right down to treetop level.

"As we came out underneath the overcast, we glided over a big tide flat and Charlie gave me that clipped-mustachioed smile of his. I had seen

Dick Bowman

soft mud on my side, and I shouted to him that we were going to nose over. He smiled again, and the old *Palomar* buried her nose in the mud, leaving us dangling upside down about 10 feet off the tide flat.

"I unfastened Charlie's belt for him and he fell into the mud on his back, uninjured. Hanging upside down from a safety belt is a bit awkward, and when I unfastened my belt I fell out too, on the back of my neck. This made Charlie feel better. It took the whole Ryan crew plus the staff two days to dig the old bird out of the mud."

That was not a good month for Widmer. Mathews later recalled this incident that occurred at Dutch Flats a few days after the forced landing:

The $5 expense for a forced landing hardly seems unreasonable by today's airline standards.

"Charlie was practicing landings with Wiley and me as passengers when we felt a hell of a jolt. He landed, and Wiley and I ran back to see what we had hit. An egg farmer was sitting in his stripped down Model T—hat knocked off, feet jammed into the three pedals, eyes glazed, and grip frozen on the wheel. The tail skid had hit the hood, the wing panel had bounced off his head, and he was in a daze.

"Wiley took his feet off the pedals, cranked up the car, put the farmer's hat back on, pushed the gear into low, and then into high gear and jumped off.

Hollywood personalities shared the spotlight on the first day of the Los Angeles–San Diego Air Line. Claude Ryan, third from right; B. F. Mahoney far left, back to camera.

"I yelled 'What are you doing? The guy's in a trance.'"

"Yeah?" Wiley answered. "What's wrong with that?"

The Model T disappeared down the road.

Between airline flights, Wiley helped rebuild a Jenny at the Los Angeles terminal. With the job near completion, he put the freshly sanded and varnished fuselage outside the shop, only to see a large cast-iron wheel from a milk truck roll clear across the field and cut the Jenny in two! "Like hot butter," Claude said.

The story may be apocryphal, since Claude was a stickler for safety, but it was said that J. B. Alexander, with only four hours of dual instruction with Widmer, loaded his wife and daughter aboard at Los Angeles and flew them to San Diego. When Wiley asked Charlie why he let him go, his response was that J. B. was the boss and he couldn't stop him.

In spite of its ups and downs, the airline paid its own way during the first months. Fares were raised to $17.50 one-way and $26.50 round trip, but the real profits continued to come from the sightseeing buses that regularly pulled up at Ryan Airport in San Diego and from the charter services.

At one time, one of the Standards was chartered by Tom Mathews to two Boston ladies for $250 a week. Joe Barrows was assigned to fly them around. The money came in for about two weeks, and then nothing—no money, no news, nothing.

Finally, a pilot came along who had seen a cracked-up Ryan Standard at Fresno. As it turned out, Barrows was flying north with his two passengers and he had planned to land at Fresno. It was dark by the time he got there, and since they didn't have lights in those days, he felt around for the field and then tried to set the Standard down. Unfortunately, workmen had been mowing the field earlier and when they finished their work for the day they left their tractor right in the middle of the strip.

Barrows managed to put the Standard down right on top of it. The plane rolled up in a ball. Barrows landed on his head and was pretty vague about the whole thing for months. Later, the plane was rebuilt and sold to a sightseeing company for $2,500.

One of the passengers was cut and lost a tooth. The other, Olga Lesh, wasn't hurt at all. She later became Mrs. Tom Mathews.

One day after a flight over San Diego, a passenger identified himself as being in the sightseeing business in Hawaii and asked if Ryan could provide him a plane and pilot for a similar venture out of Honolulu. The rebuilt Standard was sold for the purpose, and Jensen signed on as pilot. Thus Honolulu's first airborne sightseeing service was inaugurated.

The Ryan Standard created such a commotion in Honolulu that police had to be called to the scene to control traffic. People stood in line to pay $5 for a fifteen-minute flight in the big biplane, which had been named *Malolo* (flying fish).

Money from the airline and from charters helped keep the Ryan company in business, but the tourists still provided the best source of profits.

The local travel agencies pushed the program. One such was the Foster Travel Bureau at the U. S. Grant Hotel, which, according to Mathews, was run by "a personable lady I occasionally took to lunch."

"Claude introduced me to this woman, since he used to keep her rack stuffed with folders before I joined the company," Mathews recalled. "Then he got interested in somebody else and had *me* keep the rack stuffed."

In time the newness of the airline began to wear off, and passengers became less and less available. There were times when flights would leave without a paying guest aboard.

Tom Mathews

Joe Barrows and his "ladies from Boston" passengers. Olga Lesh, center, later became Mrs. Tom Mathews.

Mathews, who had a flare for mixing business with pleasure, was told to drum up a little more business. Unless they could get more passenger business or, hopefully, drum up some new type of business, there was a good chance the airline would fold.

He tried everything, hoping to build up patronage; he worked every angle for publicity.

"One time up in Los Angeles I talked a starlet into taking flying lessons and she came out for her first flight in a silk above-the-knee Charleston thing that looked pretty good climbing into the Jenny.

"We had finished the picture taking and the cameras had left when the girl said she would like to see what it was like to fly. So we stuck a helmet and goggles on her and she and George Allen took off.

"About 200 feet off the ground George put the Jenny into a steep bank and the skirt blew back and jammed the aileron pulley under the seat. George couldn't come out of the bank and a Jenny won't stay up in a 45-degree turn, so they dug in a wing and cartwheeled the plane just as Claude arrived from San Diego with a couple of passengers in the Standard.

"A front strut broke and banged George on the head and he never did remember the flight. The girl wasn't hurt, but to make sure, we took her home and explained what had happened to her mother, who then looked her daughter over very carefully for breaks, punctures, or thumbprints. When everything checked out we got down to some very serious drinking. Every few hours I would introduce George to his passenger to see if I could get a spark of recognition, but nothing.

"Finally, I got the mother to take George into the bedroom and put him to bed. Under those familiar surroundings he finally came to, but couldn't remember how he got there!"

Ryan Aeronautical Library

Businessmen board the Standard for the flight to Los Angeles. Claude Ryan is the airline "captain" on this schedule.

Glass plate negative/Walter Averett

Ryan Standards on the flight line.

They were swinging times, but they were not the best times financially for the airline. It was headed downhill.

"I tried everything," Mathews recalled later. "Spot radio commercials, pretty girls, half-fares for children traveling with adults, convention flights, thirty-day round trips, travel bureaus, everything. By the end of summer of 1926, I added it all up and told Ryan and Mahoney they should discontinue scheduled flights. But Claude was adamant."

Probably the most damaging aspect of the airline's operation was the drain it forced upon the rest of the company. It could have kept going indefinitely, breaking even most of the time and forging slightly ahead occasionally, but it robbed the small firm of some of its best pilots and most of its equipment.

Ryan had used the Los Angeles terminal as a focal point for expanding into other areas. Pilot training and charter flights were conducted out of both Los Angeles and San Diego, and there was a growing demand for more service. But Ryan's potential was limited because, oddly enough, he was saddled with the airline.

He had found an especially lucrative area in the field of real estate charter flights. His planes carried land developers and their prospects all over southern California.

But the airline had become as much a problem as an asset. Unless something could be done to make it more profitable, the door would close on the brief history of the Los Angeles–San Diego Air Line.

Ryan Airlines' new *Cloudster* is the backdrop as Claude Ryan, left, and Franklin Mahoney, front seat, host air power proponent General William E. "Billy" Mitchell, at wheel.

CHAPTER SEVEN

The Cloudster Airliner

IT WAS A LONG SHOT, but Ryan and Mahoney figured it was worth a try.

If the fledgling Los Angeles–San Diego Air Line was to survive, it would not be because of Hollywood starlets or flamboyant publicity stunts.

Survival depended upon attracting customers to the airline because of the airline itself, not because of flashy salesmanship. That meant the airline and charter business would have to offer something new, something no one else could match. And that boiled down to one thing. Ryan knew they had to come up with a new airplane, something that would make the trip between San Diego and Los Angeles a unique experience. But where, in 1925, could such a plane be found?

In Los Angeles, Donald Douglas had gone into business for himself after leaving Glenn L. Martin. He had designed his first plane, and it had already earned a significant reputation. Later he would use it as a proto-type for a new line of torpedo planes to help the Navy protect the Pacific coast from a possible Japanese attack.

Douglas had built the plane in partnership with David R. Davis, a sportsman, who had a singular goal in mind for the ship. Davis wanted to be the first man to fly nonstop, coast-to-coast.

Armed with $100 credit with a hardware firm and a $25 hand drill, Douglas had set out in 1920 to build his first plane on the second floor of the Koll Lumber Mill in Los Angeles. Early the following year, while the plane was still under construction, the race across the continent grew

T. Claude Ryan

Lieut. W. D. Coney and his deHavilland at March Field before transcontinental flight attempt.

The Davis-Douglas partners perch on the stub wing of the huge *Cloudster*. David R. Davis, left, and Donald W. Douglas. Bill Henry, Los Angeles newspaperman, and test pilot Eric Springer, at left.

Douglas Aircraft Company

Douglas Aircraft Company

hotter when Lieut. W. D. Coney took off from Rockwell Field in a special Army DH-4. Equipped with two bottles of coffee and 4 pounds of chocolate, Coney made it as far as Bronte, Texas, where he was forced down by a fuel shortage. The next night he flew on to Jacksonville, Florida, completing his transcontinental hop with only one stop.

The feat added fuel to the aviation fires in the Koll Mill. The main skeleton of Douglas's plane was completed and lowered down an elevator shaft, one piece at a time. The parts were then trucked to the Goodyear Blimp hangar on the outskirts of town, where Douglas had rented a shed. The skin was put on the framework and the gas tanks were installed. The plane was completed one year after it had been started, at a cost of $40,000.

It was a lot of money in those days, but it was a lot of airplane as well. The ship was a biplane with a wing spread of 56 feet, a length of 37 feet, and a height of 12 feet. The fuel tanks, arranged so they could be dropped from the plane, held 660 gallons of fuel. The power plant was a 400-hp Liberty.

Douglas Aircraft Company

Eric Springer, who had also left Martin to join Douglas's small staff as chief test pilot, had inadvertently given the plane its name when he told Douglas that it would be a "real cloud duster." The name was shortened, and the new ship was duly christened the *Cloudster.*

On the first flight attempt, the *Cloudster* ground-looped on takeoff and plopped into a cauliflower bed near the field. No one was hurt, and the plane was not damaged, but the farmer sued Douglas for $55.

In spite of the false start, Springer was so confident of the ship that Douglas planned an appropriate ceremony for its maiden flight at March Field. On February 24, 1921, during the drought of Prohibition, a bottle of champagne was smashed against the nose of the *Cloudster.* The act nearly generated a riot among the spectators, who lurched forward in hopes of catching a drop of the illegal beverage.

Springer took off, circled the field for half an hour, and then landed. Douglas was confident he had a winner.

The *Cloudster* made its first public appearance in March, when Springer took off in 80-degree weather and climbed to 19,160 feet to set a new Pacific Coast altitude record. On June 27, 1921, Douglas and Davis matched the *Cloudster* against the challenge for which it had been created—a nonstop flight from coast-to-coast.

The ship was loaded with enough fuel for thirty-three hours of flying. That would be good for 2,800 miles, some 300 miles more than needed to get to Curtiss Field, Long Island. Springer and Davis climbed aboard and took off. Douglas himself was not on hand at March Field for the event. He was back at the drawing boards, using the knowledge he had gained from the construction of the *Cloudster* to create a new line of planes that carried him into the forefront of the aircraft industry.

The *Cloudster* cruised easily over Arizona and New Mexico, and after 8½ hours the buildings of El Paso, Texas, were below. With the West Coast far behind them, and the history books ahead, Springer and Davis glanced down at the city below—and the engine quit.

The *Cloudster* glided to a soft landing at Fort Bliss on the outskirts of El Paso. A timing gear had stripped, an untimely event at best.

Temporary repairs were completed, and the plane was flown back to Riverside, California, near March Field, where it was stored. While the *Cloudster* was waiting further repairs, two Army lieutenants, Oakley G. Kelly and John A. Macready, succeeded where Springer and Davis had failed. They stepped from their Fokker T-2 at San Diego on May 23, 1923, after a twenty-six-hour-and-fifty-minute flight from New York, nonstop. They had made it on their third attempt.

One of the men on hand to greet them as they stepped from their plane at Rockwell Field was young Army reserve pilot Claude Ryan.

"They pulled out a big thermos jug and served all the Army officers hot coffee, direct from New York City," Ryan recalled years later.

The two pilots told Ryan that when they were investigating the possibility of the flight, they consulted Anthony H. G. Fokker, who built their plane.

"They asked him what altitude they would be able to reach carrying their heavy load of gasoline," Ryan recalled. "Fokker's first computations showed they'd have to fly 10 feet below sea level to make it! When the plane actually took off, it had to fly low, but it used sufficient gas so that by the time they reached the Alleghenies they were able to get over the mountains."

Although their course required them to buck the prevailing west winds, the two Army flyers accomplished their goal and became the first men

Above and below: Pilots of the Fokker T-2 on first nonstop flight coast-to-coast were Lieut. John A. Macready, left below, and Lieut. Oakley G. Kelly.

to fly coast-to-coast, nonstop—some twelve years after Claude had watched Cal Rodgers make the first transcontinental flight in sixty-nine hops.

If the transcontinental flight spelled victory for the Army, it spelled personal defeat for David R. Davis. Davis was a sportsman who had been beaten to the finish line. He immediately lost interest in the *Cloudster* and withdrew from the Douglas company. In the meantime, Douglas had become so involved in the production of torpedo planes that he had little time for the *Cloudster*.

The plane was sold to two businessmen in nearby Venice: Thornton Kinney, son of the founder of Venice, and Benjamin Brodsky. Both men were well-known, successful businessmen, who figured that if the people of southern California flocked to ride the amusements at Venice, surely they would rush to ride the *Cloudster*.

The *Cloudster* was redesigned into a seven-passenger plane, and the enterprise was launched with publicity and much fanfare. Thousands came to see the *Cloudster* at Clover Field, Santa Monica, but too few came to ride it. It was a losing proposition.

Meanwhile, Ryan, Mahoney, and Alexander had decided the *Cloudster* was just the vitamin needed by their airline. The ship had already achieved fame, and was the first airplane to carry the equivalent of its own weight. It had performed beautifully, and, most important, it was large enough to be transformed into an airliner the likes of which the West Coast had not yet seen.

Ryan set out to get his hands on the ship. He contacted Douglas, who gave him the names of the owners. Ryan began negotiations for the purchase of the *Cloudster,* but it seemed almost impossible from the start. He was willing to pay $5,000, but the owners wanted $7,500, and as far as Ryan was concerned they might as well have asked for a million. He flew back to San Diego to contemplate his and Mahoney's dilemma. He was convinced that the *Cloudster* was probably the only way of improving the airline and charter operation enough to make it worth the time and investment required to keep running, but $7,500 was a lot of money.

There was, of course, a way. Ryan had taken on Mahoney as a partner in the company as one means of starting the airline. Mahoney's role was to provide an economic cushion so that if the airline operation went into the red, the company would not go under. So far, the airline had held its own—unspectacularly, but it had held its own. Thus Mahoney's contribution had been some cash and the prospect of more financial backing when needed.

Ryan Aeronautical Library

Three who helped rebuild the *Cloudster* into a cabin plane were, from left, Ed Morrow, Dan Burnett, and John van der Linde.

Servicing the *Cloudster* for a flight to Los Angeles. The three workers are Hawley Bowlus, John van der Linde, and George Allen.

Tom Mathews

Claude in the cockpit of the *Cloudster* while passengers still rode in open cockpits up front.

Glass plate negative/Walter Averett

The partnership was successful in that it had widened the company's economic base through the availability of Mahoney's assets, and thus made credit easier to get. And that made it possible to borrow the money to buy the *Cloudster,* which Ryan decided to do with some misgivings. As Ryan later said, "Mahoney was the plunger of the partnership, I was the conservative." The price of the *Cloudster* was negotiated down to $6,000 and the deal closed.

The *Cloudster* became the possession of Ryan Airlines, Inc., and although Douglas had sold the plane earlier to another party, he was on hand when Ryan arrived at Clover Field to become the third owner. Eric Springer stood nearby as Douglas fondled the *Cloudster* for the last time. Finally, Ryan asked Springer to check him out in the plane. After all, it was the biggest plane Claude had ever contemplated flying.

"You just go ahead and fly it," Springer told Ryan after giving him a cockpit check. "It flies just like any other airplane."

"Egotistical young squirt of a pilot that I was, I said 'okay.'" Ryan recalled years later. "I just got in by myself and took off. I flew around a little bit, landed and then flew on down to San Diego. It was a wonderful airplane."

Back in San Diego, the *Cloudster* looked like a giant beside the Ryan Standards. Some of the fuel tanks had already been ripped out by the Venice owners and that space converted to a crude seating area. The fuselage was so wide that it was possible to seat four people across in bench-type seats in two open cockpits where the fuel tanks had been located. The pilot sat in the rear of the fuselage.

But while such an arrangement had been satisfactory for sightseeing, it would not necessarily do for airline use. And the larger aircraft would be a challenge in many ways.

On its first flight between San Diego and Los Angeles, Ryan piloted the *Cloudster,* carrying his two sisters, some friends, and a paying passenger or two. The 1,200-foot landing strip on Angeles Mesa Boulevard had been

Converting the *Cloudster* to ten-passenger cabin plane.

Ryan Aeronautical Library

adequate for the smaller planes. The area beyond the strip was overrun with weeds and light brush.

Ryan touched down, and was not surprised when the larger plane ran off the end of the strip and into the weeds. But he had not anticipated the results. The spreader board separating the wheels of the *Cloudster's* landing gear cleared the ground by about 8 inches, but it didn't clear the weeds. As the ship roared through the field, the spreader gathered a mountain of weeds. The drag increased so much that toward the end of the run, the plane nosed over and plopped onto its back. That left the passengers dangling upside down, but no one was injured.

The incident required some repairs, which were made at the nearby Douglas factory, after which Claude flew the *Cloudster* back to San Diego with the idea of making major modifications.

Ryan and his men, led by Hawley Bowlus, set out to give the *Cloudster* a touch of elegance. A two-place open cockpit for pilot and copilot was built forward of the seating compartment. The bench seats were ripped out of the passenger seating area, and the two open cockpits were combined into one large, closed cabin. Passengers were seated along a center aisle, five to a side, in the softest plush seats available. The floor was covered with carpeting, dome lights were installed overhead, and ashtrays were mounted along the seats.

The aircraft emerged from its face-lifting with sheer elegance. Although he was unaware of it at the time, Ryan had rebuilt the *Cloudster* into what became the first of the long line of Douglas passenger transports.

Cloudster Rebuild Time for October

Date	1	2	3	6	5	7	8	9	10	12	13	14	15	16	17	19	20	21	22	23	24	25
C.D. Bowlus	8	9½	8	9		8	3	10	4	5½	9	10	9	10½	8	10½	4½	4½	½			
Hawley Bowlus	9	11	8½	3½	7	7	½				2		2						2			
Henry Hunold	8½	8½	8	3½		8½		7^{10}	7½	8½	8½	8½	8½	10	8½	8^{50}	8½	8½	8½	6	1½	
Chunce Wilhite	3													7½	8½	8½	8½	8½	8^{50}	5½	5	
Daniel B. Burnett	10¾	7½	4^{55}	6^{50}		5½	4^{25}	5^{40}	5	4¾	7^{25}	6^{15}	6^{40}	9	8½	7	1^{25}	½	¾			
Stephen Varnie	9^{10}	3	5½	4½		3^{25}	3	5	½	½	4½	2¼	5¼	5¼	8½	7^{25}	2½		1^{10}	1½		
John Van der Linde							½							7¾	5			2	2^{10}		1	
J.B. Stowe	7½	8½		7¾	3	7¼		4	1		3	2	1½	8	8½	8	8	7¾	8½	8	4½	
Charley Mueller	7	3	5½	3½		5	3	8½	8½	6	7¼	2½	6	4	1			1¾	2^{20}	1¾	[illegible]	
J J Harrigan	3¾	2¼												6¾	6^{55}	[illegible]	4^{55}	5½	1^{20}			
George Allen																		1^{40}	7½	7^{10}	6½	1

Claude checked George Allen out as a pilot for the new airliner, and thereafter he and Allen, with van der Linde as copilot and chief mechanic, did most of the flying. Later J. J. (Red) Harrigan was checked out by Claude as the third pilot qualified on the plane.

Whenever there were enough passengers to justify its use, the *Cloudster* was flown on the airline route, and it became the flagship of the Ryan fleet. It was especially adaptable to charter flights, and became a favorite for real estate salesmen and their prospects who wanted a better look at new developments along the southern California coastline. It was used often for charter flights between Los Angeles and the new coastal community of San Clemente, which was being developed by Ole Hanson and Henry Hamilton Cotton.

Years later, passengers who were lucky enough to have made a flight aboard the *Cloudster* remembered the ship and the luxury it afforded far ahead of its time. And many might recall landing in an open field south of San Clemente near the Cotton home, now the Western White House of President Nixon.

But the *Cloudster* alone was not enough. The mid-twenties were difficult years for many people. The novelty of flight attracted a few customers, but passengers who remained faithful to air travel were few and far between. Perhaps the public simply was not ready.

For whatever reason, the airline began to seal its own doom, although, as Ryan said, "It was giving us a lot of advertising and helping our charter and flying school business and also carrying its own weight." There were other fields to conquer, and the airline was draining men, equipment, and energy from Ryan's small firm. No one wanted to see it closed, since it had been the first regularly scheduled, year-around airline in the country. But being first was not enough.

Ryan wanted to expand into other areas—he was working on a new plane of his own design—and he could not do that and continue to carry an airline which was doing no more than breaking even. It was either be an airline operator or an airplane manufacturer. The decision was made. And so, after a year and a half of operation, daily schedules of the Los Angeles–San Diego Air Line were discontinued.

Ryan Aeronautical Library

Above and below: With loading steps and cabin interior, the Ryan-converted Douglas *Cloudster* forecast future airline trends.

Ryan Aeronautical Library

Agnes Allen Robinson

Unfortunately the ladies have been forgotten, but not the men. Co-owners Mahoney and Ryan, left and right; San Diego Mayor John L. Bacon in the center.

These are the only in-flight pictures of the *Cloudster* known to exist. The background of San Diego waterfront is present location of Lindbergh Field.

The *Cloudster* at Ryan Field, Los Angeles terminal of the airline.

The *Cloudster* and two Ryan Standards on the flight line
at Dutch Flats, 1926.

CHAPTER EIGHT

The Beer Run

WHATEVER BECAME OF THE RYAN-DOUGLAS *Cloudster?*

For years the fate of that gallant old bird of aviation's past remained a secret. The question was generally dismissed with the simple explanation that "it cracked up somewhere in Mexico." But as time passed, and more details became known, the story of the demise of the plane that launched Donald Douglas's career, and helped Claude Ryan's along, came out into the open.

The end began on a Monday morning, two weeks before Christmas, 1926. Those were the days of Prohibition, and residents of San Diego and Los Angeles made frequent pilgrimages to Tijuana, just across the border in Baja California, Mexico. The laws of Prohibition did not apply there, and Tijuana celebrated the austerity of the United States Congress with an abundance of booze.

Mahoney was a frequent visitor to the office of the manager of the Aztec Brewing Company's Tijuana warehouse. It was during one of those visits, just a few days before the holiday rush, that Mahoney learned it would probably be a dry celebration for residents of southern California. Heavy rains had washed out 12 miles of road between Mexicali and Tijuana. The brewery was in Mexicali and the tourists were in Tijuana.

As Mahoney and the warehouse manager drank together, the manager related his tale of woe, adding that the governor was in Mexico City for the holidays and no road crew would lift a shovel until he

73

Winter 1926–27, the year of the big flood when Ryan
Airport was under water. John van der Linde is busy
picking up the pieces.

returned. The beer in the warehouse wouldn't last a week.

Mahoney was touched. The story was related years later by Tom
Mathews:

"With each mug of beer the impending crisis seemed nearer at hand,
as indeed it was. Finally, Mahoney got slowly to his feet and walked toward
the door of the warehouse, where he measured a half-keg of beer, arms
outstretched and eyes closed.

"'We can fly these barrels from Mexicali to Tijuana,' Mahoney told
the manager. 'How many do you need?'

"'A thousand barrels will carry us over New Year's,' the manager said,
ecstatic over the prospects of satisfying the needs of his clients. 'You can
do this?'

"'One thousand barrels,' said Mahoney, 'at $10 a barrel—10 percent
down and payment at the end of each week.'"

Later that day Mahoney walked into Ryan's office and tossed a check
for $1,000 on the desk.

"Tomorrow we start flying beer for the Aztec Brewing Company of
Mexicali," Mahoney said.

"I don't think we can do that," Ryan answered, but a moment later
he folded the check and put it in the drawer. He remembered that beer
was legal across the border.

Ryan called Mathews into his office and put him in charge of "the first
beer-hauling airline in history." It was the kind of assignment that appealed to Mathews, who admitted he would rather haul beer than people
any day.

John van der Linde gassed up a Standard, and Claude and Tom took
off on a survey flight. At Tijuana, they picked up the brewery manager,
and then flew over the mountains and circled the brewery at Mexicali
before landing 15 miles southwest at Laguna Salada. This was to be the
camp where Frank Wiley would be in charge of the three-tent operations
base and the five-man Mexican crew. Other pilots and planes would base
at Tijuana.

Initially, only the Ryan Standards were used for the beer run, since Ryan wanted to reserve the *Cloudster* for charter flights. But with four Standards making continual round-robin flights from the 40-mile-long Laguna Salada dry lake, the operation fell behind the tourist thirst by 100 barrels a week. The *Cloudster,* which could carry nearly twice as many barrels as a Standard, was pressed into service, with George Allen and Red Harrigan usually piloting, and from that point on the luxury ship smelled like a brewery.

In order to make more flights, the planes usually landed on a snow-covered mountain meadow just west of the break in the road, but still miles from Tijuana. As Wiley said, "We hauled beer vertically 4,500 feet and horizontally 14 miles." The climb to the mountain airstrip with a full cargo of kegs took forty-five minutes.

The beer was taken by truck over the winding road from the mesa to the warehouse. It took half the night for the Mexicans to drive from the mesa to Tijuana, but the arrangement made it possible to keep up with the demands of the thirsty tourists.

One Sunday morning Mathews was in his hotel room when the manager of the warehouse pounded on his door. He said there was only one plane at Laguna Salada and one plane at Tijuana, and he demanded to know why Mathews had allowed the beer run to slow down at such a crucial moment.

Mathews knew that if more planes weren't flying one of the pilots must be in trouble. Just about that time a truck rolled in from the mesa with forty barrels of beer. The two sleepy Mexicans had been driving most of the night. Mathews rushed out to the truck.

"Was this the last truck off the mesa?" he asked.

"*Si, señor.*"

"Was the big bird on the mesa when you left?"

"No, *señor.*"

"When you got up the big grade, did you look back and see the big bird flying?"

Frank Wiley in cockpit of the beer-hauling Ryan Standard.

Seaplanes would have been more at home at the terminal of the Los Angeles–San Diego Air Line.

The Mexican crew wrestles a few more half-kegs of beer aboard the *Cloudster*.

RYAN AIRLINES, Inc.
BUILDERS OF AIRCRAFT—SCHOOL OF AVIATION

San Diego, California

OFFICE OF
T. CLAUDE RYAN

Allen — 4 trips
6 bbls per trip.

Credit George Allen with twenty-four barrels of beer for the day.

"*Si, señor.*"

"Did it land on the mesa?"

"*Si, señor.*"

"Then why in the hell didn't you go back to meet the plane?"

The Mexican driver looked at Mathews with tired patience.

"*Señor,* we cannot turn around on the mountain, *si? El Piloto* can fly to 'Wana' in half hour? *Si?* We drive all night!"

Pilot Joe Barrows—who didn't drink or swear or smoke—must have landed the *Cloudster* on the mesa and then shut down the engine to wait for the beer to be unloaded. Unfortunately, no one was there to unload it, and no one came back to help him get the *Cloudster* started again so he could fly out. It took three good men to start the big Liberty engine, and he was all alone on a mountain meadow 4,000 feet high covered with 6 inches of snow, and nobody even knew he was stuck.

Taking full advantage of the drama in the situation, Mathews drove back to San Diego and called the local newspapers. Max Miller, a reporter for the now defunct *San Diego Sun* (who later achieved fame as author of *I Cover the Waterfront* and numerous other books) played the story for all it was worth. A pilot was missing in the highlands of Baja California!

The next morning Mahoney flew the "search" plane, carrying Miller and a reporter from the rival *San Diego Union.* He "found" the missing plane, right where he and Mathews knew it was all the time, but he told the reporters he would have to return to San Diego and the stranded plane would have to be reached by a ground party from Tijuana.

Later that day Mathews arranged for Doug Kelley in another plane to fly to the mesa, "rescue" Barrows, and return to San Diego. Back in San Diego, Mathews told Barrows to take a week off and go spend Christmas with his family. Quietly, Mathews ushered the "lost" pilot onto a bus, and then grabbed a copy of the morning paper.

There it was on the front page in bold type—"Pilot Missing, Feared Lost."

Mathews figured Joe wouldn't read the paper on the bus, and by the time he found out about the publicity escapade, it would all be over.

A few days later, the Ryan office phone rang. It was Joe Barrows.

"Hi Joe, how's everything going?" Mathews asked.

"I'm not going to talk to you . . . you . . . you . . . snake-in-the-grass. Put Mr. Ryan on so I can tell him why I'm quitting." He sounded angry.

But fortunately for Mathews, Ryan was in Los Angeles. It seems that Joe had a maiden aunt who had sent a Christmas greeting to Joe's father along with a clipping and penciled notation, "Is this our Joe?" The clipping told about a plane crash in the Sierra de Juarez mountains of Baja California. The pilot had survived the three-day ordeal by living on part of the plane's cargo—beer.

A thirsty country loved the idea of a pilot stranded on a mountain top with nothing to eat or drink but beer, and the story got good play all over the country. Unfortunately, it didn't sit well with Joe's family.

In spite of this and other fiascos, the world's first beer-hauling airline met its challenges well. But on New Year's Eve, just before the end of the tourist boom, the San Andreas fault flexed its muscles, sending shock waves through the Mexican mountains. The earthquake reduced the Aztec Mexicali Brewery to a pile of rubble. "For three days after that," Wiley recalled, "we hauled beer from our stockpile before someone remembered to come out to Laguna Salada and tell us the brewery had been destroyed!"

The beer run was over.

But that still doesn't explain what happened to the *Cloudster*.

Years later, the story finally came out. On one of the last flights of the beer run, the Ryan *Cloudster* landed at Tijuana, with Red Harrigan as

The *Cloudster* and a Ryan Standard at the Laguna Salada operations base for the holiday beer run.

pilot and John van der Linde as copilot. While the beer was being removed from the plane, a Chinese man drove up in a flashy Cadillac and asked the pilots to fly him to Ensenada, since the road there was also washed out.

The hour was late, but if the man would make it worth their time, they might be persuaded, the pilots said. They set the price at $125 and their customer didn't even flinch. He owned several gambling joints in Ensenada and Tijuana, and apparently had plenty of money.

He agreed to the price and showed up about an hour later with five other Chinese, a girl friend, and a slot-machine salesman. It was dark, but the *Cloudster* took off for Ensenada, even though neither Red nor John had landed there before.

They had been told they could land along the beach when the tide was out. They arrived over Ensenada and circled the town. There were no lights, but Red could make out the beach and shoreline and decided to set the big bird down. John pulled back on the stabilizer trim lever as the plane roared over the bathhouse and eased toward the beach. But unfortunately, darkness made it impossible to tell where the beach ended and the water began, and the crew set the plane down somewhere in between.

The wheels of the *Cloudster* dug into the incoming surf and the plane flipped over on its back, dumping the passengers into the water. Harrigan and van der Linde, though shaken up and cut, managed to help their passengers wade ashore. Fortunately, no one was seriously injured.

It was too dark to try to do anything with the plane, so the pilots secured a line to the engine and tied it to a piling on the shore to keep the plane from floating out to sea.

The next morning they hauled in the line, but the waves had chopped the plane to shreds. There wasn't anything left but the engine, landing gear, and a few stray parts.

The days of the *Cloudster* had ended. The wreckage was left in Mexico.

All that's left of the *Cloudster*. Landing gear and wing in background. Funeral services for the Liberty engine are conducted by the crew—John van der Linde and Red Harrigan.

John van der Linde Collection

CHAPTER NINE

Ryan M-1 Takes Wing

ON MAY 15, 1918, the federal government inaugurated airmail service. Major Reuben H. Fleet of the War Department made the first flight between Philadelphia and Washington. The purpose of the new service, obviously, was to improve mail delivery across the country. And while it must be admitted that airmail did enhance the Post Office Department's primary function, secondary values of the new service had at least equal significance.

In the first few years, the mail was flown as far as possible by day, moved on to the next stop by surface transportation at night, then moved again by air the following day, and so on until the mail reached its destination. But as the years passed, the system improved, and by mid-1924 the service extended from the Atlantic to the Pacific, utilizing night flying by setting up lighted airways on the level plains and prairies. Thus it became possible for mail to travel across the entire country by air—day or night.

But the airmail system did far more than merely reduce the time it took for mail to travel from one point to another. Many a young man who wanted to be a professional pilot started his career at the controls of an aging de Havilland biplane with the airmail service and later went on to perform a major role in the developing world of aviation. It was one of the few ways a man could earn a living by flying. But it was indeed risky—three out of four lost their lives during the early period. In order to survive, the pilots had to be good. As a result, those who finished their

Major Reuben H. Fleet, U.S. Signal Corps pilot, at left, was the officer in charge when scheduled air mail service was inaugurated May 15, 1918.

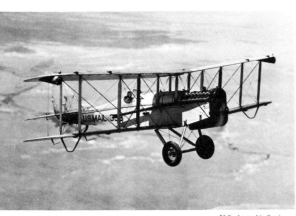

The Army was flying the mail coast-to-coast in 1924 using aging de Havilland biplanes.

time with the airmail service in one piece and then went on to bigger and better things represented the Darwinian law of the "survival of the fittest," and were well-equipped to handle the most difficult challenges offered by aviation.

The de Havillands used by the government were old, expensive to operate, and slow. They left little margin for profit. A new plane had to be found, and that fit in perfectly with Ryan's plans. He had long believed that a stable economic future for his small firm depended upon diversification, especially into the field of manufacturing. And for years he had harbored a bold dream. There was a serious void in airplane design because surplus World War I airplanes were so cheap that no one had bothered to design a new airplane for a long time.

Claude knew the market was ripe for a new concept, suitable for the expanding airmail service, and he firmly believed he had the answer. No one ought to build airplanes, he reasoned, unless he was a pilot himself, really a master pilot, and knew airplanes from the pilot's point of view.

Sometime in the fall of 1925, Ryan walked into the office of his partner, Franklin Mahoney, with a freehand sketch.

"Here's a plane we ought to build," Ryan said as he tossed the drawing on Mahoney's desk.

The drawing showed a sleek monoplane. Ryan's idea was to build a strong fuselage frame, mount a single wing atop this, then leave an area open between wing and fuselage to provide unobstructed visibility, much as in a biplane. It would have doors in the side, like an automobile, for the pilot and two passengers. Later Ryan patented his "parasol" design and assigned rights to Ryan Airlines, Inc., without receiving any payment.

Mahoney glanced out of the corner of his eye at Ryan, who stood before him, arms folded, a stubborn look on his face. Nobody was building anything like the single-engine monoplane the sketch portrayed.

"Look, Franklin," Ryan said as he leaned on the corner of the desk. "You and I fly because we love it. But aviation isn't going to survive off of guys like you and me. For most people, there's really only one reason

UNITED STATES PATENT OFFICE

April 15, 1930.

T. C. RYAN

1,754,529

AEROPLANE

Filed Jan. 13, 1927

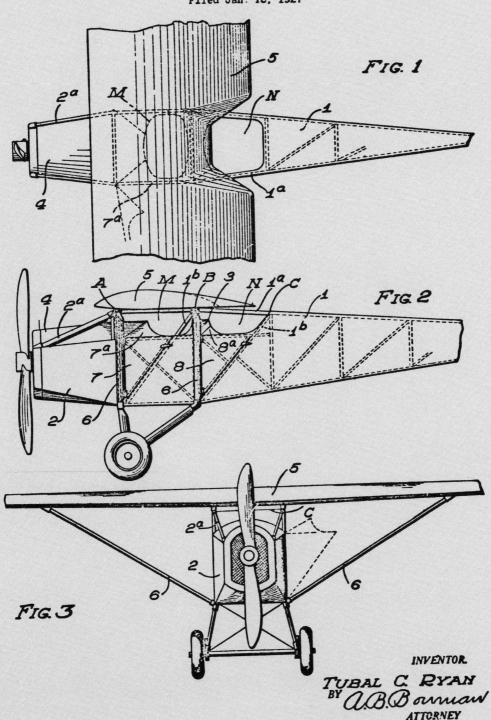

FIG. 1

FIG. 2

FIG. 3

INVENTOR.
TUBAL C. RYAN
BY A.B.Bowman
ATTORNEY

My invention relates to aeroplanes, and more particularly to the monoplane type of aeroplane.

The objects of my invention are; first, to
5 provide a monoplane in which the wing surface is mounted above the fuselage in such a manner that substantially unobstructed vision may be had ahead and downwardly without interference from the wing surface; second,
10 to provide a monoplane of this class where-

Like characters of reference refer to similar parts and portions throughout the several views of the drawings.

The fuselage 1, nose 2, cowling 3, hood 4, wing 5, struts 6, and the doors 7 and 8 constitute the principal parts and portions of my aeroplane structure.

The general shape of the frame of the fuselage 1, behind the nose of the aeroplane, is substantially the same as many now in use

Ryan Aeronautical Library

January, 1926, time card for workers building the first M-1 monoplane.

why they would ever want to fly or send mail by air, and that reason is speed. If they can't get there faster, or send mail faster, by flying than any other way, they'll find another way to get there.

"And there's something else. Flying has got to be cheaper than it is now. One of these days someone is going to build a plane that can fly faster, cheaper, and more efficiently than anything we've got today, and whoever gets there first will have an edge on the airplane market."

Ryan straightened up and motioned toward the sketch.

"That will do it," he said. "We can cruise at 115 mph with a 600-pound payload—just what the airmail contractors need."

"So what are you pushing for?" his partner asked. "I like it. I like it. But what do we do now?"

"The first thing we'll have to do is find engineers to run a stress analysis and work up detailed drawings. It will cost money, but the airline is holding its own, and we've been taking in between $1,500 and $3,500 each week, including our sightseeing flights."

"Right," Mahoney said. "Anything else we need we can borrow."

The two men talked briefly about the idea. They knew if they were going to move at all they had to move quickly. In those days, everybody in aviation knew what everybody else was doing. Although no one was building anything quite like the monoplane Ryan had envisioned, there was talk of such industrial giants as Henry Ford getting into the business with a "flying flivver." If Ryan's basic concept was correct—and he was convinced it was—the competition would be fierce.

That afternoon Ryan flew to Los Angeles to line up engineering help. The pickings were slim, since the number of aircraft engineers—most of them working at Douglas—could be counted on the fingers of one hand. But the team of Bill Waterhouse and Lloyd Royer had a sound reputation. Within a few hours after he had first discussed the project with Mahoney, Ryan was seated in the office of William J. Waterhouse, who had worked at Douglas on the *Cloudster*. Ryan pushed the sketch in front of the engineer, and outlined what he had in mind.

"Uh huh," Waterhouse mumbled after studying the sketch for what seemed like an eternity. "Sure, we can help you. We'll do the stress analysis and make shop drawings, but it will cost $1,000. You can pay us $250 down and the rest as we go along."

Ryan flew back to San Diego, and in a couple of weeks a detailed three-view drawing with general specifications arrived. Ryan called in Hawley Bowlus and spread the drawings before him.

"What do you think?" Ryan asked.

Hawley let out a low, appreciative whistle.

"Great!" he said.

Ryan grabbed his longtime friend by the arm and motioned toward the plans.

"We're going to make this work, Hawley," Ryan said. "Way back in Venice, when we were both trying to learn to fly, I knew right off the bat that you were one of the best mechanics in the world. I knew it then, and I know it now. You've done things with the Standards and the *Cloudster* that everybody else said couldn't be done. But nothing else has mattered as much as this."

Hawley looked at his boss, and felt the tense grip on his arm. In all the years he had known Ryan—from the time they both only dreamed of flying—he had never seen him so excited.

"If I've got anything to say about it," Hawley said as his eyes danced back and forth between Ryan and the plans, "this is going to be the best-built plane around."

A grin spread across Ryan's face as he relaxed his grip. Although he never doubted Hawley's ability, the verbal assurance seemed to ease the anxiety. So much would depend on the young man who stood before him, a man who from time to time would have to substitute raw talents for professional training. But Ryan was a great believer in raw talent.

"What would I do without you?" Ryan asked. For a moment they stared at each other, enjoying the friendship they had shared for so long, anticipating the excitement of the adventure that stretched before them.

In the following days, the monoplane began to take shape under the skilled hands of Hawley and John van der Linde. It was named the M-1 (M for monoplane, and 1 for the first series). The M-1 was an externally braced, open-cockpit, high-wing plane with a 36-foot span. The wings were built with mahogany plywood box spars and wooden ribs. The fuselage was of steel tubing and was fabric-covered. Each step had to be exact, from the welded tubing to the controls. Each piece had to be fitted by hand. There were few precedents, and all members of the crew knew that if they failed with their first M-1, there might not be a second.

In a few weeks a set of fairly complete wing drawings arrived, along with more details on the fuselage. And then the plans stopped coming. Ryan, who had supervised every detail of the plane himself, sent word to Waterhouse that he needed the rest of the plans, especially the tail surfaces. But nothing came.

In the meantime, Tom Mathews, the erstwhile public relations expert, had been sent to Los Angeles to drum up more business for the airline. One morning Ryan sent word to Mathews and told him to go get the rest of the plans from Waterhouse. When Mathews arrived at the small firm, he was surprised to find a plane under construction that looked just like the M-1, although not quite as far along as Ryan's. Mathews introduced himself to Waterhouse.

"He was a quiet type, more like an engineering professor," Mathews recalled years later. "He looked like he knew what he was doing. I told him I had come for some more drawings since our men were running out of work. He asked if I had brought a check. I told him that I didn't have a check with me, but that Ryan would send it.

"Waterhouse said 'No check, no drawings,' and went back to work," Mathews recalled. "I had the feeling he didn't have any more drawings, beyond those we already had and that he was building and drawing for himself, too, as he went along."

Waiting only for installation of the engine, the fuselage of the first M-1 is rolled out of the hangar.

Ed Morrow

Mathews flew back to San Diego and told Ryan about his confrontation with the engineer. When he mentioned that Waterhouse had a similar airplane about as far along as the M-1, Ryan jumped in a Standard and flew to Los Angeles.

"Claude was very easy to get along with," said Mathews. "He never showed annoyance or lost his temper. But if anything could get to him it was a challenge involving honesty."

In a few days Ryan returned to San Diego, grim but determined. He called Hawley and Mahoney into his office and laid it on the line. No one could say for sure whether there had been a misunderstanding with Waterhouse over payment, or design rights to Ryan's concept, or whether there had been a breach of faith. But whatever the cause, Waterhouse was trying to put out his own version of the new monoplane design.

"He's got a lot in his favor," Ryan told the two men. "He obviously has the backing, and his reputation as an engineer is good. If he gets that plane out ahead of us, it's going to hurt."

The three men sat quietly for a moment, and finally Ryan turned toward Hawley.

"Can you finish it up?" Ryan asked.

It was a difficult decision. Without engineering drawings, the plane would have to be finished with the same type of "fingertip aerodynamics" that Hawley had used on the conversion of the Standards. But in the case of the Standard, he had been working with a plane already in wide use. Now, it was a brand-new baby.

"Do you think I can?" he asked Ryan.

"Yes."

"Then let's go."

From that point on, the construction of the M-1 reverted to the tried and true methods that Ryan's crew had used in developing the Ryan Standard. The workmen followed the basic drawings as carefully as possible, allowing an extra margin for safety whenever there was any doubt.

It was a long, uphill climb. And always, there was the fear that Waterhouse might beat them out with his own plane. There were rumors that he was going to sue to get the rest of his money, to recover the drawings, and to stop construction by Ryan. But the men kept working, relying on intuition and natural ability when the drawings seemed lacking. By early February the first M-1 was nearing completion.

Finally, on February 14, 1926, the bird was rolled out in front of the small hangar of the Ryan Flying Co. The signs above the hangar door read "Operators of Los Angeles–San Diego Air Line," "School of Aviation," and now, most importantly, "Builders of Air Craft."

Ryan walked slowly around the plane, buttoning his leather jacket as a brisk wind whipped across Dutch Flats. As he rounded the nose he paused briefly in front of Hawley Bowlus. The two men grinned nervously, and then reassured themselves as Ryan climbed into the open cockpit of the M-1.

Ryan fondled the controls as Bowlus pulled the prop through a couple of times.

The critical moment finally came. Ryan pulled the stick back and peered

The Ryan Flying Co. fleet, March, 1926. From left, two Ryan Standards used on the airline run, the first Ryan M-1 monoplane (Claude Ryan under left wing tip), Mahoney's Thomas-Morse Scout, the *Cloudster*, and a Jenny.

Tom Mathews

Contact! Claude taxis out in the Hisso-powered M-1 for the first flight of the new Ryan monoplane.

Ryan Aeronautical Library

around the cowling, trying to catch a glimpse of Hawley.

"Contact!"

Hawley pulled down on the wooden prop. It whipped around, caught, and the Hispano-Suiza engine roared to life. Ryan fed in the throttle and the tail skid swept around. The young pilot nosed the plane into the wind, and it scooted down the field. In less than 50 feet the tail skid lifted out of the dirt. Moments later, the plane rose over Dutch Flats.

"She's up," Bowlus howled, and then said softly to himself, "Beautiful. . . ."

Some of the crewmen danced an inventive version of the jig on the apron in front of the small firm as the plane rose over San Diego. Somehow, the taste of victory seemed especially sweet. It might not have seemed so if the plane had been entirely the product of engineering specifications, rather than partially a result of personal resourcefulness and determination.

Moments after takeoff, Ryan settled down on the strip at Rockwell Field, where some of his friends were waiting. Lieutenant Lowell Smith—commanding officer of one of the Army forest patrol units, who later achieved fame for an around-the-world flight and in-flight refueling—walked around the M-1.

"You sure that thing can stay up?" he asked, grinning.

"Like a dream," Ryan answered as he climbed out of the cockpit while the plane's engine continued to run smoothly.

"Looks kind of naked with just one wing," Smith snorted. "I think if someone has to fly that thing I would rather it be you than me."

Ryan took the kidding in the good-natured manner it was intended, and then climbed back into the M-1. He waved goodbye and headed off across the field.

Smith yelled to his mechanic and climbed into his de Havilland, the Army's old reliable. The twelve-cylinder Liberty roared and Smith blasted down the field after the speck climbing out over Pt. Loma. Meanwhile, Ryan began putting the M-1 through its paces, unaware of Smith's pursuit.

"Perfect," Ryan whispered to himself as the plane responded to his touch.

He drifted off into a private world, basking in the special joy of having achieved something few other men would ever achieve. This was his bird, a product of his own inventive spirit, something the world would not have had if it had not been for Claude Ryan. That is a satisfaction known to few men, and Ryan was enjoying every minute of it as he guided the M-1 through the clear winter skies above San Diego.

Out of the corner of his eye he caught a glimpse of the blunt nose of Smith's DH. The Army pilot grinned at Ryan as he pulled alongside, and then motioned for a race.

Ryan shoved the stick forward, dropping the nose of the M-1 to pick up speed. The huge wooden prop of the DH clawed at the air as the two planes shot downward. Smith's DH inched forward, the powerful engine spitting flashes of exhaust from its bowels.

Then the M-1 closed up, and the two planes ripped nose to nose toward San Diego Bay.

Ryan watched his airspeed indicator climb to 109 as the altimeter needle wound around and around—6,000—5,000—4,000.

Suddenly the M-1 shuddered a protest and a series of vibrations shot through the plane. Something began to bang, and the noise grew louder and faster. Ryan eased back on the throttle.

He reached up with one hand and grasped the parachute ring, thankful it was there, but wondering silently whether he had the courage to use it and watch his M-1 plunge to earth. As the future of his fledgling company hung in the balance, he checked frantically to see if he could determine the source of vibrations.

He found it. The aluminum strut fairings between the wings and the fuselage had distorted, causing the sleeves to shudder against the internal steel strut they were covering.

If silence really is golden, Ryan was the wealthiest man alive when the plane was throttled back to 84 mph and the clattering stopped.

"That was close," Ryan mumbled. "Won't be needing you after all," he said to himself as he patted the parachute ring.

Ryan circled over the bay and landed at Dutch Flats, a happy and wiser man. On the ground, he leaped from the cockpit and grabbed Hawley's outstretched hand.

"We've done it, Hawley," he yelled, grinning.

After appropriate celebrations over the success of the flight, some hard facts floated to the surface. It was true that the M-1 had flown, and flown reasonably well, but the plane needed some refinements that were beyond the technical expertise of Ryan and his staff of mechanics and pilots.

A few days later Ryan called an old friend, John K. Northrop, and asked for help. Jack was one of the best of the pioneer aircraft engineers and later he achieved fame in his own right. At the time, however, he was working for Donald Douglas. Ryan briefly explained his problem.

"How about doing a bit of moonlighting for me on weekends, Jack?"

"If it's okay with Doug," Northrop said. "I can sure use the money. But I've got a young fellow named Art Mankey who works with me and I'd like to bring him along."

This time Claude's new M-1 design sports a Super Rhone engine.

Forty-three years after the fact, Jack Northrop explains to commentator Clete Roberts how he "moonlighted" on Donald Douglas to work for Claude Ryan (both at right). Another pioneer, Allan Lockheed, is at left.

A call from Claude to Douglas turned the trick but with the proviso: "Remember now, Claude, just weekends."

Ryan agreed, and in a week or so Northrop and Mankey joined the operation, coming to San Diego to work Saturdays and Sundays, redesigning the wing to take out excess weight and otherwise refining the design details.

The box-spar wing construction of the Waterhouse-engineered M-1 was changed over to an I-beam design by Northrop. This, with other changes, reduced the weight by 200 pounds.

The wing got a working over.

When the first production order for the M-1 was received, Claude realized that manufacturing would have to be moved from the cramped operations hangar at Ryan Airport. The handiest factory space available was an abandoned fish cannery on the bay, not far from where he had first set up business with his old surplus Jenny four years earlier.

The cannery reeked with the smell of fish, but it afforded more room and represented a substantial improvement over the operations hangar. Completed fuselages and wings were hauled out to Dutch Flats, where Ryan and Mahoney kept their offices, and final assembly and test flights were conducted there. As with the first M-1, Claude continued to test-fly each new airplane himself.

The plane was flown with a variety of power plants, from 90-hp to 200-hp, made possible by a quick-change engine mount. Among these were the faithful 90-hp OX-5, the 110-hp LeRhone and the 120-hp Super Rhone. But most significant was the new Wright 200-hp J-4 engine, which, with the 150-hp Hisso, became standard equipment on the M-1s. The Hissos and OX-5s were available in abundance from war surplus stock at Rockwell Field.

Meanwhile, in Los Angeles, Waterhouse introduced his Cruzair monoplane. It didn't surprise Ryan that the Cruzair bore a marked similarity to his M-1.

Waterhouse's plane was in direct competition with the M-1, and as a result of promotional attempts for the Cruzair, the dispute between Ryan and Waterhouse became known. Since Waterhouse had withdrawn from the M-1 program before the plane had been finished, the Professional Pilots Association of Southern California raised questions about the airworthiness of the M-1. Waterhouse indicated that his contract had ended before he had completed the stress analysis on all parts of the plane.

Ryan, who was a charter member of the Professional Pilots Association, moved in for the kill. He announced that his plane had been completely engineered to military aerobatic requirements and verified by Northrop. The documentation convinced the association and helped spread the word about a new breed of airplane being built in San Diego.

Waterhouse built three of his monoplanes and then abandoned the venture.

And, in Chicago, a dealer in Ryan planes hired air race pilot Art Chester to produce, hopefully at less cost and with better performance, a plane like the later Ryan M-2. While the appearance was quite similar, the new Yackey monoplane was no match for the M-2. Though the two prototypes did well in a long-distance race, the dealer was killed soon after in an accident resulting from structural failure. That pretty well ended competition from "copies" of the Ryan monoplanes.

The men who made the M-1 go—Claude Ryan and Franklin Mahoney with sales manager J. B. Alexander in the middle (pun intended). John van der Linde is on the wing gassing the first Wright Whirlwind-powered M-1.

Tom Mathews

M-1 with 150-hp Hisso engine for Colorado Airways.

CHAPTER TEN

M-1s for the Air Mail

THE RYAN OPERATION IN SAN DIEGO had been watched from afar with much interest by Vern C. Gorst, of North Bend, Oregon. Gorst had been in the transportation business for years and had done some flying with Silas Christofferson. He had bought his first airplane as early as 1913, and owned six struggling bus lines which operated over short routes all the way from Medford, Oregon, to Santa Monica, California.

Although Gorst had little capital to expand his business, he recognized aviation as a potential threat to his bus lines, particularly with the inauguration of commercial airmail service. But it was primarily his interest in learning about operations such as the Los Angeles–San Diego Air Line which took him to San Diego while the first M-1 was under construction.

Although Ryan was skeptical of Gorst's financial capabilities to organize a company to bid on the Los Angeles–Seattle airmail route, he was not one to pass up any possibility. He convinced Gorst that if he really meant business about getting into aviation, the first thing he should do was learn to fly.

"You've got to know enough about flying for others to have confidence in you," Ryan told him. "You can't run an airline unless you know something about airplanes. You ought to have a pilot's license yourself."

This appeared reasonable to Gorst. He stayed to take flying lessons, given "at the regular rates" by the company's top pilot—Claude Ryan himself.

Ryan not only taught Gorst to fly, but helped him lay out the airline

91

For new Los Angeles–Seattle night mail route, Vern C. Gorst, center, bought Ryan M-1 monoplanes. Claude Ryan, left, flew survey flight. Partner B. F. Mahoney, at right.

Claude Ryan's pocket memo in which he entered during winter 1925–1926 the names of Contract Air Mail award winners. This became his "prospect list" for selling Ryan M-1 monoplanes. A pilot for C.A.M. 2 later made aviation history.

CAM 1.
Colonial Air Transport Inc.
Boston, Mass.

CAM 2
Robertson Aircraft Corp.
Anglum, Mo.

C.A.M. 3.
National Air Transport. Inc.
310 So. Michigan Av.
Chicago, Ill.

C.A.M. 4.
Western Air Express Inc.
810 W. M. Garland Bld.
Los Angeles.

C.A.M. 5
Walter T. Varney
154 Pine St
S. F. or
Boise, Idaho.
Elko, Nevada or
Pasco, Wn.

route and prepare his proposal to the Post Office Department. And he saw to it that Gorst watched the M-1 while under development and learned of the advanced design concept which made it suitable for his proposed contract airmail operations.

But still Gorst lacked the financial backing necessary to be regarded as a potential customer for the M-1.

One day, while Gorst was in San Diego, Claude piloted one of the scheduled Ryan Airlines flights to Los Angeles. Moments after landing, a chauffeured Pierce Arrow rolled alongside the plane and a well-dressed man in a fur-collared coat stepped out. The man, obviously affluent, introduced himself as C. N. Comstock, a retired Eastern banker.

"I read in the *Los Angeles Times* here recently about the new airmail contracts," Comstock said. "Do you suppose the company trying to get the route here on the Pacific Coast needs some additional financial backing? If so, I'd like to buy in."

Ryan wondered for a moment if he was dreaming, then set about to make full use of the ready-made opportunity. He arranged a meeting between Gorst and Comstock, and out of that grew the formation of a new company, Pacific Air Transport. In time, PAT would become a part of the nationwide United Air Lines network, but nobody had such bold thoughts in 1926.

Gorst regarded Claude Ryan as his aviation "adviser," although no formal agreement had been made. He returned to North Bend, and before long contacted Ryan again with word that he had been awarded the Pacific Coast airmail contract on January 26, 1926, and would be in the market for six or seven planes to start his operation. Contract Air Mail route no. 8 was the longest awarded by the government, and Gorst needed all the technical assistance available. Gorst said that although he personally favored the M-1, he felt he should make a tour of the United States to see what else was available, and he wanted Ryan to go along as his adviser.

It was out of the question for Ryan to leave the business at that time, and so he convinced Gorst to take along the sales manager Claude had recently hired—J. B. Alexander, a Los Angeles automobile man. Ryan explained to Alexander that Gorst liked planes so much he would want to buy every one he saw during the tour. Therefore, Alexander had only one assignment as far as Ryan was concerned—keep Gorst from buying anyone else's planes.

Comstock accompanied Gorst and Alexander on the trip around the country. Following the tour, Alexander reported back to Ryan. He had managed to keep Gorst from buying the competitors' equipment, but in the process he had been forced to bend the facts a few times, and the relationship had become somewhat strained. To make matters worse, Alexander said he had allowed himself to be pressured by Comstock into pledging $16,500 of Ryan's money to PAT to help get the operation off the ground.

"They're a bit mad at me," Alexander said. "I think you better take it from here."

Ryan told Comstock that Alexander was not authorized to make such a commitment, and that the company did not have $16,500 to invest in PAT. After all, Claude's objective was to get money from potential airline operators, not give it to them to finance their operations.

For awhile the whole thing hung in the balance, but Gorst was on hand the day the M-1 went through test paces requested by Comstock—carrying a 600-pound load of sandbags, the payload required for the airmail service. The sparkling performance of the M-1 reenergized Gorst, who had asked Ryan to demonstrate the plane with a Wright J-4 Whirlwind 200-hp engine installed instead of the 150-hp Hispano-Suiza. Then the plane was to be flown by Ryan on a survey flight of the Los Angeles–Seattle route to prove the ship's superiority.

C.A.M.6. Ford Motor Co...
Dearborn Mech

C.A.M.7. Ford Motor Co
Dearborn, Mich.

C.A.M.8.
Pacific Air Transport
509 Balboa Bd.
S.F.

C.A.M.9.
Charles Dickinson
Rm. 132 Autetoria Hotel
Chicago, Ill.

C.A.M.10.
Florida Airways Corp
50 E. 42nd St.
New York City

C.A.M.11
Clifford Ball
503 Standard Life Bd.
Pittsburg, Pa.

C.A.M.12
Colorado Airways Inc.
1227 Broadway
Denver, Colo.

Ryan Aeronautical Library

First Ryan M-1 with Whirlwind J-4 engine gets a final check at Dutch Flats before leaving on survey flight.

The Seattle Daily Times

SEATTLE, WASHINGTON, THURSDAY, MARCH 18, 1926.

PLANE SETS RECORD FOR S. F. TO SEATTLE FLIGHT

Newsreel footage from Tom Mathews

Refueling at an intermediate stop with a sandwich and a bottle of milk, Claude is off on the next leg of his survey flight for Pacific Air Transport.

In March, 1926, just a month after the first test flight in his new plane, Ryan set out from Los Angeles for Seattle with Gorst and Comstock, their luggage, and a token amount of airmail. Clouds socked in the airway over the Tehachapi Mountains to Bakersfield. In those days, before instrument flying, you flew over, under, or around clouds, but not into them. After several unsuccessful attempts to get through, Claude decided to land for fuel on a Mojave Desert lake bed near the borax works where the co-operative manager topped off his tanks. By the time they flew around the cloud cover and landed at Bakersfield, Comstock—not exactly the outdoor type—had decided to return to Los Angeles.

Ryan and Gorst flew on to Fresno for the night. Approaching the small field which was set in a grove of orange trees, Claude knew he would have to make an unusually short landing. There was no wind, the field was hard as concrete, and the plane had no brakes. The M-1 rolled on and on, finally crossing a road and going into a small ditch at the edge of the trees. Then something on the landing gear let go. A fitting had failed.

United Air Lines

Pioneers Gorst and Ryan on the PAT survey flight arrive in Seattle after record-setting flight.

The man whose ranch the plane had landed on and his son came over and offered the hospitality of their home for the night and the use of their blacksmithing equipment in the barn the next morning. With repairs made, the intrepid airmail pioneers were again on their way.

After leaving Crissy Field at San Francisco, Claude was flying over ground familiar from forest patrol, and Gorst knew Oregon and the Pacific Northwest well, so pilot and copilot breezed into Seattle in the record time of seven hours, three minutes. Other intercity records had been broken along the way, and at nearly every stop postmasters anxious to promote the new airmail route had been on hand to greet the fliers.

Bolstered by the performance, Ryan allowed himself to get into an argument during a stop at Pearson Field, Vancouver, Washington, on the return trip. Ryan insisted that his M-1 would do 135 mph and could beat the DH in a match race. Not just any de Havilland, but the special two-place 400-hp craft—considered the fastest and most powerful in the Air Corps—piloted by the famed Lieut. Oakley Kelly, then commanding officer of Pearson Field.

It was a bold claim.

Kelly was one of the nation's aviation heroes at the time. After all, he had made the first nonstop transcontinental flight in May, 1923. One of the men who greeted him when he arrived at San Diego had been a young pilot by the name of Claude Ryan. Now, a mere three years later, Ryan was challenging Kelly to a race, and Ryan would fly a plane he conceived and built, with half the power of the DH.

The race would consist of three laps over a 2½ mile course.

Ryan had expected a friendly bout, but it began to shape up as something else. All through the night Air Corps mechanics swarmed over the DH, tuning it up and pouring special fuel into its tanks. Ryan had no mechanic. The M-1 sat to one side. It would use ordinary automobile gas as fuel.

There was a big crowd on hand the next morning, and it was a field day for bookies. Most bettors took the DH, by far the odds-on favorite.

The bookies will long remember that day: The de Havilland lost.

It was an easy victory for the M-1. Claude got off the ground in half the distance Kelly took to get the powerful de Havilland in the air, and with each lap the M-1 widened the gap between the planes. One of the biggest winners insisted on giving Ryan part of his winnings.

In an article in the Portland *Oregonian*, Kelly cited the race as an indication that the Air Corps had failed to keep pace with commercial aviation.

"Here's my machine with a 400-hp motor with less speed than Ryan's with a 200-hp motor," Kelly said. "I'm dragging around a lot of struts and wires that aren't necessary to the modern planes. My machine was built by the government in 1917, and Ryan's was built this year."

Kelly took the loss more gracefully than some of his superiors. Ryan was warned by one Army general that he had greatly embarrassed the Army and would live to regret it.

It mattered little to Ryan at that point, but, as he observed long afterward, "It was years before I ever got a government contract!"

Gorst immediately ordered six M-1s equipped with Wright engines. The airframes were priced at $2,400 each, a total of $14,400; the engines were an additional $5,000 each.

Later that year Ryan introduced the M-2, a refinement of the M-1 with the improved wing engineered by Northrop. A group was sold to Colorado Airways of Denver. Others went to air-service operators back east and

95

AIR RACE STAGED AT PEARSON FIELD

T. Claude Ryan Defeats Lieutenant Kelly.

BIG ARMY PLANE DISTANCED

Officer Declares Military Airship Outclassed.

NEW VEHICLES WANTED

400-Horsepower Liberty Engine Unable to Pull Craft Fast as Small Machine Goes.

VANCOUVER, Wash., March 21.—(Special.)-T. Claude Ryan, flying the Ryan M-1, a monoplane and the first machine built for the Pacific coast air mail route from Seattle south, won a match race from Lieutenant Oakley G. Kelly, command-

Portland Oregonian

First southbound airmail from Seattle is handed to Los Angeles postmaster J. J. O'Brien, right, by C. N. Comstock of PAT. Survey flight pilot Claude Ryan at left.

Illustrated Daily News, Los Angeles

Ryan Aeronautical Library

Hawley Bowlus, builder of the air mail planes.

one more to PAT. Occasionally a Hisso-powered M-1 would be used by Ryan for passengers between San Diego and Los Angeles.

By late August, Claude had seen the advantage of having full-time engineering talent "to make a rounded-out airplane manufacturing organization," and was corresponding with Giuseppe M. Bellanca, then affiliated with Wright Aeronautical, about joining the Ryan company. At that time, Claude reported that three M-1s were being produced each month and that fourteen had already been delivered.

Whether or not the record of twenty-three sales the first year is accurate is questionable at this late date, for Mathews recently observed that "Alexander had the orders and deposits, but in many cases the buyers' enthusiasm outran their available credit."

Nearly six months elapsed before PAT started service, on September 15, 1926. Careful preparations were made before venturing over the rugged terrain at night. Additional trial flights were made by George Allen and other pilots to check emergency landing fields and to arrange for location of thirty lighted beacons.

Gorst asked Ryan to join the company as operations manager for the airline, but Claude maintained the position that his future lay in the design and manufacture of planes. However, PAT did sign up Dick Bowman, who was to become a senior United Air Lines captain, George Allen, Charlie Widmer, and Lee Schoenhair as pilots.

Considerable night flying was necessary on the new route. Departure from Los Angeles was at midnight to permit arrival at Seattle at 2:00 the next afternoon. The southbound schedule called for leaving Seattle at 3:45 A.M. and arriving in Los Angeles at 5:00 P.M.

PAT became the first privately operated line to be flown at night. There was no radio navigational assistance, and in the frequent fog and overcast sky, the only aids were the company's own beacons that illuminated the Los Angeles–San Francisco and Portland–Seattle legs of the airway.

George Allen left Ryan in May to fly one of the new M-1s on a PAT charter to Seattle to pick up pictures taken by Roald Amundsen and the dirigible Norge over the North Pole. The flight was a preview of the difficult weather PAT pilots would face in year-around operation. Then

Toughest assignment on PAT was the midnight mail north out of Los Angeles. Ryan veteran George Allen is the pilot.

United Air Lines

Allen began additional survey flights to select emergency fields and locations for the night beacons.

His bride Agnes, a former Ryan secretary, rode in the front cockpit, following their flight on a road map. When there was a location to be marked, George would gun the engine to attract Agnes's attention. One finger held up by George was the signal to make a red mark on the map location; two fingers was a blue mark. When they landed, the Allens would get in their car, drive as near as possible to the marked locations, and then proceed on foot.

"In many places," Allen wrote, "it was impossible to bring equipment in by truck. We often had to depend on sheer manpower to move in the steel, cement, sand, and water used to erect the beacons. Once we started flying over the mountains, though, we found the beacons were worth their weight in gold."

Agnes Allen Robinson

Pilot George Allen, second from left, and his bride spent months installing beacons to guide mail planes at night.

Seely V. Hall

Inaugural flights on PAT were made September 15, 1926, this one out of Medford, Oregon.

For the first two months the "service was 98 percent perfect," Gorst reported to the stockholders, but soon there were frequent delays and several accidents because of the inability to obtain adequate weather information for the pilots. Winter storms over the Siskiyous, south of Medford, and Tehachapis, north of Los Angeles, made flying extremely hazardous.

"We never knew when we started out whether we'd get there or not," Bowman recalled. "There was no weather service. Before taking off on a run we would telephone one or two places along the route and inquire of the police chief or constable, or anyone we could arouse, what the weather was like. Then we just guessed the best we could and flew accordingly."

97

Seely V. Hall

PACIFIC AIR TRANSPORT, Inc.

FORM 12 10M 6-26

RADIOGRAM

COPY

Wednesday, October 26

no Los Angeles mail due to Bowman #7 cracking up near Bakersfield.

Vuden 18 Frisco section of todays (and 25ths mail from Bake, Fresno, and L.A.) arrived 9:17 am off 1 wgt 3#8 oz.

Miller 4 left 9:25 am. on 3 wgt 6#15 oz. Part cloudy. no passengers.

Dick Bowman had to get out and walk.

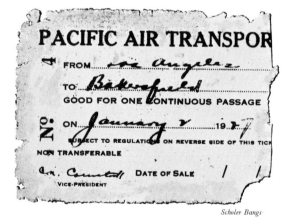

The pilots knew the risks and took them. Ralph Virden, on departing Medford, Oregon, observed that "the weather in the canyon is impassable to anyone but a darn fool." But everyone was so imbued with the commitment "the mail must go through" that no one thought of himself until the mail had reached its destination.

Charlie Widmer had to bail out after leaving Ryan Field at Los Angeles one midnight, and Jim Rutledge had to "hit the silk" in bad weather near Bakersfield. Eddie Neher crashed in a storm front west of Fresno. Allen met a squall line on the Ridge and came into Bakersfield with mesquite brush in his landing gear.

One night in October, 1927, Bowman took off from Saugus, north of Los Angeles, with a storm moving in. At 9,000 feet over the Tehachapi Mountains his carburetor and wings iced up, the plane lost altitude, and the instruments bounced around, "so I had to get out and walk." Bowman landed by parachute at 2:00 A.M. on a 5,500-foot peak, walked to civilization after dawn, and phoned in at 11:00 A.M. to report the accident. They found the remains of the M-1 about a week later.

PAT discouraged passengers traveling in the open-cockpit planes during winter months, but 102 hardy souls had been carried between mid-September and the end of 1926. These pioneer air travelers were willing to pay $132 for the doubtful privilege of being crammed among the mail sacks for the 14-hour journey between Los Angeles and Seattle.

Although mail and passenger revenue totaled $62,600 as of December 31, 1926, Gorst did not achieve the profit level which had been anticipated because the coastwide mail loads were not as heavy as those on the transcontinental route serving Midwestern and Eastern cities.

Seeking financial assistance from the Wells Fargo Bank of San Francisco, Gorst found himself dealing with banker William A. Patterson, a man who later played a vital role as the guiding hand of United Air Lines.

Aircraft mortality the first year of operation was high, according to Bowman, mainly because airway aids were inadequate, and by 1928 the Ryan M-1s were phased out due to attrition.

Ernest L. Smith, one of the airline's pilots, bought one of the M-1s and modified it. In July, 1927, he and Emory B. Bronte, navigator, became the first civilians to fly from California to Hawaii.

Early in 1928, Boeing Air Transport, operators of the Chicago–Salt Lake City route, purchased PAT; both then became part of United Air Lines. By then, the Ryan mail planes had accomplished their pioneering task on the rugged West Coast route.

Ryan and Mahoney remained confident that they could sell all the planes they could build, and they continued to produce even when no orders were on the books. Within a short while they found themselves with five planes nearing completion, deeply in debt, and not a buyer in sight. The future was beginning to look bleak when a man showed up and introduced himself as the owner of a hardware store.

"I've got a contract with an advertising and promotional firm in Pasadena," he said. "They've got big plans for promoting some new product through a nationwide air tour. I'll need five planes. Can you deliver?"

The man offered to put up a deposit, with the balance on delivery within a few days. It was a ready-made deal, since five was exactly the number of planes the company had nearly completed. He showed up about a week later with a down payment and formally placed the order.

The day before the delivery date the planes were finished and polished up, ready to fly. Mahoney and Ryan went down to the local restaurant for breakfast and, as usual, picked up a copy of the morning paper. The

Five Hisso-powered M-1s on the flight line. Four at left were "Mexican Revolution" planes; that at right was mail plane for Colorado Airways.

headline blared that a Mexican revolutionary plot had been uncovered, and the story reported that several trucks had been captured along the border. The agent of the revolutionary band was an American—the same man who had placed the order for five M-1s.

Somehow, breakfast didn't taste so good after all. Ryan and Mahoney returned to the plant, but of course no one showed up to claim the planes. The loss of the sale hurt, but what really troubled Ryan was the fear that he might be suspected of contributing to the revolution. He sat in his office, waiting for the call he knew would come.

Finally a man from the Justice Department showed up.

"Do you know this man?" the investigator asked as he showed Ryan a picture of the man who had placed the order.

"Yes I do," Ryan answered.

"Did he give you a deposit for some planes?"

"Yes he did."

"He's in jail," the investigator said. "He's up on a very serious charge, and the Justice Department intends to prosecute. We will have to attach those planes."

Ryan had expected trouble, but not that. The company was heavily mortgaged, and loss of the five planes could be disastrous.

"This is going to put us under," Ryan said.

"That's not my end of the business. Talk to the United States Attorney."

Ryan and Mahoney immediately went down to see the Attorney, who turned out to be a woman. She admitted that it would be a hardship on the company, but made no concessions.

Ryan hired a local attorney, William Mirow, who managed to convince the woman to release four of the five planes. They were sold over a short period of time, but the fifth plane was held as evidence and rolled across the field from Ryan Airport to be locked up at the Marine Corps Recruit Depot on the other side of the airstrip. The trial dragged on and on. When it finally ended, the man who had placed the order was sent to jail. And Ryan and Mahoney got a dirty, rusting airplane back, the sad remains of the "Mexican Revolution" fleet of M-1s.

RYAN M-1

Ryan Airlines, Inc.
SAN DIEGO

A. ESSIG

CHAPTER ELEVEN

The Plane That Pays a Profit

"THE PLANE THAT PAYS A PROFIT," READ THE HEADLINE on the new Ryan Airlines, Inc., brochure, "designed and executed by Thos. P. Mathews, Adv. Mgr." The sales pitch reflected Claude's own persuasive enthusiasm. Like famed designer William B. Stout, he believed that a plane had to support itself financially as well as aerodynamically.

Tom's literature and a series of trade magazine advertisements featured a monoplane "lighter, faster, and more efficient per horsepower than a similar biplane." The ads attracted attention, but what was needed was a convincing demonstration of the monoplane's safety.

"The trend was toward monoplanes," Ryan explained years later, "but pilots were very skittish of them. While engineers made good stress analyses, they weren't too familiar with aerodynamic loads. Wings did come off, and the record of monoplanes was a checkered one.

"I knew the monoplane was most efficient, but the problem was not only to make it strong enough but to get away from the stigma that monoplanes weren't safe.

"We asked Waterhouse to stress for a load factor of 8, the same as for pursuit aircraft. This permitted acrobatics of all kinds. I had a pursuit pilot's rating, which required proficiency in aerobatics, and I enjoyed doing them, particularly when demonstrating the M-1. I did everything in the book. We went around to air meets and proved that here was one monoplane that the wings would stay on."

101

Vance Breese, beside cockpit, turned the first M-1 inside out demonstrating its excellent aerobatic qualities.

Tom Mathews/Frank Wiley

Ryan ads of the day told the story, too.

> Loop it, barrel-roll it, dive it a thousand feet, and pull back quickly on the stick. Try to whip-stall it, try to spin it. Wind it up in a tight spiral, full throttle, kick top rudder. Give it everything, then float it down and look it over. A biplane would probably need rerigging. But the Ryan M-1 will be just as tight as the day it left the factory.

The Ford Reliability Tour, a sophisticated form of nationwide barnstorming, provided a ready-made audience of knowledgeable pilots. Claude tried to get one of his old instructors at March Field, Ned Shramm, then stationed at Rockwell Field, to make the tour in the M-1, but Ned could not get a leave of absence from the Army. Instead, Claude hired a young pilot named Vance Breese, whom he had seen do some fine stunt flying at San Francisco.

Accompanied by J. B. Alexander, Ryan's sales manager, Breese did an outstanding job on the tour, establishing himself as a fine aerobatic pilot

San Diego-Made Plane Wins Spectacular Honors In East

Sept-10-26

Ryan M-1 Back After Capturing Ford Reliability Grand Sweepstakes and Mile-High Honors

Bringing a silver cup that stands a yard high and also prize money, the Ryan M-1 monoplane, made in San Diego, returned today from two national competitions.

The monoplane has been absent a month durin... ...me it...

the fact it was the only stock-production plane in the event. The others were all specially made with racing equipment.

J. B. Alexander, relief pilot who accompanied Vance Breese, pilot, on the long stretch, state today that the only expenditure in ... of gas an... ...

Ryan Aeronautical Library

Ford Motor Company Archives

Flown in the 1926 Ford Reliability Tour by Vance Breese, the new Ryan M-1 attracted much attention because of its monoplane design.

and the Whirlwind-powered M-1 as an outstanding airplane capable of the most difficult flying maneuvers.

Breese was young, but a natural, and what he lacked in experience he made up for by a passion for flying. Ryan didn't catch the act until the end of the tour at Santa Monica, and then he understood why the M-1 had attracted so much attention.

Breese put the plane through a series of grueling acrobatic stunts, including diving the plane toward the field, rolling over 90 degrees until the wings were vertical, and then flying across the airport, getting enough lift from the side of the fuselage to maintain altitude.

The message got through. The M-1 could take it.

After the tour, Breese was hired by Gorst as a pilot for PAT.

Orders for the M-1 continued to come in, though not exactly at a staggering rate.

Mathews thought he could do something about it.

"Alexander talked me into thinking I was a salesman, so I went to Claude and asked him to send me out on a trip with Joe Barrows. I also did a little talking out in the shop; I told them to keep building because I would probably sell a flock of them. I really wasn't going out there cold because we had at least fifty inquiries about the M-1 from central and northern California."

Claude agreed, but not without some misgivings. "By golly, you'd better sell some M-1s, because if you don't, don't come back!" The comment was only half in jest.

The first stop was Merced, California.

"I remember Merced," Mathews recalled. "I had the name of a Mr. Hunt who had inquired about the M-1. We landed at dusk (it was always just getting dark when Joe decided to land) on the high school practice field and went to the hotel in town. I called Mr. Hunt, who turned out to be a ten-year-old boy. Enthusiastic though! I told him if he would bring his father out the next morning, we would give them a ride, which we did, and so on to the next stop.

"In Sacramento, our prospect was staying at the Senator Hotel. It was about 10:00 P.M. when we finally knocked on his hotel room door. It was opened a crack and then we heard a lot of scurrying around and finally we were let in. I introduced Joe and myself to our prospect and explained

Tom Mathews Collection

Tom Mathews, glib promotion man and raconteur, shown at nose of Whirlwind-powered M-1, still builds and flies racing planes although pushing seventy years.

This ski-equipped M-2 found its way to Canada where it was eventually lost after landing on an ice floe which drifted out to sea. The crew was saved.

National Museum of Canada

Frank Wiley Collection

Among early users of M-1s for business travel was Westland Oil Co. of Montana. Pilot is Frank W. Wiley, veteran of the Ryan Airlines beer run in Mexico. The last remaining M-1 in existence, this plane is now in the San Diego AeroSpace Museum.

we had the plane out at Mather Field. There were four other men in the room—a state senator, a big shot lobbyist, and a couple of our prospect's friends. As soon as they discovered we weren't the house dicks, out came the girls—from closets, under the beds, behind sofas. I wanted to back away, but there were plenty to go around so we joined the party.

"It was shortly after this party that I had to wire down for more money."

Tom and Joe stayed out and their expenses kept running up. "The weather was bad," Claude recalled, "and they had a terrible time—not a single order. Finally I told them to come on home.

"In a few days I had a telephone call from a service station near La Jolla, north of San Diego. There was a nice barley field up there, kind of flat. Tom Mathews was on the phone.

'Your airplane is up here in the barley field. Perfectly okay—we haven't cracked it up. Nothing's the matter except it's just a little worse for wear and tear. A little dirty, a little oil on it, but it's okay, and so . . . we'll see you later.'

"And, you know," Claude recalled, "that's the last I saw of either Mathews or Barrows for years. They just took me at my word that if they didn't sell any planes, not to come back!"

But sales were made, and the plane continued to attract attention. . . .

Not long after Claude's survey flight to Seattle for PAT, Lee Schoenhair flew in the reverse direction—950 miles nonstop from Portland to Los

Frank W. Wiley

To store the former Westland Oil M-1 in his barn, the farmer-owner cut off the wings. Plane was saved from oblivion by Frank Wiley of Montana Aeronautics Commission, by the Northwest North Dakota Historical Society, and by personnel of the Minot Air Force Base.

Angeles in eight hours and fifty minutes.

When "kidnapped" evangelist Aimee Semple McPherson was found on the desert in Arizona, Claude flew an M-1 charter flight for newspapers to bring pictures back, flying at night from Douglas, Arizona, to Los Angeles. He had no parachute and the plane was not equipped for night flying, but he was the first back with the pictures.

At the 1926 National Mile High Air Meet in Denver, the M-1 won every event for airplanes in its class.

Westland Oil Company of Montana was an early buyer. Ryan pilot Frank Wiley, a veteran of the beer run, signed on to fly for Westland. Today, the Westland monoplane, the last known M-1 in existence, is a prize display at the San Diego AeroSpace Museum.

Its cockpits enclosed against the northern Montana cold, Westland's M-1 is enroute from Billings to Scobey.

R. J. Coughlin, Jr./Westland Oil Co.

Later Wiley returned to San Diego for a second Ryan, an M-2, for state senator John Schnitzler. After a forced landing in Nevada caused by a broken copper oil line, Wiley took off, only to have another one because of the bad weather. In a crosswind, the plane drifted off a wagon road where he was trying to land and into the mesquite. It was time to send for help.

"I phoned Hawley Bowlus," Wiley said, "and he and John van der Linde sneaked a new propeller and hub, and a right landing gear, out of the stockroom without the stockroom boss knowing about it.

"They shipped me the parts, prepaid express, and charged them off to engineering—just as aircraft factories have been doing ever since. After all, I found out for them that you just can't fasten a copper oil line rigid to a motor bed and expect it to last very long!"

Except for the usual "incidents"—greatly embellished in the telling by most pilots—all went well for a while.

Orders for the M-1 continued to come in, and the plane was dubbed a great success. Meanwhile, the Los Angeles–San Diego Air Line had been phased out to free more men and funds for production of the M-1.

Claude Ryan's "parasol" wing concept for the M-1 proved to be so flexible that it would be a relatively easy step to enclose the two open cockpits and convert the plane into a cabin craft. Space and horsepower available were adequate for carrying additional passengers, and obviously it would be more comfortable for them to ride in a cabin. Even the rugged, leathery pilots of PAT complained that the open cockpit in bitter winter was a bit too spartan.

The general consensus around the Ryan shop by late 1926 was that the company had better get busy on a cabin model. Again the versatile craftsman, Hawley Bowlus, was called upon. His task: take the first M-2, then under construction using the first Northrop-engineered wing, and

First Ryan "brougham" cabin plane, carrying four passengers and pilot, was the *Bluebird,* an enclosed version of the M-2 powered with the larger 200-hp Hisso-E engine.

make it into a cabin plane. By this time a recent Massachusetts Institute of Technology graduate, Walt Locke, had joined Ryan, and he provided some engineering assistance, although Hawley, as shop superintendent, figured out most of the changes without any drawings.

In the M-1 the pilot flew from the rear cockpit, but in the cabin model the controls and pilot seat were moved forward under the wing in order to provide seats for four passengers in the aft cabin, with a baggage compartment farther to the rear.

The power plant selected was the largest of the Hisso series of water-cooled in-line engines—the 200-hp E model built under license in this country by Wright, makers of the Whirlwind radial engine. The *Bluebird,* so-called because of the color scheme of the cabin plane, retained the 36-ft wing of the M-1.

"It was a nice flying airplane," according to Claude Ryan, who flew it more than anyone else, "although a little hotter on landing and takeoff than the other planes." Everyone agreed that the cabin arrangement was a giant step forward, but Tom Mathews says this particular plane left something to be desired aerodynamically.

In any case, only the one *Bluebird* cabin plane was built, although some M-2 owners later closed in their planes, but it paved the way for subsequent cabin models. A plane in that series was destined to become the most famous plane ever built, but no one in Ryan's shop suspected it in the fall of 1926.

The *Bluebird* came to an ignominious end—with Doug Kelley at the controls and sales manager A. J. Edwards as passenger. In landing at Rogers Field, Los Angeles, Edwards opened the right-hand door to wave to a friend—something you just don't do! Possibly the celebration of the landing of another Ryan plane that day in Paris was a factor.

In any case, the plane went into a side slip, which Doug simply couldn't right. The *Bluebird* flew into the ground and flipped over on its back. The remains were gathered up, trucked back to San Diego, rebuilt into an M-2, and sold. Edwards was trucked to a Los Angeles hospital for treatment of head cuts.

But no one could deny that, overall, the company was moving steadily ahead, particularly in its ability to come up with new and better airplane concepts.

106

PHOTO BY ERICKSON.
2749
5786

H. A. Erickson

Forerunner of the *Spirit of St. Louis*, the Ryan *Bluebird* shows a remarkable similarity to Lindbergh's transatlantic craft.

With 180 Hisso motor, $5100; with Wright Whirlwind motor, $9700.

All prices at San Diego — Wire or write for convincing performance details.

RYAN AIRLINES, Inc., - SAN DIEGO, CALIFORNIA

Aviation Magazine May 2, 1927

Bluebird, first Ryan cabin monoplane, was used to promote the future "Brougham" series. Left to right, Claude Ryan, secretary Georgia Mathias, and salesman Bill Bodie.

CHAPTER TWELVE

Response to a Wire

ALL APPEARED WELL AT RYAN AIRLINES, INC., but all was not as it seemed to be. Friction had developed between Ryan and Mahoney. "They were," Dick Bowman later said, "a mismatch as partners."

As a man of means, Mahoney had developed a taste for the good, casual life, and he enjoyed the role. However, it was with divided loyalties that he started slipping away from business in his mid-twenties—an age at which he somehow worshipped two opposing virtues, hard work, and anything goes.

He knew his marriage to Helen Post was waning. Although his inlaws were leading citizens of San Diego, he found it hard to live up to their expectations.

He was a dapper young man, two years younger than Ryan but already married and the father of two sons. He had a taste for good clothes, and usually wore imported tweed suits. He was a tall, handsome man of medium build, who parted his hair right down the center of his head, and he often wore a tweed cap to match his tweed suit.

If he appeared pompous to some, most people forgave him for it. Years earlier he had learned the fundamental fact that men will forgive most anything if, while trespassing against their nature, you also make them laugh. Thus his friends and associates found him an extremely likable man, one for whom life never seemed dull.

He drove around town in a flashy Templar roadster, which he thought

Ryan Airlines' partners and crew: Standing, from left, Claude Ryan, Charlie Widmer, Hawley Bowlus' father; from right, Franklin Mahoney, Dan Burnett, Bowlus. Kneeling, from right, John van der Linde, Red Harrigan, Gordy Boyd.

Ed Morrow

Mahoney's Thomas-Morse Scout.

appropriate for a man of his calling. There was a hole in the center of the windshield, reportedly made by a bullet. Most people would have had the windshield repaired as soon as possible, but not Mahoney. He left the hole there as a symbolic badge of courage.

Since the environment at home was rather hostile, Mahoney preferred spending his time hanging around the Ryan operations at Dutch Flats. Ryan and Mahoney had struck up a friendship. They were drawn together partly because of their differences, and partly because of the loneliness that showed beneath Mahoney's facade. In spite of his faults, he was an extremely likable man. Ryan did not shun fun, but it was obvious that he cherished his work more. He and Mahoney offered a sharp contrast.

Ryan had taught him to fly, and soon Mahoney had added a Thomas-Morse Scout sport plane to his collection of accessories. He often showed up near closing time, just in time for dinner, and Ryan frequently joined him in a local restaurant. Later they shared an apartment. On the surface, he didn't appear the sort of fellow who would envy another, but he seemed to see in Ryan something he sensed he would never match, a sense of purpose, of dedication, of meaning—things the lack of which must haunt many men in the lonely hours of morning when they are left with no one's company but their own.

Mahoney had had sense enough to know that aviation was more than a fad. It had also been obvious to him that although Ryan was doing well, he did not have the capital to expand as fast as he wanted to. This opened the door that had intrigued Mahoney, and with money as his special asset, he had chipped away at Ryan's seemingly self-sufficient foundation. Now he was an equal partner with Claude. They had started an airline together and bought the *Cloudster,* and under Claude's leadership they had launched the M-1, the first all-Ryan design.

Through a friend of Mahoney's, twenty-year-old Georgia Mathias learned of a job at Ryan Airlines and was hired as secretary to both Mahoney and Ryan. She was in a unique position to see the difference in basic personality between the partners.

"Mr. Mahoney was an easygoing, happy-go-lucky individual, very liberal with money," recalls Georgia, now the wife of San Diego banker

M-2 wing being fitted to fuselage in fish cannery factory.

Anderson Borthwick. "He was pleasant and well-liked by everyone, but didn't have the serious attitude about the business that Mr. Ryan had, or the determination to work problems through."

Mahoney was not devoid of ability. It was just that he had never learned to apply himself. Perhaps, with the passing of time, he would improve. Or so Claude reasoned.

While the uneven partnership may have weakened the company in some ways, it did let Ryan achieve his ambition. Still, the main source of day-to-day income for nearly three years was not Mahoney, as some people thought, but the tour buses that brought sightseeing passengers to Dutch Flats.

Soon after the first M-1 made its debut, Ryan knew he had a winner and that the company's future lay in manufacturing—not airline operation.

The company continued to grow. With the order from PAT for six planes, the firm expanded into the nearby cannery, which was leased for $200 a month. Fuselage and wings were trucked to Ryan Airport, and the planes were assembled and test-flown there.

Mahoney enjoyed the growing reputation of a successful industrialist. He had equal authority in the affairs of the company, though he seldom

Ryan Airlines leased left half of abandoned fish cannery. Though not its legal name, sign at door reads "Ryan Aircraft Mfg. Co."

Benjamin Franklin Mahoney.

showed much concern over routine business matters, a fact that left Ryan constantly disturbed. The company was closing the Los Angeles–San Diego Air Line, the venture which had opened the way for the partnership in the first place. It was still paying its way, but it was draining the company of men and equipment which could be put to better use.

The different life styles of the two men caused growing friction. Although they had managed to remain friends, people wondered where it would all end.

That was a question Ryan didn't like to face. But there was another problem that worried him even more. The company had prospered well on Ryan's business ability and Mahoney's daring and credit. As it turned out, however, Mahoney wasn't as wealthy as some had thought. Ryan's banker never got over the hole in the windshield. "That's some partner you chose!" the banker said, when Claude first told him of their partnership.

In time it became clear there was only one solution, and that was to incorporate and bring in new capital. "All this time," Ryan related later, "we were badly undercapitalized, and were going on Mahoney's credit, which had its limits, too. We needed to incorporate and take in some more stockholders and get some additional capital because we were extended way beyond good business limits."

Mahoney agreed, but he kept dragging his feet. Ryan had the papers drawn up, but they collected dust on top of Mahoney's desk. He just didn't sign them, although symptoms of economic disaster were growing stronger every day.

General William Mitchell, the great champion of air power, was a visitor in the summer of 1926. In forecasting that significant long-distance flights would be made with planes like Ryan's new monoplane, he brought into focus the divergent views of the partners.

Mitchell told Ryan and Mahoney that they'd gotten onto a sound, basic design that would lend itself to being scaled up, both in size and production volume. "You could make a bit larger version of the M-2," Mitchell said, "and it would be capable right now of flying nonstop from here to Honolulu."

Claude thought the idea of increasing production was all well and good, but you still had to build planes a few at a time and sell the ones you built. But Mahoney liked the idea of expanding out of the fish cannery into a real aircraft manufacturing plant. Here again was potential conflict—between the advocate of careful management and the enthusiastic expansionist.

As the days passed, the situation got worse. To hedge his bets, Claude had been looking into the possibilities of the aircraft engine business. The partnership had reached the point of no return.

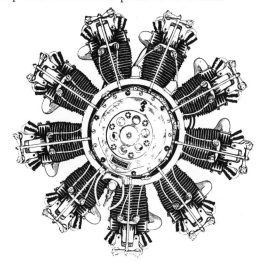

In the latter days of 1926, while still trying to get the improperly named Ryan Airlines, "Inc.," legally incorporated, Ryan approached Mahoney with a proposition. The two men faced each other, their friendship strained by the friction which had plagued the company for more than a year.

"This arrangement won't work any longer," Ryan said.

Mahoney shrugged his shoulders. He had known for some time that this part of his world was slipping out from under him, but decisions weren't his line. He had known also that if he waited long enough, Ryan would probably make the first move.

"One of us has got to get out," Ryan said. "Either you buy me out or I'll buy you out."

"I'm not interested in selling," Mahoney answered. And, of course, Claude was ill-equipped financially to take on the indebtedness of buying out Mahoney. That left only one course open. The price was set at $25,000 and one new M-2, for, as Claude said, "I was determined that I would never be without an airplane for my own use."

Mahoney agreed that the $25,000, though in excess of half the struggling company's book value, was hardly a high figure. He—some said his mother—paid $10,000 in cash in addition to the M-2 and gave Claude a second mortgage on property Mahoney had in downtown San Diego.

It was a mixture of relief and personal tragedy for the twenty-eight-year-old Ryan. He had first set out in business in San Diego a little over four years earlier. With nothing more than the money from the sale of his Model T Ford, he had started out on his own, on a narrow strip of land he didn't own, using a small plane the Army had sold as surplus.

NOTICE OF DISSOLUTION OF PART-NERSHIP.

Notice is hereby given that the copartnership heretofore existing between the undersigned B. Franklin Mahoney and T. Claude Ryan, under the firm names of "Ryan Airlines", "Ryan Flying Co." and "Los Angeles-San Diego Airline", and doing business at San Diego, California, and at Los Angeles, California, and elsewhere in said State, has been this day dissolved by mutual consent. Said T. Claude Ryan has retired from said firm and business and has sold all his interest therein and in the assets thereof to said B. Franklin Mahoney, and said B. Franklin Mahoney will continue the business at the same place and under the same firm names. All debts due and owing to said partnership are to be paid to and received by said B. Franklin Mahoney, and all lawful demands on the said partnership are to be presented to him.

Dated at San Diego, California, this 23rd day of November, 1926.

B. FRANKLIN MAHONEY.
T. CLAUDE RYAN.

Date of first publication, Nov. 29, 1926.
(19109)

Tom Mathews Collection

It seemed a long time ago that he had stood across the desk from Joe Brennan, San Diego's harbormaster, and wondered out loud if he could pay $50 a month for the lease on the strip.

"Hell!" Brennan had shouted, "Get out there and make a success. Then we'll worry about paying the lease."

Ryan chuckled to himself as he thought of Brennan. Somehow, Ryan *had* made it, but was he losing out now by default?

"Claude, I want you to stay on and run the business for me," Franklin said as they concluded their agreement to dissolve the partnership. "I'll pay you $300 a month until we can find a competent manager to take over from you."

Although the company no longer belonged to him, Ryan felt responsible for the men he had hired, most of whom viewed the change in ownership as a dubious turn of events. It was mostly that concern which led to his reply.

"Okay, I'll stay for a few months. But you can't afford the $300 salary. Make it $200 a month."

On November 30, 1926, the legal documents that ended the Ryan-Mahoney partnership were filed.

Despite some problems in the front office there was a lot of down-to-earth ingenuity among members of the Ryan crew. One unschooled but practical

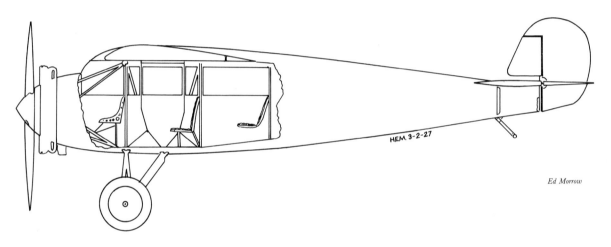

HEM. 3-2-27

Ed Morrow

draftsman-designer was Ed Morrow, who, like the others, saw the possibility of improving on the *Bluebird* and came up with some fairly detailed drawings for a similar but larger cabin plane.

In any case, everyone recognized that it would be advantageous to have a full-time engineer if the company was going to move ahead.

In early 1927 when Ryan landed from a charter flight, Mahoney walked out to the plane.

"Claude," he said, "I want you to meet a young man who's a graduate of the Pratt Institute in New York. Maybe it would be a good idea to have our own engineer. And he's not asking for much by way of salary."

Thus Donald A. Hall joined the Ryan organization on January 31, 1927. After graduation from Pratt, Hall had worked for Curtiss Aeroplane Company, and then under Art Mankey at Douglas.

Ideas for the larger cabin plane were already beginning to crystallize. The scaled-up version would have a larger and longer fuselage and a 42-foot wing span. The power plant would be either the 200-hp Hisso E or the new Wright J-4 radial. The first of the new B-1 Broughams—a name suggested by Mathews—was to be built on special order for a young San Diego hotel owner, Richard T. Robinson. Then the order for Robinson's so-called "gold bug" Brougham was switched to speed flier Frank Hawks, who wanted it for the Ford tour.

"I did some preliminary general and structural design work," Hall recalled years later, "on the first B-1 Brougham airframe during the interval between February 7 and 24, 1927."

At the same time the first cabin plane ads were making their appearance, describing the Ryan Brougham for 1927 as "A Modern Closed Airplane destined to predominate the commercial and pleasure plane field as an ideal type." Ryan Airlines, it said, was offering a complete line of open and closed models in the passenger, mail, and express types. The ad illustration was of the *Bluebird*.

During an Eastern delivery flight of a Douglas military transport cabin plane similar to the *Cloudster,* Claude had met A. J. Edwards, President of the Aviation Club of Muskogee, Oklahoma. A private pilot, Edwards was an automobile distributor there. Early in 1927, when in San Diego, Edwards accepted an invitation to visit Ryan if he ever got to the Coast. As a result, Edwards signed on with Mahoney as the Ryan Airlines sales manager—and only salesman—after J. B. Alexander left and just before Donald Hall joined the firm.

Ryan was working in his capacity as general manager on the morning of February 3, 1927—just two months after he had sold out to Mahoney—when a messenger from the telegraph office arrived. Georgia Mathias opened the yellow envelope and spread the telegram on his desk. It read:

"CAN YOU CONSTRUCT WHIRLWIND ENGINE PLANE CAPABLE FLYING NONSTOP BETWEEN NEW YORK AND PARIS STOP IF SO PLEASE STATE COST AND DELIVERY DATE"

The telegram was from Robertson Aircraft Corp. in St. Louis. It appeared that the intent of the telegram was to locate a vehicle capable of meeting the greatest challenge aviation had faced to that date. The competition was heavy to fly the Atlantic, and someone had apparently decided the Ryan monoplane could do it.

But who could take such an inquiry seriously?

"Everyone thought the wire was a joke," says Georgia. "They were just about ready to tear up the telegram and throw it in the wastebasket. But Mr. Ryan refused to dismiss it as a prank."

Claude said, "Sure we can do it." He called in Donald Hall, who had been hired the week before as the company's engineer, to study Robertson's requirement.

"By carrying what would normally be considered a great overload," Ryan related later, "Don and I agreed it could get off the ground." The next day Ryan filed an answer:

"CAN BUILD PLANE SIMILAR M ONE BUT LARGER WINGS CAPABLE OF MAKING FLIGHT COST ABOUT SIX THOUSAND WITHOUT MOTOR AND INSTRUMENTS DELIVERY ABOUT THREE MONTHS."

Later Ryan and Mahoney talked about it, and Franklin was not quite as enthusiastic about having given Robertson Aircraft a favorable answer.

Although he didn't know it, Ryan's price of $6,000, plus the cost of the engine, was well within the small budget of the Robertson Aircraft Corp. The next day another telegram arrived:

115

Don Hall at the drafting board.

Sales Manager A. J. Edwards.

That afternoon, on February 5, 1927, Ryan Airlines answered the telegram:

"GAS CAPACITY THREE HUNDRED EIGHTY GALLONS CRUISING SPEED ONE HUNDRED MILES PER HOUR LOADING ONLY TWELVE AND HALF POUNDS PER FOOT AND TWENTY POUNDS PER HORSEPOWER STOP CAN COMPLETE IN TWO MONTHS FROM DATE OF ORDER IF NECESSARY STOP WILL REQUIRE FIFTY PERCENT DEPOSIT".

In St. Louis, a young man laid the telegrams in front of his backers. "I've never heard of the Ryan Company," said Harold M. Bixby.

"Do you think they can build a plane with enough performance, Slim?" asked Harry F. Knight.

"All I know is that Ryan mail planes have a pretty good reputation," Slim answered.

"Well, I certainly wouldn't turn them down because we haven't heard of them," Bixby said. "They probably haven't heard of us either."

The Ryan organization was ready for business when a tall, slender airmail pilot arrived in San Diego.

The young man was, of course, Charles A. Lindbergh.

H. A. Erickson/Missouri Historical Society

CHAPTER THIRTEEN

"Spirit"— Sixty-day Wonder

THE BEST AIRCRAFT MANUFACTURERS IN THE COUNTRY had turned a deaf ear to Charles A. Lindbergh, a twenty-five-year-old airmail pilot who had decided he could do something no one else had been able to do. The obscure Lindbergh was a complex youth who had tamed his restless spirit with a singular goal. The lanky pilot, with the experiences of barnstorming, parachute jumps, wing-walking, and military flying already to his credit, had become obsessed with a desire to fly the Atlantic and thus attain one of the most coveted goals in aviation.

Lindbergh had never flown more than 500 miles at a stretch. He had never flown over water. He knew virtually nothing about long-range flight. He did not have a plane capable of flying 3,600 miles nonstop, and it had not been demonstrated that such a plane existed anywhere in the world. Lindbergh had backers, but his financial resources—$2,000 of it his own money—ended at a mere $15,000. Most manufacturers would have required several times that amount to build a plane for Lindbergh.

Like most men who change the course of history, Lindbergh had a vision. He had thought carefully about flying the Atlantic and each time he guided his airmail plane along the St. Louis–Chicago route, he had drilled himself for the challenge he was determined to meet. He would deliberately fly through foul weather, and at night, thereby mastering the use of the few instruments available to pilots in those early days of aviation.

Several seasoned pilots with substantial backing had tried to fly the

117

Atlantic, attracted by the $25,000 prize offered on May 22, 1919, by hotelman Raymond Orteig, for the first nonstop flight between New York and Paris. The prize had gone unclaimed for seven years.

The first man to try it was René Fonck, the World War I French ace. His burdened Sikorsky crashed and burned on takeoff at New York's Roosevelt Field on September 21, 1926. Fonck and a crew member escaped, but the remaining two crewmen burned to death.

His failure did not stop others. The famed thirty-nine-year-old explorer, Comdr. Richard E. Byrd, planned to try the hop in a Fokker trimotor. His ship, the *America,* would carry a crew of three. The year before, Byrd had flown to the North Pole behind three Wright Whirlwind engines, and was regarded as one of the foremost figures in aviation.

Lindbergh had studied each failure, and his conclusions were so unorthodox that they gave birth to some of the strange but unjustified myths about the young airmail pilot and his role in aviation, myths that would portray him as nothing more than a lucky daredevil.

Most of the pilots who had tried and failed had used expensive multiengine planes equipped with the best navigation and communication equipment available. Lindbergh decided they had failed because they had loaded their planes with so much fuel and equipment that they were unable to remain airborne for the long flight. In some cases they had been unable to get off the ground, often crashing at the end of the runway with disastrous results.

In the early twenties Lindbergh was a barnstormer and flight instructor, then became chief pilot on Contract Air Mail route no. 2 in April 1926 when service was started between Chicago and St. Louis. That's "Slim" in white coveralls.

Missouri Historical Society/St. Louis

Lindbergh decided success rested in simplicity—a single-engine monoplane powered by the newly developed, but highly successful, Wright Whirlwind air-cooled engine.

He concluded that a multiengine plane would be so heavy with the enormous amount of fuel it would have to carry that if one of the engines failed, the plane would be unable to maintain altitude and would crash anyway. He would be better off with one good engine and less weight.

Communication equipment was heavy and would not contribute significantly to the success of the flight, he reasoned. He would eliminate the radio.

And finally, and perhaps most important, he reached a decision that was to leave most spectators shaking their heads and concluding that the young pilot was mad. A copilot, Lindbergh reasoned, would mean more weight and would not contribute substantially to the success of the mission.

Lieut. Charles A. Lindbergh, U.S. Air Service, Kelly Field, 1924.

He would rather swap the copilot for another fuel tank. The world simply was not ready for a picture of a young man flying the Atlantic in a single-engine plane, alone.

Nor were the major aircraft manufacturers. One by one, they rejected Lindbergh's reasoning and refused to become involved in a mission they regarded as foolish. Others who could have provided the plane wanted too much money, or too much control over the project. One insisted on reserving the right to select the crew—leaving no role for Lindbergh.

Because of his airmail experience, Lindbergh had heard of Ryan Airlines, Inc., and of the successful little monoplanes Ryan was building for PAT and other airmail contractors. He didn't know much about the company itself, but time was running out. After a brief exchange of telegrams, and one final, futile trip to New York to obtain the Whirlwind-powered Bellanca used as a showcase by Wright to promote its new engine, he hopped on a train for the trip West.

He arrived in San Diego on Thursday, February 23, 1927, and was far from overwhelmed by his first impressions of the Ryan plant. As he recalled years later in his book, *The Spirit of St. Louis,* the factory was in an old, dilapidated building near the waterfront. The building had housed a cannery, and the smell of dead fish did nothing to increase his expectations.

Just how precarious the Ryan company's situation was at that time is indicated in a letter to his publisher written a few weeks later by Frank E. Samuels, Western Representative of *Aero Digest* magazine:

> While in San Diego I took up the matter of their bill with Mr. Edwards. They are going to recapitalize at once and expect to be able to pay all outstanding bills inside of the next thirty days. I know that they are very short of money and that they must be recapitalized or close their doors. They have plenty of orders for ships, but no money to build them with, which seems funny as they should be able to secure money on their orders. Mr. Mahoney bought out Ryan, paying $35,000 for his interests and I think that has crimped his bankroll. Edwards is trying hard to get the company on a sound basis. Mahoney does not know that Edwards has gone into this with me, and has not said a word about being short. Let us hope that they pull out in good shape, as I believe they will, especially if the *Spirit of St. Louis* makes the trip.

On the day Lindbergh arrived in San Diego, Claude was in Los Angeles trying to retrieve an M-1 that Charlie Widmer had "sold" but which had not been paid for. Taking a taxi from the train station, the newly arrived airmail pilot came to the Ryan factory office. The door opened to the small, dusty, paper-strewn office where he was met by Donald Hall, the twenty-nine-year-old engineer who had joined the firm shortly before the first telegram arrived. Franklin Mahoney introduced himself and asked Lindbergh to tour the small factory before getting down to business.

Mahoney led the way through the back of the small office and onto the factory floor, with evidence still around of the days when the factory had been part of the adjacent cannery. The firm employed only about thirty-five persons, most of whom were working on planes already in production.

Hawley Bowlus, factory manager, joined Mahoney, Lindbergh, Hall, Edwards, and Locke as they moved through the building. Workers paused as the group passed, sizing up the prospective buyer. But none of them knew of Lindbergh's bold plans.

Mahoney led the way upstairs to a loft where men were working on a wing. Finally, the group returned to the small office and got down to business. Mahoney made a sales pitch, but backed away from Lindbergh's

Wing Department in Ryan's fish cannery factory.
Dan Burnett, far left.

suggestion that if he believed in the plane he should be willing to guarantee the plane's cruising range.

"I don't see how we can do that. The risks are too high. It isn't as though we were a big company with a lot of money in the bank," said Mahoney in a candid burst of truth.

Lindbergh turned to the young engineer and decided that his decision over whether he should place his faith in the company rested primarily with Hall. The two men left the group and went to Hall's office, a small room in the loft with a bare bulb hanging from the ceiling.

Hall and Claude Ryan had based their first wire to Lindbergh on the expectation of using features from both the M-2 and the new Brougham cabin plane under development, but as Hall talked with Lindbergh he realized that additional modifications would be necessary. In fact, much of Lindbergh's craft would have to be built from scratch. As the discussion progressed, it was obvious that what Lindbergh needed was a flying gas tank.

Primarily, the plane would be an extension of existing Ryan monoplane design philosophy. Hall noted that the wingspan would have to be increased from the projected 42 feet of the as-yet-unbuilt B-1 Brougham to 46 feet, and the fuselage would have to be longer.

"Even with Hall's stretched-out wing, we left the struts in the same location," Claude recalled. "There was just that much more overhang, which was all right for a one-purpose flight. This brought the wing loading down to where it could handle the huge load."

Additional fuel tanks could be provided in space which would have been used for a copilot, Lindbergh reasoned. Hall was startled. It was the first he had heard of Lindbergh's plans to fly alone. But while he may have been jolted initially, the idea had its merits. The extra storage space would provide reserve fuel, something that had been worrying Hall since the first telegram had arrived.

120

"But are you sure you can stay awake for that long?" Hall asked. "It's going to take about forty hours."

Lindbergh wasn't sure how long it would take. Then it dawned on them that neither really knew exactly how far it was from New York to Paris. So they climbed into Hall's rusting old roadster and drove to the public library. Stretching a piece of string across the library's globe, they concluded that the distance was about 3,600 miles.

Lindbergh had already selected the Wright Whirlwind engine for whatever plane he would use for the transatlantic flight. But which model? Claude pointed out the good experience and reliability of the J-4 model flown by PAT in the M-1s. However, Wright had the new J-5 model in production, with some design refinements and a 220-hp engine instead of the 200-hp of the J-4.

"I questioned whether the J-5 would be the best choice," Ryan said, "because it was a new model and the old one was well proved, had been debugged, and was highly reliable. Lindbergh, however, insisted on the J-5. Wright provided an engine and spares, with every part specially inspected. Lindbergh's choice was good and the extra power was certainly worthwhile."

After looking over the factory that first day in San Diego, Mahoney drove Lindbergh out to Ryan Airport at Dutch Flats, where an M-1 demonstrator was put at Lindbergh's disposal.

John van der Linde, who was chief mechanic on the flight line, talked years later about the time he was told to warm up the M-1.

"But instead of one of our pilots getting in, this young boy got in and I wondered if it was all right for him to fly the airplane," van der Linde recalled. "So I walked over to Red Harrigan, who was chief pilot at the time, and I asked if the kid was supposed to fly it. He said 'yeah' and told me who he was.

"He flew that ship for about an hour, wrung it out like nothing I'd ever seen. He could fly it all right!"

Public library globe was used by Lindbergh and Hall to lay out route for New York-Paris flight. Globe is now in San Diego AeroSpace Museum.

On arrival in San Diego, young Lindbergh flew Ryan M-1 monoplane for the first time and really "wrung it out."

H. A. Erickson

Originally Hall had wanted a week's time after his first talk with Lindbergh for making basic design specifications final, but Lindbergh insisted on an answer within twenty-four hours—by 2:00 P.M. on Saturday.

"We did not want to bother the engineers and planners," reported A. J. Edwards. "So on Saturday we invited Lindbergh and Bowlus to join us for lunch aboard Mahoney's cabin cruiser. On our return Hall and Locke laid the plans for the job before Lindbergh and with his approval the order for $10,580 was signed and a deposit made on the plane." Earlier that day Lindbergh had visited the U. S. National Bank and opened his account with the $15,000 check from his St. Louis backers.

Lindbergh was pleased with what he had found in San Diego. "I'm ready to cast my lot with the Ryan organization," he wrote years later. "I have confidence in the character of the workmen I've met. This company is a fit partner for our organization in St. Louis. They're as anxious to build a plane that will fly to Paris as I am to fly it there."

The company had sixty days to build the plane, an overwhelming challenge under the best of circumstances. And if there had been problems between Ryan and Mahoney, and if the company's financial footing was precarious, it must be said that the difference was more than made up in other areas. The small group of men Ryan had assembled was ready to tackle history, although in the early days of the project only a few knew of the magnitude of the undertaking. What they did know was that a young man from St. Louis wanted a plane, and he wanted it to be perfect.

"As factory manager, Hawley Bowlus was very much the driver—but he led, not pushed," Ryan related. "His drive was contagious and Lindbergh added greatly to the morale. It became a team. Lindbergh saw to it that employees felt the project was as much theirs as his. And he was such a likable, boyish fellow that they all fell for him."

"Every man and woman connected with Ryan Airlines," said Edwards, "devoted every waking moment to the job of finishing the plane on time."

Hall had rightly said the plane would be a flying fuel tank. It could carry 450 gallons of fuel—one 209-gallon tank in the main fuselage, one 89-gallon fuel tank in the nose, and three in the wings. The pilot

Specifications

Span - 46 ft.
Chord - 7 ft.
Length - 27 ft. 3 in.
Wing loading 15 lbs.
High speed 130 M.P.H.
Cruising speed 105 M.P.H.
Range - 4300-4500 Miles
Weight 4750 lbs.
Gas Capacity 450 Gal.
Wing Area 320 Sq. ft.

Missouri Historical Society

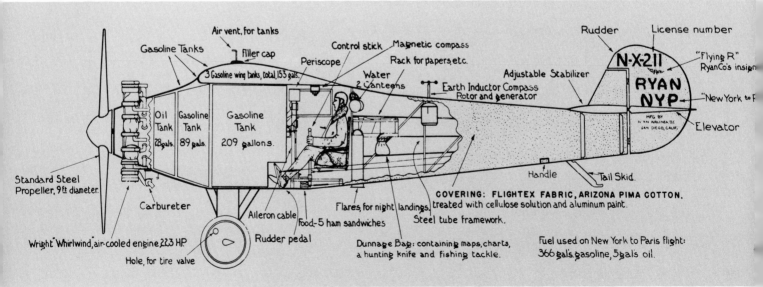

could shift fuel from one tank to another through a small hand pump in the cockpit.

The main concern was weight. Owing to the amount of fuel the small plane would have to carry, every ounce of unnecessary weight would endanger the mission. Lindbergh made his own flying boots to save weight. He even tore out the parts of his charts that he would not need.

To provide a structure capable of handling the tremendous takeoff load, Hall came up with a new, wide-wheel-tread landing-gear design. This outrigger-type gear—similar to that of the Fokker *Universal*—carried loads not only to the lower fuselage structure, as in the M-1, but also through struts to the upper fuselage and wing structure.

"We put the pilot's cockpit in the aft position instead of forward, like it was to be in the Brougham," Ryan recalled. "This was Lindbergh's choice; he wanted to be back of the main fuselage tank, not sandwiched between the engine and tank where he would be crushed in a takeoff accident. As a pilot I shared Lindbergh's view that it would be better to be located aft for safety, even at the sacrifice of forward vision.

"The greatest danger of the flight he felt, and I agreed with him, was the hazard of the takeoff with an extremely heavy load."

Lindbergh didn't see any great disadvantage to his restricted visibility. "What difference will that make. I will be flying by instruments and there will probably be no one I will run into out over the Atlantic Ocean," he said.

Lindbergh was a quiet, intense man who hovered over every detail in the construction of the plane, which had been labeled NYP (New York to Paris). But he enjoyed a practical joke. "No college kid," said Edwards, "could outdo Charlie in pranks." And if he seemed abrupt at times, the men realized it was because of his preoccupation with the project. His lanky frame earned him the additional nickname of "Slim."

Conscious that his $15,000 provided little in the way of living expenses, Lindbergh got an inexpensive room at the U. S. Grant Hotel. It fell to Edwards to shepherd Lindbergh, the new and very special customer.

"Our work and plans brought us so much together in the evenings," Edwards recalled, "that I insisted on his moving into my bachelor quarters at the Palomar apartments and living with me. He agreed providing I would let him pay his half of the rent."

The proposal appealed to cost-conscious Lindbergh, who was spending $2.50 a day at the Grant Hotel.

"During all the time I knew Lindbergh," wrote Edwards in 1937, "he never took a drink and there was only one occasion that he even had what you might call a date with a girl."

During this period the federal government began giving aviation the kind of attention it deserved, and for the first time the U. S. Department of Commerce started issuing licenses to pilots. The program was launched on the West Coast by a team of examiners who set up shop at Rockwell Field. One of their first customers was Charles Lindbergh, who took time off from the construction of the *Spirit* to take the test. He passed and received one of the department's first licenses—everything from private pilot to transport rating. It was presented in Claude Ryan's office, and Slim went back to work.

"Lindbergh was truly a master pilot," said Ryan. "He had a perfect feel for an airplane; he had good judgment; he had experience. If there was ever a natural pilot, it was Lindbergh.

"We'd both had our flight training as Army Air Corps cadets. We had something in common and we talked the same language. One day we were

Donald A. Hall

Lindbergh at the drafting board in Hall's office.

Lindbergh meticulously planned every detail of the flight.

Charts, Maps, and Forms

Maps of N.A. & Europe
with course plotted

Charts of North Atlantic
with course plotted
and variation recorded
both east and West.
Also containing vector
chart. Also hourly positions
on S.D - St. L. Maps.
Hourly report form

Map of Paris Airport.

comparing notes as to his chance of success. He turned the question back to me and said, 'What do you think the percentage is?'

"Well, I made it a little better than I really believed, so as not to be discouraging. I said, 'I think you've got a 75 to 25 percent chance of making it.' He said, 'That's just about what I figured.'"

Although his planning revealed an aeronautical sophistication rarely seen in those days, Lindbergh remained naïve about the impact his mission would have on the rest of the world. He once asked Mahoney how much his fare would cost to get from the airport into Paris at the end of his journey.

Mahoney, delighted, replied in all seriousness that he could catch the interurban for only a few francs.

Most of the men in the plant worked for about 65 cents an hour, and overtime pay was out of the question. The firm also employed several women, some as office workers and some in the fabric department, who worked for about 35 to 40 cents an hour. Yet it wasn't always easy to meet the factory payroll.

Most of the workers had been with the company for several months, at least, and they were proud of the reputation the firm had achieved with the M-1 and M-2. In the beginning, there was some resentment over the lanky pilot who hovered over them. But the project remained shrouded in secrecy.

"We were working out at the mud-flat airport (4 miles from the cannery) but we didn't even know what we were working on," recalled Fred Magula, who did sheet-metal work. "All at once we were told to build a great big old gas tank out there and we didn't even know what for. I thought it was a gas tank for a doggone fishing boat.

"It was a mammoth thing, and we were told to be particularly careful about how we built the thing. They didn't want a scratch on it because they figured vibrations would set in and create a leak. Talking to the other fellas while we were building it, we wondered why we should take so much care with a gas tank for a fishing boat. Then it finally leaked out what the tank was for."

One of the men working with Magula was Fred H. Rohr, the sheet-metal foreman, who later founded the huge company which bears his name.

Everyone developed an early respect for Lindbergh as the full story became known. And as the workers began to understand what was at stake, their respect for Lindbergh grew. The hours became longer and longer, many working until midnight every night. But no one worked longer and harder than Lindbergh and Hall.

"Slim would walk around the plant, studying problems," recalled "Dapper Dan" Burnett, who was in charge of part of the woodshop. "He had the habit of whistling without making any noise. He'd pucker his lips and the air would come out, but no sound."

Hall was especially dedicated to the job. He would arrive at the factory several hours before the work day was scheduled to begin because he wanted to have his part completed so he would not delay the others. At one point he remained bent over his drafting board for thirty-six hours, working out the details of the construction which was largely done from rough shop sketches. As with the *Bluebird,* detailed engineering drawings were not completed until after the *Spirit* was built.

The results proved that Hall was several years ahead of most aeronautical engineers of the time. He set rigid limits on the amount of solder that could be used, thereby holding down the weight. The NYP was perhaps the best streamlined plane up to that time. Hall required all joints

Ed Morrow Collection

Four who helped: A. C. Randolph, periscope idea man, and Fred Magula, sheet metal craftsman, standing. Kneeling, Fred Rohr and Walt Crawford.

to be faired with balsa wood, something few engineers would have required, not fully aware of the drag created by rough seams and exposed edges.

Throughout the long days of construction, most eyes focused on Lindbergh. He took long walks along the shore and in the foothills east of San Diego. Some said it was because he liked to be alone, but others said it was in preparation for the long ordeal ahead. If he was to be the only man aboard the plane, he would have to stay awake for thirty-five to forty hours. On one such hiking trail he remained awake for forty-nine hours.

On occasions, Hall and Lindbergh were seen sitting on the beach, going over specifications for the plane. And when he wasn't hovering over the construction of the *Spirit*, Lindbergh spent long hours preparing for the flight, struggling to master the techniques which would permit him to guide his plane, alone, across 3,600 miles of water.

The long days in San Diego became a race against time.

Soon after Lindbergh had arrived, the story broke that Byrd had received the backing of aviation enthusiast Rodman Wanamaker, who had announced he would finance Byrd's attempt with $100,000.

A few days later, word was received that the American Legion had put up $100,000 to finance the flight of Lieut. Comdr. Noel Davis, who planned to make the trip with a big Keystone Pathfinder, powered by three Wright Whirlwind engines.

Lindbergh's $15,000 bankroll looked more meager than ever.

Meanwhile, on the other side of the Atlantic, Captain Charles Nungesser, one of the top aces of World War I, announced that he would pilot a French-built plane from Paris to New York. His copilot would be the famous one-eyed airman, Lieut. François Coli. They had been preparing for the trip for two years.

Indeed, time seemed to be running out, but Lindbergh continued to push for perfection, refusing any compromise which might endanger the mission later by saving time during the critical days of construction.

"We had been working for about three weeks getting the engine installed in the fuselage," recalled O. L. Gray, an installation mechanic. "We had it pretty well installed and were fitting our oil lines and controls when a man up in the rafters dropped a 10-inch crescent wrench."

The wrench hit one of the air-cooling fins on the number one cylinder and chipped off a piece about the size of a quarter.

"Lindbergh almost cried," Gray said. "I told him we could smooth it out with a file and a little paint and never know the difference."

"I'll always know the difference," Lindbergh responded. "I want another engine in there."

The workers thought at first he had been joking. But they soon knew otherwise, much to the disgust of at least one man.

"Why does this damn thing have to be so perfect," the disgruntled workman mumbled under his breath.

"For two reasons," Lindbergh shot back. "The first is I'm not a good swimmer."

The response eased the tension, and the men chuckled among themselves. Then Lindbergh grew serious again.

"The other reason," he said, "is that I've always been taught that perfection pays off."

The men went back to their work, and another of the four "super-inspected" engines made available by Wright for the flight was installed.

Lindbergh insisted on other changes as well.

"We were cutting and fitting oil lines one day, running them back from

The cruising range will be well over 4200 miles. C.A.L.

Nungesser (right) and Coli, Paris-to-New York aspirants.

the engine through the nose section, when Lindbergh came up," recalled van der Linde. "In those days, you couldn't just draw a precut preformed oil line out of the stock room and install it. We drew out maybe 25 feet of straight copper tubing and then cut it right at our benches and beaded it and strung it to fit.

"Lindbergh was wearing a baggy blue suit and a felt hat that was, as usual, battered out of shape. He stood there for a few minutes, rocking back and forth on his heels."

"Don't make any oil line more than 18 inches long without a joint and a hose connection," Lindbergh blurted.

The mechanics were astonished.

"Break the oil lines every 18 inches and reconnect them with a rubber hose," Lindbergh insisted.

Some of the workers groaned.

"What for?" asked mechanic Ed Morrow.

"Well," answered Lindbergh, "most forced landings I've heard about on long hops were caused by a break in the oil line. From vibration. If we put rubber hose connections in, they'll absorb the vibration."

It was done, and few engineers today would question his judgment. Frank Wiley's forced landing in Nevada with a broken oil line proved the point.

Wires for the engine controls were carried inside quarter-inch steel tubing. With the twists and bends around the engine to contend with, Lindbergh felt that the controls might bind for lack of clearance. At the expense of several days work, the tubing was replaced with a size one-sixteenth inch larger.

If Lindbergh was hard on the workers, he was even harder on himself. Often he would work on the plane with a sandwich in one hand and a wrench in the other, unwilling to stop for lunch. His enthusiasm was matched, however, by the men and women of the small factory. As time wore on, they became more and more dedicated to the task that stretched before them. Some were skeptical, but many were confident that the end result would be success.

That optimism was not found in all quarters, however. In San Diego, the venture was regarded with substantial doubt by many residents. Lindbergh shied away from public meetings, and only occasionally allowed himself to get trapped into making an appearance.

On one such occasion he was asked what would happen if somewhere over the Atlantic his single engine stopped.

"That would be too bad," he observed with due candor.

Lindbergh was constantly bombarded with questions, especially from Navy pilots who stopped out of curiosity. He could provide a ready answer for most of the questions, but when he was stumped, he would pull a worn notebook from his pocket and write down the question. Eventually, he would find the answer.

It was during those days that one of Lindbergh's bitterest and longest feuds began—an undeclared war with the press. At first, the San Diego press, as well as newspapers across the country, paid little attention to Lindbergh. When references were made to the project, they frequently were inaccurate, sometimes owing to uninformed reporting, and sometimes owing to Lindbergh himself. He resented the prying questions of reporters, and at times they were forced to seek their information elsewhere, not always from reliable sources.

Lindbergh never forgave the press for the one thing he could not tolerate—imperfection.

Mar 26, 1927

We are progressing rapidly in the construction of the Monoplane and prospects for a successful flight appear brighter as time goes on and information comes in.

Charles A. Lindbergh

But the newspaper problem was unique. In general, the construction of the *Spirit* was not marked by bitterness or feuds. Some specific qualities which permeated the entire project were dedication, hard work, careful planning, and humor.

Mahoney brought out Lindbergh's inherent delight in practical jokes and horseplay. Lindbergh took great delight in connecting a booster magnet to the wire fence that encircled the flying field. Whenever anyone touched the fence while he was around, Lindbergh would crank up the mag with shocking results.

The men at the plant reciprocated. Someone dreamed up an alarm-clock rig to keep the Lone Eagle awake during his long flight. The rig was supposed to jab Lindbergh in the seat of the pants with a sharp needle every fifteen minutes. He didn't take it.

In a more serious vein, A. C. Randolph, one of the men who worked at the plant, came up with an invention that he was too shy to present to the young pilot for a long time. Randolph, who had served many years in the submarine service during his Navy career, had developed a periscope which he figured would help Lindbergh see around the fuel tanks that would block his view.

After coaxing by his fellow workers, Randolph eased up to Lindbergh one day and thrust the drawings before him. The young pilot liked the idea, and the periscope was installed aboard the *Spirit*. It had little practical application, however, since it could be used only on the ground, and Lindbergh preferred to stick his head out the window and peer around the tanks rather than through the periscope.

Construction on the plane had reached a feverish pitch by early April, but reports of other pilots and their successes continued to pour in. On April 9, Davis completed his maiden flight in his Keystone Pathfinder and described it as "beautiful." Byrd's Fokker trimotor was also nearing completion.

On April 14, Clarence D. Chamberlin and Bert Acosta landed their Bellanca in New York after an endurance flight of forty-one hours, eleven minutes. They immediately announced plans to fly the Atlantic.

Byrd's Fokker crashed on landing at New York on April 16, damaging the plane substantially, but not beyond repair. Byrd was still in the race.

Meanwhile, work continued at the small Ryan factory.

Other pilots joined the race, and there were a few mishaps, but on April 26 the most disturbing news of all came through. Noel Davis and his copilot, Lieut. Stanton Wooster, had been killed in the last of their trial flights when their plane crashed near Hampton, Virginia.

In San Diego, the news was shocking. It brought home the inescapable fact that the life of a young man rested in the hands of thirty-five men and women who were struggling to build a plane—in a brief span of sixty days—to do a job that four men had already died trying to do.

Even some of those who were building the plane admitted later they were skeptical. Most, however, were confident they would succeed, although their confidence was rarely shared by those not directly associated with the project. With a sly sense of humor, and destiny, Mrs. Evangeline Lindbergh, then teaching school in Detroit, wrote her son that "for the first time in my life I realize that Columbus also had a mother."

Dan Burnett took Lindbergh to a church supper one night and introduced him as "the man who's going to fly the Atlantic."

People smiled and asked Burnett if he had managed to get his 1918 Maxwell running right.

The whole thing brought mixed emotions to Claude Ryan. It gave him

Wide World Photos

Clarence Chamberlin, right, with Charles A. Levine, owner of the Bellanca.

Wide World Photos

Comdr. Richard E. Byrd and his North Pole Fokker trimotor.

French war ace Capt. René Fonck, whose own flight had ended in disaster, wishes Lindbergh Godspeed.

Missouri Historical Society

an intense sense of pride to realize that the workers he had brought together were capable of the kind of devotion and teamwork so evident in the construction of the *Spirit of St. Louis.* Yet to a large degree he was left detached from one of the most exciting ventures his company had attempted; the financial aspects of the firm were in such sad condition that Ryan was forced to devote almost his full attention to keeping the firm solvent. Thus he had little time to become personally involved in the construction of the *Spirit.*

Tom Mathews perhaps best, and not unkindly, described the key figures. "Mahoney, the gambler; Hall, the eccentric engineer; Lindbergh. These three personalities created the *Spirit of St. Louis.* They were the catalyst. And Claude Ryan's brainchild, the Ryan M-1 in its Cinderella role, was about to become the most famous plane in history."

Although the press remained skeptical of Lindbergh's chances, the name of Ryan Airlines, Inc., appeared in newspapers and aviation journals around the world. Ryan knew that if Lindbergh succeeded, the company would be worth many times what Mahoney had paid. The future, with any luck, would be golden, but Ryan would be left out as the company he built moved on to bigger and better things.

Yet in spite of his own personal disappointments, Ryan could not help but be proud of the company and the men he had assembled. They were caught up in something that demanded their finest performance, and each was giving his best to the project. The work was demanding, the pressure was intense, and toward the end of the project the tension began wearing through.

One night, while the finishing touches were being added to the wing, someone showed up with a jug of cheap red wine. The jug made the rounds a number of times, and as the evening wore on the workers grew happier, partly because of homemade wine and partly because of the feminine gender of some of the workers.

Hawley Bowlus, who had shouldered much of the responsibility for building the *Spirit,* partook perhaps too freely of the wine; at one point

Fuselage of the *Spirit* emerges from the fish cannery factory. One side of landing gear had to be removed to get plane through door. Left to right: O. R. McNeel, Doug Corrigan, Bert Tindale, Hawley Bowlus, and Shirley Morrison.

H. A. Erickson

Using Claude's Studebaker roadster, the *Spirit* fuselage is towed to Dutch Flats airport for final assembly. Ed Morrow is in front seat looking back to watch the plane.

he leaped up behind one of the seamstresses, Peggy DeWitt.

"You've been working too hard, Peggy," Bowlus said, and picked her up and sat her on top of the wing.

There was a sickening cracking sound. The workers sobered up in a hurry. Several ribs in the wing had been cracked. By morning, however, they were patched as good as new, and Lindbergh didn't find out for years about the time Peggy cracked his ribs.

Most of the workers desperately wanted to be a part of the plane they felt was destined to cross the Atlantic, but they resisted the temptation to slip personal items aboard, thus adding more weight. Instead, just before the wing was covered, they gathered around and signed their names on the front spar.

Then they added the finishing touches to the plane. On April 27, the fuselage was hauled out of the shop, tied to the bumper of Claude Ryan's 1925 Studebaker, and pulled down the road to the airport on Dutch Flats.

The wing had presented special problems. The workers had overlooked a minor detail. It was too big to get through the door and down the stairs. Fortunately, railroad tracks ran alongside the factory, so the men pushed

From vantage point atop boxcar, Charlie Lindbergh, in dark suit, watches as wing is moved from second floor to railroad car, then lowered by crane.

H. A. Erickson/Ed Morrow Collection

FOR THE "FIRST TIME", THE WING IS TRIED ON.

M – MAHONEY   S – SHIRLEY MORRISON
X – LINDY   J – JOHN VON DER LINDE
Y – DOUG. CORRIGAN   Mᶜ – McNEEL
Z – ED. MORROW   D – DAPPER DAN

a boxcar to the side of the building. The large double doors left over from the cannery were opened, and the wing was pushed out and onto the top of the boxcar. It was then lowered onto a wing dolly for the trip to Dutch Flats.

The following day, exactly sixty days after work had started, the *Spirit of St. Louis* was ready for its first test flight. Everyone showed up for the occasion. A cheer went up as van der Linde stepped up to pull the big metal prop.

"Contact!"

The engine caught, roared, and Lindbergh motioned for the chocks to be removed.

Douglas Corrigan, a young man who later flew across the Atlantic himself (after filing for a flight West, thus earning the nickname "Wrong Way" Corrigan) darted under the wing and pulled the chocks free. Within moments the plane was airborne. Years later, van der Linde recalled the scene like this:

"We yelled, slapped each other on the back, kissed all the girls, then stood there rather awkwardly but proudly, watching him circle overhead. A Navy Hawk, a fighter plane, dropped down to nose up to this rather strange new bird and Lindbergh rolled over in a bank to dog-fight with him. The big Hawk had more speed, but Lindbergh cut inside him over and over. Then he brought her back to earth."

The Spirit lacked inherent stability, a fact which both Hall and Lindbergh had anticipated when they decided to increase the wingspan without changing the M-2 tail surfaces. But Lindbergh wanted it that way. If the plane required more attention, he reasoned, he would be less likely to fall asleep.

The first flight was a success.

The following day Lindbergh made three more flights, each about six minutes long.

"Charlie took off very early one morning," van der Linde recalled, "to make a run over the measured course at the Silver Strand to get an accurate check of his speed under different engine operating conditions.

The first takeoff. April 28, 1927.

H. A. Erickson

130

H. A. Erickson

Ready for the first engine test. In golf knickers at far right, A. J. Edwards.

About seven o'clock the fog rolled in and Lindbergh hadn't returned in the *Spirit*.

"Red Harrigan got concerned and suggested we fire up an airplane and go look for Charlie. We took off and about halfway across the bay we got fouled up in the fog, too, and decided to head back. As we approached the field, feeling our way along at very low altitude, we had to pull up over the telephone wires. Just then along came Lindbergh in the *Spirit*, only 15 feet away from our wing tip. In the fog, we hadn't seen him, and he hadn't seen us. That's how close Charlie came to almost not getting to Paris!"

Lindbergh continued to test the plane over the next few days at the Camp Kearny parade ground, gradually building up the fuel load toward the 400 gallons he would have to carry if he was to make it across the Atlantic.

But on the 300-gallon test, the wheel bearings smoked, the tail skid broke, and the shock absorbers hit bottom. Lindbergh studied the plane carefully and finally said he was satisfied with the tests. Repairs and some minor modifications would have to be made, but he would not try a maximum fuel load test until he took off on his way to Paris. New York's Roosevelt Field was 500 feet lower, and he would count on that to give him the extra margin he would need.

On May 8, Nungesser and Coli took off from Paris. "It was," Lindbergh said, "the first time a plane loaded for the flight between New York and Paris had actually taken off." Anticipating the possibility of their success, Lindbergh spent most of the day studying a transpacific flight plan! The

The whole crew. Mentioned in the text are (1) O. R. McNeel, (2) Walter O. Locke, (3) Charles A. Lindbergh, (4) Georgia Mathias, (5) A. J. Edwards, (6) Dapper Dan Burnett, (7) Peggy De Witt, (8) Fred H. Rohr, (9) A. J. Randolph, (10) Walt Crawford, (11) Doug Corrigan, (12) John van der Linde, (13) Donald A. Hall, (14) J. J. Harrigan, (15) Hawley Bowlus, (16) B. F. Mahoney.

H. A. Erickson

"We Built the Ryan New York to Paris Plane"

world waited, but Nungesser and Coli died somewhere in the Atlantic.

A day earlier, Mahoney had left for Los Angeles to catch the Western Air Express night plane as far as Salt Lake City. He would go on by train to be with Lindbergh at the takeoff from New York for Paris.

On the afternoon of May 10, after a two-day delay for the weather, Lindbergh shook hands with bystanders at Rockwell Field. Then, quietly, the Lone Eagle climbed into the cockpit of the *Spirit of St. Louis* and took off.

Harrigan and van der Linde "chased" him as far as the mountains to the east of San Diego in an M-2. But in time, the silver plane disappeared into the east.

The following days nobody did much around Ryan Airlines, Inc. They were entitled to some relaxation from the pace of the past two months. The men just laughed when they were told to get back to work.

One man never did relax. Claude Ryan, the man who had built the company and nursed it into what it had become, had left his temporary job as general manager and gone East on personal business before the *Spirit of St. Louis* began its epic flight.

Running the fuel load tests at Camp Kearny. Lindbergh in center on gasoline drum. Atop pyramid is Ryan chief pilot Red Harrigan.

At North Island, ready to leave for St. Louis. At right, Lindbergh, Hall, and Edwards. Holding banner, O. R. McNeel and George Hammond. Fueling the plane, John van der Linde, chief flight mechanic.

Lindbergh landed in St. Louis after a fourteen-hour, twenty-five-minute nonstop trip from San Diego. It was a new record. He flew on to New York after a one-day layover, and arrived there tired but happy on May 12, setting another record. Those who had scoffed at the former airmail pilot took another look. The success of his cross-country flight made the skeptics reassess him, and what they found was not what they had expected.

The *Spirit of St. Louis* had already proved what Lindbergh would later reiterate over and over. Some reports would claim that the plane was a rickety bucket of spare parts that the pilot managed to hold together through daredevil zeal and extraordinary luck. Of all the erroneous impressions that would grow out of his adventure, that remained the most irritating to Lindbergh. He regarded the *Spirit* as the best existing plane for the flight, equipped with the best engine and the best instruments available.

Lindbergh was anxious to get started as the competition grew keener every minute. Byrd was on hand. Chamberlin and Lloyd Bertaud were

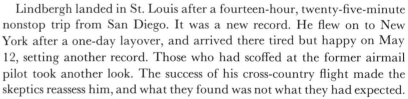

The famous Lindbergh grin in perhaps the most widely printed of all photos of the famous flier.

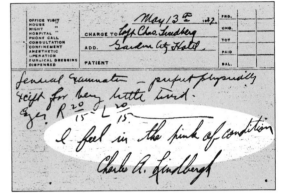

A confident Charlie Lindbergh adds a postscript to Dr. David Dooman's examination on his arrival in New York following record-setting flight from San Diego to St. Louis to New York.

ready to go in the Bellanca but Bertaud got into an argument with Charles Levine, their backer, over the expected prize money, and their takeoff was delayed.

Then the weather closed in and everyone was held up.

Mahoney arrived on the 19th, looked up Lindbergh, and took him on a tour of the Wright plant. After dinner and a Broadway show, they returned late to the hotel. Slim was unable to sleep.

Early on the morning of May 20, Lindbergh was driven to the airport. Despite local raw winds and intermittent showers, Lindbergh had decided the weather over the Atlantic would be favorable. This would be the day. At 4 A.M., the *Spirit* was pulled out of the hangar. Almost 500 persons watched the silver plane roll out, shivering in the wind and rain. The plane was rolled onto the field and fuel was added, bringing the total to 451 gallons.

Byrd, who shortly before had taken his plane on a test flight, walked up and grasped Lindbergh's hand.

"Good luck to you, old man," Byrd told the young pilot. "I'll see you in Paris."

Lindbergh climbed into the plane. He carried no parachute. His provisions included five sandwiches and a few candy bars. He had a fishing line and a couple of hooks, just in case he was forced down at sea.

It was a murky and otherwise depressing morning. A short distance from the field lay the burned, twisted wreckage of René Fonck's plane. The crash a few months earlier had claimed the lives of two men, and the blackened spot served as a cruel reminder of Fonck and others who had thought they could succeed, but failed.

At 7:51 A.M., with a final wave, Lindbergh ordered the chocks removed. The *Spirit* lumbered forward, one man pushing on each wing; it lurched

Ready for takeoff. Next stop, Paris.

The *Spirit* heads out over the gray Atlantic.

and bounced as it plowed across the rough field. It bounced into the air once, and then hit the ground again. It took off again, and came down once more.

Lindbergh had passed the point of no return. It was either now or never. The *Spirit* lifted off the ground for a third time. This time it stayed in the air. It cleared a tractor at the end of the strip by a mere 10 feet. Its huge wing and rugged landing gear had met the test.

In San Diego, Edwards was awakened at 5:00 A.M. by a phone call. "A. J.—It's Franklin. He's off! Everybody went wild. He's on his way. If he makes this flight, we won't be able to build planes fast enough and I'm sure he'll make it!"

As Lindbergh had anticipated, the Lone Eagle flew much of the way on instruments, blinded by low visibility. The long hours he had practiced on his airmail run and while waiting for the *Spirit* to be completed paid off. Fortunately, the plane was equipped with the best engine and best instruments available.

When the weather permitted, he guided the *Spirit* closer to the water to estimate his drift by watching the waves. He ate only one and one-half of the sandwiches.

At about 4:30 P.M., European time, the second day, most of the trip lay behind him and Lindbergh was growing ever more confident. He spotted a fleet of small fishing boats and nosed down for a closer look. He circled, made a low pass, and shouted to a startled fisherman:

134

Louis Bleriot, first to fly the English Channel, in 1909, is flanked by Lindbergh, the new aviation hero, and U.S. Ambassador Myron G. Herrick.

San Diego AeroSpace Museum

"Which way to Ireland?"

There is no record of the fisherman's answer.

For more than thirty-three hours the Lone Eagle guided his tiny ship across the Atlantic, while those he had left behind voiced both optimism and pessimism.

Shortly before dusk he looked across the horizon and saw "the most wonderful looking piece of natural scenery I have ever seen." It was the coast of Ireland. And he was only 3 miles from the point he had expected to be by dead reckoning.

In Paris, word flashed that Lindbergh was going to make it. Huge crowds thronged to LeBourget Field. At 10:00 P.M. Lindbergh circled the field and landed—exactly eight years after Orteig had offered the $25,000 prize—amid a screaming mass of 100,000 persons. He had 85 gallons of fuel left over, more than enough to get a young man to Paris.

On the other side of the world, in the small city of San Diego, a handful of men and women set out to take the town apart, one piece at a time. They rigged up a homemade cannon by welding a pipe to Ryan's Studebaker. They filled the pipe with acetylene gas and set it off with a blow torch.

"It made a helluva racket," van der Linde recalled.

The workers paraded down the main streets of San Diego, setting off explosions that shook the downtown area. Army and Navy guns took up the salute. American flags appeared as if by magic along the principal streets. Clanging trolleys, automobile horns, factory whistles, backfiring engines, joined the jubilation. The police finally silenced the Ryan workers' improvised cannon, but the celebration continued, a little quieter than at first, but it continued.

And when the shouting finally died down, a young man by the name of Donald Hall, who had met the greatest challenge of his life, walked quietly along the beach, alone.

B. Franklin Mahoney, who had gone to New York for the takeoff, began making immediate plans to travel on to Paris, where he would bask in the reflected glory of the Lone Eagle.

And still another young man, T. Claude Ryan, marveled at his own sense of incredible timing. The company he had built had earned the world's most lavish praise, and he stood on the outside looking in.

135

CHAPTER FOURTEEN

Epilogue

CHARLES LINDBERGH HAS BEEN DESCRIBED VARIOUSLY AS The Last Hero, The Lone Eagle, Lucky Lindy, and other lesser known titles—some, like Flying Fool, not overly complimentary.

Had the circumstances been only slightly different, he might have been none of those. As one of the men who helped build his plane recalled years later, if Ryan Airlines had been better established, with a team of full-time engineers, Lindbergh's request would have been denied as impractical, and the *Spirit of St. Louis* would not have been built.

But as it was, a group of men and women who had everything to gain and little to lose set out to do something others had said could not be done. Improvisers of the Ryan and Bowlus type, a risk-taking gambler like Mahoney, an engineer of Hall's devotion, and a small group of dedicated employees made it possible.

The Lindbergh story caught the imagination of the American public as few stories had done before, and not until astronaut Neil A. Armstrong set foot on the moon in 1969 has the world been so enchanted with a single aeronautical feat.

It has been nearly half a century now since Lindbergh climbed from his silver monoplane before throngs of hysterical Parisians, and much has happened. The world clamored at his doorstep, but in time the Lone Eagle turned away, determined that his life would not revolve around a single act by a twenty-five-year-old pilot. Above all, he cherished his privacy,

137

Colonel Lindbergh appears less than pleased about his induction into Ancient Egyptian Order of Sciots after return to San Diego.

Lindbergh in the South Pacific with Marine Corps ace Major Joe Foss, left.

H. A. Erickson

Sensor Studio

Wide World Photos

and except for the months immediately following the flight to Paris, he shunned the spotlight with a determination rarely seen in public figures.

Years later, he summed up his feelings over the continued publicity of the 1927 flight when he told a friend: "I devoted time to that in 1927 and 1928, and I've written two books about it. Now I am most anxious to continue living and working quietly."

But like it or not, the flight secured Lindbergh a permanent place in history at a price he certainly never expected to pay. His fondness for seclusion became an obsession after the kidnap and death of his first child, which Lindbergh blamed largely upon invasion of his family's privacy by the press.

Public suspicion during World War II that he was sympathetic with Germany because he had been privileged to fly Luftwaffe planes during a visit there—whether justifiable or not—injured him deeply. For a while the Lindberghs fled from their own homeland and took up residence in England. But in 1944 as a "tech rep" for Vought he flew combat missions against the Japanese in the Pacific.

If Americans misunderstood their hero and occasionally were harsh in their criticism, the passing of time healed most wounds and Slim resumed his role as one of the nation's most beloved figures. During his later years he has devoted most of his energy to the preservation of wildlife and to other conservation matters—dedicated as in his youth to making this a better world in which to live. Typically, he was way ahead of his contemporaries in concern for the environment.

But all that is only part of the story of the *Spirit of St. Louis*. The story of what happened to the men who built the plane has never been told fully, and it is a story which is long past due. It offers a rare commentary on the high price often exacted by success.

Benjamin Franklin Mahoney, the playboy turned businessman, traveled to Paris immediately after Lindbergh's flight to join America's idol. By the time he returned to the United States with the aviator, the success of the flight had thrust Ryan Airlines, Inc., into the forefront of aviation. It was a position the company was ill-prepared to accept, but this fact

Bust of Lindbergh, now in main passenger concourse at Lindbergh Field, San Diego's international airport, is photographed against *Spirit of St. Louis II.* This only exact duplicate, flown at Paris Air Show in 1967 on flight's fortieth anniversary, is main attraction at San Diego AeroSpace Museum.

After success of transatlantic flight, company's
name was changed to B. F. Mahoney Aircraft Corp.

Gold Bug, first B-1 Brougham, owned by pilot
Frank Hawks, was completed just after Lindbergh
plane.

escaped Mahoney, who rarely had time to think about such practical
matters.

After Lindbergh landed in Paris, the company was swamped with orders.
Everybody wanted a plane like Slim's. Mahoney was in Paris and Edwards
was in a Los Angeles hospital with a fractured skull. Edwards called the
plant and had Hawley Bowlus fly Georgia Mathias up there with the
telegrams and mail so some kind of answers could be sent to the deluge
of customers.

When the shouting began to die, Mahoney made his way back to San
Diego. He changed the name of the company to B. F. Mahoney Aircraft

Pride of San Diego flew east to greet Lindbergh on return from Paris. Pilot Frank Hawks in golf knickers. Next to him A. J. Edwards, sales manager, still wearing patch on forehead from crack-up in Bluebird.

Bunnell Photo

Corporation and launched into expanded production of the B-1 Brougham, the five-place plane that was being developed at the time production was shifted to the *Spirit of St. Louis*. Frank Hawks received the first B-1—the *Gold Bug,* which was rushed through to completion and renamed *Pride of San Diego.* Hawks and his wife made a speedy trip East, flying out to sea to greet Lindbergh as the cruiser *Memphis* neared Washington with the returning hero.

Later a few more M-2s were built and three Hisso-powered B-1s and B-2s came off the production line before the Wright Whirlwind B-1 "sister ships" of the *Spirit* became standard.

Those anxious to duplicate Lindbergh's success were among the buyers of Broughams for a variety of stunt flights. The Japanese newspaper *Mainichi* ordered a copy of the NYP for long-distance flights. Later it was

Three B-1 and B-2 Broughams, left, powered with the 200 hp Hispano-Suiza "E" engine were built. The early Wright B-1 Brougham, below right, flew mail out of Whitehorse in Yukon Territory.

H. A. Erickson

Ryan Aeronautical Library

Ryan Aeronautical Library

Sheer Hollywood press-agentry was behind purchase of special Brougham (below) to carry MGM's trademark lion on nationwide tour. Pilot Martin Jensen discusses details with Franklin Mahoney, above.

virtually duplicated, at twice the size, but the pilot died in a fiery crash on takeoff. Emilio Carranza, the Mexican ace, suffered a similar fate in a special Brougham.

Metro-Goldwyn-Mayer hired Martin Jensen to fly Leo, the MGM trademark lion, in an iron cage built into the fuselage of a Brougham. They crashed in the mountains of Arizona. Fortunately the cage remained intact and Jensen walked away unscratched either by the crash or by Leo's paws. A long-distance plane for a California-Rome flight was ordered, but the pilot refused to cooperate with the lady sponsor when she appeared more interested in him than in the flight.

One of the first Broughams was displayed and flown at the Cleveland Air Races. The pilot who owned the plane, the service crew, and the salespeople were staying at one of the big hotels.

"About 2 A.M.," Mathews related, "we set up a bowling alley with bottles and a round hassock in the hall on the sixth floor. The management came up and singled out the pilot as the ringleader.

"'We want everything out of your room in half an hour; you are no longer a guest in this hotel!'

"So Frank went in and tossed everything out the window: bureau, bed, rugs, pictures, the whole bit (we may have helped a little), then got his stuff and walked out."

In August of 1927, Mahoney was quoted as saying that for every order the company accepted, five others had to be turned down. "We could be selling five planes every day now if we could only build them," he said, announcing plans to turn out one plane a day by May 15, 1928.

Thus it appeared that the future was sound for the fledgling company, but the actual situation was quite different. Mahoney still had his zest for life, and he found the lure of his many diversions overwhelming. He would not appear at the office for days at a time, leaving the factory unable to meet its promises, pay its bills, or fill its orders.

"Mr. Mahoney was really catapulted into trying to run a big company," Georgia Mathias recalled. "He was willing to go along with it as long

Martin Jensen Collection

Fumio Habuto in NYP-2 duplicate of Lindbergh's plane set new nonstop record for Japan in 1928.

Mexican newspaper *Excelsior* sponsored goodwill flight of Capt. Emilio Carranza.

The pilot of this potbellied flying gas tank, built for flight to Rome, refused to cooperate.

". . . my good Irish friend, Benjamin Franklin Mahoney"—*Lindbergh.*

as it was going all right, but he was not really a businessman."

"The company was on the verge of bankruptcy before Lindbergh, during Lindbergh, and after Lindbergh," Mathews said. "Some of the transactions to keep the plant going were weird indeed. As an example, Wright would send out five or six Whirlwind engines but required they be placed in bond and released to the factory for production only upon payment of $5,000 apiece when they were taken out to be put in the Broughams for delivery.

"The flying operation always carried itself with something left over for the production end. One Saturday afternoon Mahoney wrote the payroll checks and then asked me how much cash I had from Dutch Flats. I counted out about $650 and he said to bring it along. We drove to Tijuana. There he won about $2,500 and gave it to me to deposit first thing Monday to cover the payroll checks.

"And Franklin dug into his own pocket, too, when necessary, selling personal securities to see that everyone got paid."

"I can't vouch for the reports," Lindbergh wrote. "I can only say it would have been in keeping with the character of my good Irish friend, Benjamin Franklin Mahoney."

These are among last Broughams built by Mahoney company before production in San Diego stopped in September 1928.

Peter M. Bowers Collection

Old newsphoto shows roll-out of special B-1X Brougham which was a gift to Colonel Lindbergh in April 1928.

Although he was having trouble meeting his commitments, Mahoney and the various suppliers of equipment for the *Spirit* built a new B-1X Brougham, the only one with a 46-foot wing, and presented it to Lindbergh in April, 1928, as a gift.

But Mahoney moved to make the best of the circumstances, recapitalizing the firm at $500,000 and preparing to sell shares to the public. Hawley Bowlus continued as factory superintendent and A. J. Edwards as director of sales. Both served on the board of directors along with Mahoney, his mother, Mrs. Jennie L. Mahoney, and hotel owner Richard T. Robinson.

The application form for shares in the new company listed assets of $74,185.73 and liabilities of $84,051.37, for a deficit of $9,865.64. Intangible assets were estimated at $285,510.00 and for this, after deducting the deficit, Mahoney was to receive 2,756 of the 5,000 authorized shares with a par value of $275,600.00. The public would have the other 44.9 percent of the stock.

Shortly after the firm was recapitalized, a group of St. Louis businessmen, including several of Lindbergh's original backers and Phil DeC Ball, owner of the St. Louis Browns, offered not only to buy the company but also to give Mahoney a two-year employment contract at $1,000 a month.

The stock certificates had been printed in the fall of 1927, and key employees were supposed to get busy and sell all they could. "When the St. Louis crowd came in, they wanted all the stock or no deal," recalls Mathews. "They were paying Mahoney a cool million dollars for 5,000 shares of stock and they wanted every last share. Fortunately we had only sold about 75 or 80 shares, and in a couple of weeks we had them all back except for one share I had sold to a bartender in Tijuana. After I had tried for a couple of weeks to get it back, I think Mahoney went down and closed that deal, too."

So on December 31, 1927—little more than six months after Lindbergh's success—the B. F. Mahoney Aircraft Corporation of San Diego became the Mahoney Aircraft Corporation of Missouri, but it continued to produce

Notebook of employee Lloyd M. Best records completion of wings of planes no. 167, 168, and 169 as San Diego Brougham production nears end.

SEP 14 1928 *Fri.*
W 167 SDT

SEP 18 1928 *Tues.*
W 168. SDT.

SEP 18 1928 *Tues.*
W 169 SDT.

Lloyd M. Best

145

Lindbergh's new B-1X Brougham at Grand Canyon airport with St. Louis backers Harold M. Bixby, left, and Harry H. Knight, right.

B-1s and some B-3 Broughams in San Diego. Then the decision was made to move headquarters to St. Louis, and yet another company was formed, the Mahoney-Ryan Aircraft Corp., with the Ryan name being restored apparently to bolster the company's dwindling image.

A new factory was opened in St. Louis in November, 1928, to begin construction of a six-place B-5 Brougham powered with the larger Wright J-6 engine. Only a handful of employees moved to Missouri, most preferring to remain in San Diego after the last plane was completed in the old fish cannery.

The new St. Louis plant used the best production techniques available, and soon the planes were rolling off the lines at a rapid rate. The company led the nation in exports, with approximately 20 percent of its planes shipped out of the country to China, Japan, Australia, New Zealand, Italy, Guatemala, Mexico, and Canada. The company also set up one of the first distributor chains in the nation, with nineteen franchises covering the entire United States. Others were established in foreign countries.

Deliveries kept going up, but financial results were down, and at the height of its operations the company was sold once again, this time to Detroit Aircraft Corp. Coming full circle, in June of 1929 the name again

Many B-5 Broughams built at St. Louis plant by Mahoney-Ryan were for export market.

became Ryan Aircraft Corp. when it introduced the B-7 Brougham and C-1 Foursome models, the latter designed by Art Mankey. But fate took yet another turn. The Great Depression set in, and Detroit Aircraft and its subsidiaries, including Lockheed Aircraft Company, folded.

Thus ended the saga of a company which had answered a request from an unknown airmail pilot and soared into the ranks of the nation's major corporations for a brief struggle with success.

A fascinating era in the life of a unique corporation had ended. For a while the spotlight of the world had focused upon the people who built the *Spirit*. What happened to them?

For some, the light was too intense, and it impaired their vision for the rest of their lives. For others, the spotlight became an illusive beacon which they chased for years but never again recaptured. A few stood in the light briefly, and then went on to live normal lives, proud of the role they had played in history. But none of these descriptions fits B. Franklin Mahoney.

Estimates of Mahoney's profits on the sale of the company to Lindbergh's backers ranged as high as $1 million. Whether it was more or less matters little. Early in 1929 he moved to New York City and started living it up on Park Avenue with Tommy, the second Mrs. Mahoney. Within months, he reportedly lost nearly all his holdings in the stock market, apparently having bought heavily on margin in the hopes of making a killing. Then he dropped out of sight. No one in San Diego heard from him for years until a man who had worked as a pilot in California stumbled across him. The pilot was in New York on a business trip for an aircraft engine company. He stopped briefly at Roosevelt Field, where Lindbergh's transatlantic flight had begun. Here is his story:

"I don't remember the name of the man who had the lease on the hangar, but I'd met him before. This particular evening, after I hangared my plane with him, he said, 'By the way, aren't you from the West Coast?' I said I was, so he asked me if I recalled a fellow by the name of Mahoney.

"'You mean Franklin?

"'Yes, if he's the man who built Ryan planes.'

"'That's him. I'd like to see him.'

"'Well, he's living in my hangar, up there in the storage area.'

"Climbing up the stairs, I found Franklin sitting on an Army cot. He hadn't shaved for at least a week. We talked for about an hour. He appeared to be living in the loft, probably the only place he had to hang his hat.

"I was just a kid at the time—twenty-one years old. He had been living

Twenty-year-old Marvel Crosson, sister of famed Alaskan bush pilot Joe Crosson, flew Mahoney-Ryan B-3 Brougham to new women's altitude record.

Left, below: Again bearing Ryan Aircraft name, a few B-7 Broughams were built after company became subsidiary of Detroit Aircraft. Below: This C-1 cabin plane, assembled in August 1930, was last aircraft built by the original Ryan Airlines and its unfortunate successors.

plenty well the last time I had seen him. I was terribly upset and shocked. I never saw him again."

Mahoney did, however, manage to pull out of it for a while. He became a salesman for an aircraft company in Los Angeles, married again, and for some years lived a relatively fruitful life. Ten years after the Lindbergh flight he was reportedly working as a glider salesman for Hawley Bowlus. A former Ryan worker who saw him in San Francisco when Mahoney was selling airport lighting equipment said that his recent boss "had aged twenty years." Mahoney died in 1951 in a sanitarium near Los Angeles where he spent the last years of his life with a heart ailment.

And thus ends the story of B. Franklin Mahoney, with this reflective observation by Tom Mathews: "He may have lived the Roaring Twenties somewhat in the F. Scott Fitzgerald manner, but he was a pretty smart Irishman, who, unfortunately, had his share of human weakness."

Charles Lindbergh gave as much credit to Donald Hall for the success of his flight as anyone else. It was Hall who labored day and night over his drafting board to make the necessary modifications to the Ryan design that permitted Lindbergh to complete his journey. It was Hall, along with Lindbergh, who saw that quality was built into the plane at every step.

Hall's last official contact with Lindbergh's flight came on June 16, 1927, when, seated quietly near Lindbergh at a banquet in New York City, he heard the Lone Eagle describe him as "one person to whom great credit belongs."

Hall stayed on with Mahoney after the flight, and during the first few months designed a new low-wing monoplane. Mahoney hoped to build them by the hundreds for the surging post-Lindbergh market.

The plane had no elevators. The horizontal tail was a small airfoil that could produce lift in various amounts according to its angle of attack. The angle was controlled by two levers—one was the conventional stick in the cockpit and the other was at the side of the cockpit to control a 50-pound weight which traveled on a track the length of the fuselage, thus influencing the pitch of the craft.

Mahoney reportedly invested $50,000 in building one of Hall's planes.

Don Hall's radical monoplane design featured a movable aft wing in place of the normal horizontal stabilizer-elevator combination. Aft wing was controlled in part by a "gearshift" lever.

H. A. Erickson

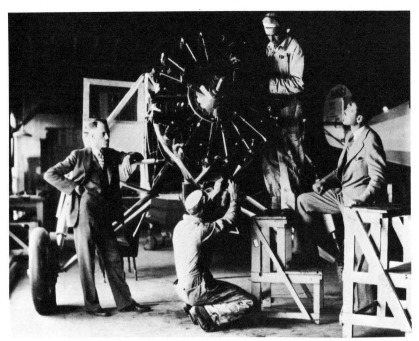

W. A. (Art) Mankey, left, who had worked on M-1 engineering for Ryan, returned in 1928 as chief engineer for Mahoney. Publicist Tom Mathews, far right.

Red Harrigan, the company's test pilot, was assigned to try the plane out. Here is what happened, in the words of Mathews, who had stayed on as Mahoney's public relations manager:

"Ex-Navy pilot Harrigan was qualified in flying boats, pontoon planes, balloons, dirigibles, fighters, bombers, transports, and utility planes, but he was the first to admit that his first flight [in Hall's plane] was completely unrelated to any previous flying experience. On takeoff the tail kept getting higher than the nose. In his first turn the plane crabbed sideways and started to slip toward the ground. For a little while it appeared that the plane and pilot—bouncing like a kangaroo—were going to disappear over the horizon. Harrigan finally got the ship headed back to the field and landed. It was then Hall explained the function of the second lever—the speed shift—on the side of the cockpit.

"The flight tests continued, and as Harrigan gradually taught himself to fly the plane and gained confidence, he manipulated the weight fore and aft under good level flight control, made sweeping turns, ran a few speed runs over the field at 135 mph, and completed a variety of landings.

"Harrigan refused to spin the plane because he wasn't sure but what it would spin tail first, and as he explained, he didn't want to be the first guy in the world to find out about that."

Mahoney later dropped the project as "having more problems than possibilities," Mathews recalled.

It was during this period that Hall's role changed from chief engineer to chief experimental engineer. Mahoney had hired W. A. (Art) Mankey, the Douglas Aircraft engineer who had helped Jack Northrop in redesigning the M-1 wing, as the company's chief engineer. Mahoney never got around to telling Hall of the organizational change, and it came as quite a surprise to Hall when Mankey told him he had taken over the top engineering job.

In spite of Harrigan's poor assessment of the X7621, Hall considered his role in designing it as important as the role he played in the *Spirit*

Hall's X-1 Special not only had a controllable aft wing but the rudder "weather-vaned" as there was no vertical fin. Lindbergh made several flights in it at St. Louis.

A happy mood prevails as old friends Hall and Ryan witness 1967 first flight of duplicate of *Spirit* piloted by Frank Tallman, right, its builder.

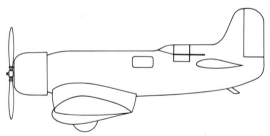

Hall's 1931 design for a "Super Speed Mail-Express" featured his controllable aft wing.

of St. Louis. He struck out on his own, determined to prove the success of his design. He took a job at the YMCA, where he also lived, but he soon learned that his dream was so costly he could not even afford the YMCA standard of living. He was given permission to move back into his former office at the old Ryan Airlines plant in the fish cannery. He put a cot and a hot plate on one side of the room, and it became his laboratory, office, and home.

He washed his clothes in a bucket and hung them in the wing loft to dry. He cooked his meager meals on as little as 10 cents a day, buying only the cheapest foods.

The City of San Diego bought the old Ryan plant in the early thirties, but Hall was allowed to live and work there, rent free, while some laughed quietly at his struggle. Occasionally he did some engineering consultation work for Claude Ryan, who was constantly trying out ideas for new aircraft design.

In 1931 he found business partners who helped him organize his own company, and this brought a little financial relief. Brighter prospects gave him the courage to propose to Elizabeth Walker, a girl who had waited in silence as he struggled to recapture the thrust he had once known. But the business arrangement did not work out, and it was dissolved in 1936.

By then, the Halls had a one-year-old son, and the responsibility became too much to bear. In the quietness of their home, Hall and his wife finally decided to abandon their dream. He went to work in 1937 for Consolidated Aircraft Corporation, which its founder, former airmail pilot Major Reuben Fleet, had moved to San Diego two years earlier. In December, 1949, Hall was hired as an aeronautical engineer at the Naval Air Station on North Island, formerly Rockwell Field. His last job was with the Navy's air rework facility there.

Throughout his years of employment after 1937, Hall remained a good engineer, although his career was not marked by brilliance. He was highly regarded by his fellow employees, and he did his work well.

But never again did the call to greatness summon the response it had

150

in the early years of his life. He was in many ways an ordinary but dedicated man who had risen to meet an extraordinary challenge. And when that challenge was over, he became once again an ordinary man.

On May 2, 1968, at the age of 69, Donald Hall died. His widow, for reasons of her own, told only a few friends about his death. Two months later, his death became known when a story appeared in the San Diego *Evening Tribune.* It began like this:

"The fleeting finger of fame touched his life briefly and then moved on, and when he died in his home here a world which had sung his praises scarcely knew he had gone."

But Lindbergh would never forget Hall's great contribution. Even thirty years after the flight he wrote a friend that "Hall deserves most of the credit for the high standards of design and careful inspection of engineering requirements that went into the *Spirit.*"

Belatedly learning of Hall's death, Lindbergh wrote that "I never see the *Spirit of St. Louis* without thinking of the magnificent engineering job Don did in its design and construction—sixty days to create such a record-breaking plane! Hanging there in the National Museum, it will always be a memorial to his fortitude and genius."

Others associated with the *Spirit* also sought to carve their own niche in history. Three of Ryan's former employees, headed by O. R. McNeel, moved to Los Angeles and established their own firm—Ryan Mechanics Monoplane Co.

They designed the Lone Eagle, a small monoplane engineered by William J. Waterhouse, who had worked on the Ryan M-1. The new plane used steel tubing throughout, in the wings as well as the fuselage. In time, the company moved to San Bernardino, but because of Ryan's objections over use of his name, it changed its name to Federal Aircraft. At least two planes were built, and then the design was modified. In 1929, the company received an order for fifty planes through Dick Bowman, a former Ryan pilot, who was then flying for PAT. But the small firm was unable to muster the resources to meet the order, and it was finally forced to close its doors.

Missouri Historical Society

Besides developing their own design, Ryan Mechanics Monoplane Co. modified a Waterhouse Cruizair for a projected New York-Portland, Oregon, flight. Pilot is O. R. McNeel.

Ryan Aeronautical Library

Ryan Mechanics formed a new company to build cantilever wing monoplane which, with Lindbergh's permission, was called Lone Eagle. Former Ryan Airlines employees who formed company included O. R. McNeel, president, center; Henry Hunold, vice president, on McNeel's left; and Fred Ayars, secretary-treasurer, in business suit.

Bowlus rejoined Claude for a while in the Ryan-Siemens engine business when the Mahoney group moved to St. Louis. Always a glider enthusiast, Bowlus in 1929 taught Lindbergh and his bride, Anne, the art of sailplane flying. The Bowlus Albatross manufactured by Hawley was the leading sailplane of its day. During World War II, he developed a cargo glider capable of carrying more than forty troops when towed behind a flying "tug." Later he made precision-built model trains; he headed Bowlus Engineering, Inc., up to his death in 1967. But Hawley was always a better innovator than businessman and wouldn't have had it otherwise. Though he hadn't flown for years, Hawley wanted one last fling at flying. Ten days before his death he trucked an Albatross sailplane out to the desert and was towed aloft. He hadn't flown for many years, but he hadn't lost the touch.

In Albatross sailplane of his own design, Hawley Bowlus taught Charles and Anne Lindbergh fine points of powerless flight.

Title Insurance Collection

The colorful, short-term sales manager A. J. Edwards, who took the self-assumed role of Lindbergh's "manager" after the flight, was another playboy type—he had an affection for the fair sex but was without addiction to the fruit of the vine. A flamboyant promoter both of himself and any product he represented, Edwards had a colorful career as a race car and stunt driver, in competition against Lincoln Beachey, and as automobile salesman and distributor.

Just how many times A. J. was married not even his eldest son was able to compute. Edwards could, his son recalls, arrive in any city and within fifteen minutes have a date lined up. Money was for spending, not saving. "One time," his son recalled, "Dad made $15,000 on a deal and three days later didn't have a cent left. He could live on $5 a week or $5,000—it didn't make any difference."

Even when Lindbergh made his headquarters at Edwards' apartment, Edwards' twenty-one-year-old son, employed by a San Diego finance company, paid the rent. When the decision was made to move the Mahoney operation to St. Louis, Edwards remained behind and joined a new firm, Prudden–San Diego Airplane Company, as sales manager.

152

Lindbergh visits with San Diego aviation group in 1928. Left to right, O. R. McPherson, chamber of commerce; B. F. Mahoney; George H. Prudden, builder of all-metal planes bearing his name; Lindbergh; A. J. Edwards, Prudden sales manager; and Major Thomas Lanphier, flying companion of Lindbergh.

He was succeeded at Mahoney-Ryan by tire salesman Sam C. Breder. Later Edwards job-hopped to Los Angeles, then to Wichita, and on to Cincinnati as sales manager with various aircraft makers. Finally, back in San Diego, he at last settled down in the automobile business as a used-car salesman, his promotional ability exhausted. In 1953 his death went virtually unnoticed.

Just as the *Spirit* in a broad sense altered the lives of all America—and the world—so too did the *Spirit* syndrome affect the participants in a very personal way, although not so greatly—or, in one area, so tragically—as in Lindbergh's case.

Mahoney was finally conquered by heart trouble. Hall's undeniable engineering capability never again reached public notice. Many workmen on the plane, who came to believe that Lindbergh would have failed without some minor contribution of theirs, lived in the past for the rest of their lives. Edwards, the car salesman briefly thrust into the limelight, went back to being a used car salesman.

Others who had been involved in the *Spirit* continued to cling to that remnant from the past, often bickering among themselves over who had played the greatest role.

A few like Hawley Bowlus, John van der Linde, Walter Locke, Fred Rohr, and Red Harrigan rejoined Claude Ryan and lived productive lives, proud of their past but able to look to the future.

In 1940 Rohr formed a successful company of his own—a story in itself—but then his role in the construction of the *Spirit* was of less consequence than the roles of Hall, Bowlus, and Locke.

Through all the eddying currents Claude Ryan flew a steady course. Over the years he, virtually alone, gave continuity to the spirit of adventure, of pioneering, and of dedication to aviation he had engendered in his original company.

For years, T. Claude Ryan had struggled to build a sound company. His success was not astonishing. Like many others of that era, he began with little and forged ahead, one small step at a time. It was the story of America in the 1920s, a young nation on its way to world leadership.

153

Sam C. Breder succeeded A. J. Edwards as Mahoney-Ryan sales manager. In 1935, Breder joined Claude Ryan and was key sales executive for over two decades.

On twenty-fifth anniversary of Lindbergh flight, five Ryan Aeronautical Company employees relive days when they worked on *Spirit of St. Louis*. Left to right: Fred Magula, Red Harrigan, John van der Linde, O. L. Gray, and Walter O. Locke.

By a stroke of fate Claude had missed aviation's greatest business opportunity. He had seen his original company go bankrupt through neglect, ineptitude, and the egotism of those scrambling for credit in the reflected glory of Lindbergh's great accomplishment.

One of the great jealousies of the Lindbergh years grew out of the fact that the *Spirit* carried the Ryan name to world prominence. The press and the public identified the man bearing that name as the man "who built Lindbergh's plane." This oversimplification caused some to resent Ryan, claiming he sought for himself the glory of the Lindbergh achievement. But Ryan knew the role he had played, and he never accepted more of the credit than he deserved.

Aware of the problem, and the reaction of his contemporaries, Ryan was meticulous in pointing out that he had only "founded" the company. Lindbergh phrased it best: "Claude Ryan . . . built the company that built the *Spirit of St. Louis.*"

Georgia Mathias, secretary to Ryan and Mahoney, put it in other terms. "If Claude hadn't been there and seen to it that Lindbergh's wire was taken seriously, there would have been no *Spirit of St. Louis.*"

One San Diego newspaperman went out of his way to gratuitously denigrate Claude with the comment: "Contrary to general opinion, T. C. Ryan, who founded the company that bears his name, is not affiliated with the concern and had absolutely nothing to do with the success of Lindbergh's flight."

Less than two years later, this same reporter, who covered the story of the sixty-day miracle in building Lindbergh's plane, wrote Edwards to complain: "While Lindbergh attained worldwide honors in his Paris flight, virtually every person even remotely connected with his achievement fell heir to misfortune or plain damn hard luck. In other words, you, Mahoney, Hall, Bowlus, the shop foreman, and even myself, lost our jobs."

Only twenty-six years after the great events of the spring of 1927 did Ryan unburden himself in a letter to Lindbergh.

They built the *Spirit of St. Louis*—Bowlus, Mahoney, Lindbergh, Hall.

"Although I no longer owned a financial interest in the company during the period your plane was being built, I had the satisfaction of knowing that I had developed the team which had the ability, confidence, enthusiasm, and energy to do the job.

"I spent much of my time, during the period Franklin asked me to continue in a managerial capacity, on some of the company's pressing business matters. The reason our partnership was dissolved was because Franklin would not settle down and face the business problems.

"I was glad to see you give Hall, Bowlus, and all the others the credit you did. I had originally picked every one of them and they were personal friends.

"I could see the undreamed-of opportunity that was dropped in the lap of the company which had been virtually my whole life, and was concerned that it had no serious-minded management in authority to run it. Franklin, with all his lovable qualities, had always just enjoyed the sporting thrill that his original investment made possible. He liked it that way and until he acquired full ownership did not participate much in running the operation.

"During that period of high excitement, I was in the ironical position of being on the outside while the little company I had started, built up and operated until shortly before the flight, was suddenly in the middle of world attention. I am sure now that that trick of fate was a most fortunate circumstance for me because otherwise, at the age of twenty-nine, I too might have been deluded into believing I was something which I definitely was not."

History had played a peculiar trick on Ryan. Fate came to the aid of his company when it was small and struggling, and success opened unlimited possibilities. But it came too late for Ryan, who was forced to begin anew while the company he had founded fumbled the unparalleled opportunity thrust upon it by the success of Lindbergh's flight.

155

Claude Ryan built the company that built the *Spirit* as Lindbergh noted in autographing his book about the flight.

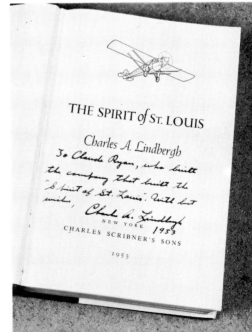

Dutch Flats airport, 1928, with former partners Mahoney
and Ryan now in business side-by-side.

CHAPTER FIFTEEN

A New Beginning— and Tragedy

"HONEST, MR. PERKINS, I NEVER TOOK ANYTHING FOR IT," Russ Saunders said as he eyed his high school principal across the desk.

Glen Perkins knew the big burly youth was telling the truth. Russ was too frightened to lie. The strapping lad towered over the desk, and Perkins thought for a moment the kid looked like a giant, which indeed he was to many of the students at San Diego High School.

Young Saunders had captured the imagination of just about every male in town, student or otherwise, and the undying devotion of most females. There weren't many high school students around who could handle a football the way Russ could. And with the season's championship game just hours away, the principal and the gridiron star faced a real crisis. Russ had been accused of accepting money for a boxing match, thus disqualifying him from the game.

The problem went beyond the scope of the single football game. Although Perkins was a fan himself, he might have been inclined to let the whole thing go had it not been for the husky youth who stood before him.

Russ was tough, and before his reputation was established he had often expressed his convictions through the strength of his hands. But he wasn't a liar. And he wasn't a cheat. Perkins couldn't just sit still and watch a promising youth suffer because of an unsubstantiated claim.

"Your dad's up in Hemet?" the principal asked, finally breaking the agonizing silence.

157

Gridiron star Russ Saunders.

"Yes sir," Russ answered. "And he knows I didn't take any money. He can vouch for me."

"We'll have to get him to sign a statement and get it back here before the game."

"But Mr. Perkins," Russ interrupted, "That's better than a hundred miles from here. We can't get up there and back before the game. It's just no use."

"I think I know how we can do it," Perkins said as he bounded out of his seat. "Come on."

The principal dashed through the door of his office with Russ at his heels. Within ten minutes they were at Dutch Flats, over by Mission Bay. Russ stood aside while Perkins talked with a young man near a small airplane. He watched while the principal motioned toward him and the other man looked his way.

Finally, the two men turned and walked across the mud flats.

"Russ," Perkins said, "I want you to meet Mr. Claude Ryan."

The youth realized the name was familiar as he reached out and shook Ryan's hand. Russ thought he had seen him at some of the games. He knew he was a flyer who had built some airplanes, and he was sure he had something to do with the Los Angeles–San Diego Air Line.

"I'm one of your fans," Ryan said. "And I've been looking forward to today's game. Maybe I can help."

About an hour later Ryan's M-2 settled on a field near the farming community of Hemet. Russ's father met the plane and signed a statement saying his son had never accepted money for a prize fight. He barely had time to get out of the way before the plane whipped around, taxied down the field, and took off.

Russ played that afternoon like he had never played before. The arch rival was beaten miserably. During a post-game rally that evening, Perkins got up and told the whole story.

It was the first time Gladys Bowen had heard the name of Claude Ryan. As a drama teacher at San Diego High School, she was vaguely aware of some of the early aviation history in her community—dates going back to the days of Glenn Curtiss—but the name of Ryan meant nothing to her.

The story about how the day was saved for Russ and the football team was an exciting one, and that night Gladys talked about it for awhile with her roommate, Lois Perkins, the principal's sister, but it was several months before Ryan's name came up again.

One day Perkins was driving the two girls across town. At the airport, he turned the wheels of his car sharply and skidded to a halt.

"How would you like to have an airplane ride?" he asked.

Without waiting for an answer, he jumped out of the car and disappeared into a small hangar. There were several planes clustered around the field. Gladys had paid little heed to the operation at Ryan Airport, but she knew a lot of people went there on weekends for flights over San Diego.

A few moments later Perkins emerged beaming from the hangar and rushed to the car.

"We're in luck," he said. "Claude Ryan himself is going to take you up."

"Claude Ryan himself, huh," Gladys said as she climbed out of the car. It sounded like a pretentious buildup for a young upstart who spent his time flying airplanes.

The ride in the cabin plane was fun, she admitted later, but she just couldn't see why Perkins was so excited about Ryan. He seemed awfully intense to her, and he paid so much attention to the airplane that he scarcely spoke to either of the girls.

As far as Gladys was concerned, that was it for Claude Ryan. But weeks later, after Lindbergh's flight, his name came up again when Perkins asked her to attend a party. Perkins was trying to interest Ryan in a business deal, and he had promised the flyer a blind date with a pretty schoolteacher if he would come to the party.

The offer was hardly flattering, but Gladys finally agreed. She couldn't even remember what Ryan looked like, since she had seen him only once, and he had spent most of his time babying his airplane.

Meanwhile, Ryan himself was having second thoughts about the party. He never had been able to get along with schoolteachers. They just didn't talk the same language. Why had he let Perkins talk him into a blind date? But it was too late to back out.

That night, Ryan learned the real reason behind the party. Perkins had lined up a few men for some sort of a joint business venture, and he wanted to get Claude into the same deal. But Ryan just wasn't interested. Still, the night wasn't a total waste.

That Gladys Bowen was quite a girl, Ryan decided as the evening wore on. She was quiet, friendly, refined, and sincere. And she was a very good-looking woman, even if she was a preacher's daughter.

Reed Studio/Ryan Aeronautical Library

Claude just went for the good-looking gals like schoolteacher Gladys Bowen.

"I didn't go for the swinger types," Ryan recalls, "but I did want my girls to be good-looking."

Gladys also did a little reassessing during the evening. Sometime during the party Claude got a business call. A company had ordered three airplane engines. Ryan came back from the phone call like a kid. Three motors in one whack!

While a purchase order for three airplane engines is not the sort of thing most girls would get excited about, Ryan's reaction left an impression on Gladys she would carry for the rest of her life. He was absolutely irrepressible, and Gladys was drawn to his boyish enthusiasm.

"If you believe in love at first sight," Gladys recalled, "that was it!" Neither of them dated anybody else after that evening.

They saw more and more of each other as the days passed, and slowly Gladys helped piece together the fragments of the life which had come to mean so much to her.

Ryan was twenty-nine years old. Years later, he would say that perhaps he was better off for having missed the boat in the Lindbergh deal.

Success would have come too easy; money would have been too plentiful. It would all have been too simple, and perhaps easy success would have been accompanied by arrogance, as it so often is. The post-Lindbergh years revealed that few men were able to cope with the pressures of instant triumph. Perhaps for Ryan, too, the burden would have been too heavy.

But there must have been moments in those early days when he had to struggle to keep his disappointment from turning to bitterness. Apparently, even before the Lindbergh flight, Ryan had sensed the challenge he would have to face. While still working as general manager of the company he had sold to Mahoney, he was following up on ideas he had earlier developed for a way to invest his resources and time. Idleness would have led to personal disaster.

After careful study he decided, in mid-1926, that there was a void in the engines available for private flying that should be filled. Those that were available were either too expensive or too scarce. He considered trying to manufacture what he thought was needed, but that would have taken a tremendous investment, one that he simply did not have the means to make.

RYAN *Siemens*

APPROVED BY UNITED STATES GOVERNMENT FOR AIR MAIL LINES

The Motor is the Heart of the Airplane

He discussed it with his mechanic, John van der Linde, who suggested he look into the Siemens-Halske Co. of Germany. Siemens was a huge, diversified firm among whose products were radial aircraft engines. The engines were far superior to anything in this country except the Wright and Pratt & Whitney radials. The Siemens featured ball bearings throughout, and interchangeable parts for five-, seven-, and nine-cylinder engines. They had already established a record of 5 million miles in service as standard equipment with twelve German air service operators.

Ryan contacted the company a couple of weeks before Lindbergh's flight. Accompanied by writer Max Miller, he hitched a ride in an Army plane to Dayton and then on to New York to talk with the firm's representative. While there he nailed down an agreement to become the sole distributor and manufacturing licensee in this country. He then purchased a used Chevrolet to give his father and began the long drive across country.

Somewhere along the way he heard about the success of Lindbergh's flight, but he was already looking forward to his new venture. Back in San Diego, he rented a downtown office, set up shop under the name of Ryan Aeronautical Corporation, and arranged to borrow a secretary from the attorneys next door. His total investment in the engine business was $12,500. The next step was a trip around the country by train, lining up orders for what was billed as the Ryan-Siemens engine. He also leased part of the field at Dutch Flats, adjacent to Mahoney's operation, as an operating base for the engine business.

The cross-country sales trip was so productive that more orders began coming in than the manufacturer could fill. "It was," Claude said, "a slick deal. I'd signed up half a dozen aircraft manufacturers for engines. The warehouse in New York would change the engine nameplates from Siemens to Ryan-Siemens and I'd simply wire directions for reshipment from New York in the original boxes."

H. A. Erickson

A Ryan-Siemens engine powered this enclosed version of the M-2 monoplane.

161

H. A. Erickson

Powered by three 125-hp Ryan-Siemens engines, the huge Albatross carried two-and-a-half times its own weight.

H. A. Erickson

San Diego-built Prudden all-metal trimotor was Ryan-Siemens equipped.

Waco biplane was among twenty American planes powered by Ryan-Siemens engines.

Two new southern California aircraft manufacturers—among those trying to ride the crest of the wave of enthusiasm following Lindbergh's flight—were purchasers of Ryan-Siemens engines.

One was Zenith Aircraft of Santa Ana, whose trimotored Albatross, flown by Charles Rocheville, carried 2½ times its own empty weight during endurance flights when powered by three Ryan-Siemens 125-hp engines.

Another user was the Prudden-San Diego Airplane Company, whose all metal trimotor was similarly powered. The firm's managing director was George H. Prudden, formerly chief engineer of the Stout Metal Airplane Company, originator of the famed Ford trimotor.

Ryan had been promised that the Siemens company could deliver all he could sell, but the firm came through with only about fifteen engines a month, just about one-third the number Ryan had sold.

Ryan complained bitterly to the firm's New York representative, but to no avail. He decided the only answer would be to go to Europe and talk to the top officials in person. But he didn't want to go alone.

During the difficult months following the success of Lindbergh's flight, Claude's bond with Gladys Bowen had grown deeper. When Lindbergh returned to San Diego in September following his flight, it was the pretty drama teacher who sat beside Claude Ryan on the platform in the high school stadium as the city officially paid its respects. That evening at a formal dinner, Ryan was not asked to sit with the dignitaries. He bought his own ticket and sat in a corner of the dining hall, virtually alone.

As he began to regain his lost momentum, Gladys was frequently at his side. She too enjoyed flying, and she joined him on many flights around the San Diego area.

"I've never felt he had any regret about what had happened," she recalled years later. "He was happy to be back in business, especially under his own name, and he had a lot of enthusiasm for starting over again. True, it was a step back to the kind of business he had started five years earlier, but he tackled it with real drive. He's never lost that enthusiasm."

But Gladys realized early in the game that Claude could get a lot more excited about selling airplane engines than considering matrimony. When their third date rolled around, he had just returned from Long Beach,

Claude equipped his own M-2 with the imported
Siemens engine marketed under the Ryan name.

Ryan Aeronautical Library

where he had attended the wedding of his sister, Louise.

"Was it a nice wedding?" asked the drama teacher.

"It was all right, but I don't know why on earth she wanted to get married," Ryan said.

"What's the matter, don't you like the fellow she married?"

"Oh sure, he's all right, but I don't know why anybody would get married."

Perhaps that should have been enough to compel any beautiful young woman to direct her attention elsewhere. But Gladys Bowen was not just any young woman.

She had learned much about her flyer, and she bothered to look deeply enough to see beyond his superficial objection to marriage. He had watched while Mahoney nearly cracked up over an unsatisfactory marriage. The same was true with J. B. Alexander. Edwards' marriages, too, were a shambles and all was not well in the personal lives of several others in the business. Ryan had reason to be skeptical, she concluded, but his skepticism did not constitute grounds for her dismissing him as a prospect.

Claude was a flashy pilot—in the sense that he was a superb one—but that flashiness did not extend to his personal habits. Although he managed to have plenty of girls around, he was essentially, according to his own description, "a pretty hardworking pilot," and his personal life was uncomplicated.

Time has a way of curing most skeptics, especially when helped along by a woman who has met her man. Gladys was a real contrast—a refreshing, sensible, attractive woman—to the wives and girlfriends of his flying friends.

"We were engaged by Thanksgiving," Gladys recalled later.

They planned to get married the following summer after school was out, but Ryan's plans to go to Europe offered a great chance to combine business with pleasure. They were married in Los Angeles on February 18, 1928, and were soon on their way to Europe. En route to New York, Ryan stopped in Muskegon, Michigan, to try and sell the manufacturing rights for the Siemens engine to Continental Motors Corporation of Detroit for $100,000. He was turned down. Years later, the Ryan company was to purchase Continental as a majority-owned subsidiary.

Ryan Aeronautical Library

The honeymooners head for Europe.

Dr. Hans Frank, the Siemens representative in New York, accompanied Claude and Gladys to Germany. While in Berlin, Ryan called on the top officials at Siemens-Halske to pound the table in hopes of getting more engines. But instead of promising to meet his demands, the officials tried to raise the price of the engines. After two weeks in Berlin, Ryan managed to talk them out of that, but he couldn't get them to promise to deliver enough engines to fill his orders.

"When it came to travel, we were babes in the woods," Gladys recalled of the trip after leaving Berlin. "We had a wonderful time in Lucerne, and then we took the trip down the Rhine to Cologne. After flying from Cologne to Paris, we went to England to visit some of my relatives. We were on our own."

Ryan and his new bride returned to San Diego, disappointed over the lack of progress in the Siemens deal. In his absence, two business associates who were to join Claude in organizing a flying school under his name moved ahead far too rapidly, committing Claude's money to their rather grandiose ideas. "When I left for Europe I didn't have a flying school," Claude recalls. "When I got back I had one, as well as some debts I hadn't

164

bargained for." Ryan was not ready to take that big a step so soon. He severed his relationship with the two men, but kept the school open on a more realistic basis.

About that time an old friend returned. Hawley Bowlus, a man with whom he had shared triumph and disappointment, rejoined Claude's team.

In the meantime, Ryan built up his small air fleet, adding planes as good deals came along. After Mahoney sold out to the St. Louis buyers, Ryan bought the old company's entire flying operation at Dutch Flats through a third party, combining it with his own operation. Thus he was back in business where he had started.

Like Bowlus, many others who had worked with him before came back.

One of the planes included in the purchase of the Mahoney flying service operation was a practically new Brougham, which Ryan tried to sell for $15,000. No one was particularly anxious to buy it, but finally a man came along and asked to make a trade.

"Will you take an oil well?" the man asked.

"Will it produce oil?" Ryan wanted to know.

"Yup," came the answer. "It's pumping right now. And what's more it's right on the edge of Long Beach, so if the oil runs out you can use the land for a subdivision."

That oil well stayed on the Ryan books for years, steadily producing enough oil to make it worth keeping around.

Within a few weeks after his trip to Europe, Ryan received word that the Siemens Company wanted to send its own representative to the United States, thus killing his contract to distribute the engines. He offered the company the chance to buy him out, provided he was paid for the good will and intangibles his association had earned for the firm. That deal, including the money he had made by selling engines, netted Ryan about $75,000, forming the nest egg for expanded operations in other areas.

Midsummer 1928 found Claude back again in the flying service business at Dutch Flats.

Title Insurance Collection

For the first time, Ryan had the resources to establish a sound economic footing for his own enterprise. $75,000 was not a lot of money, but, together with the experience Ryan had gained from the Mahoney debacle, it was enough to get him through the great national tragedy that lay in the years ahead.

In the fall of 1929, just a few months after Ryan had dropped out of the Siemens deal, an economic blight crept across this country with disastrous results. The stock market plunged to the bottom, taking with it the investments and savings of millions of Americans.

It was the kind of disaster the United States had never known. Businessmen who had once ruled vast enterprises stood on street corners selling apples, struggling to feed their families.

And each day the sickness grew worse. At the height of the Depression more than 16 million Americans were out of work. Men and women roamed the streets and back alleys of cities; they haunted the silenced workyards of the nation, and they watched as their children went hungry.

The tragic cry of "Brother, can you spare a dime?" became a theme for a song.

Every bank in the country was forced to close its doors. Many never opened again.

Through it all Ryan managed to keep his small company solvent, and even pushed ahead in some areas. But "Those were difficult days," Gladys Ryan recalled years later. "The highlight of the week would be if the school sold a flying course. We'd go out and celebrate. Maybe have dinner out."

During the Depression Gladys gave birth to the first of their three sons. They named him David Claude, and, of the three sons, he was the one

William Wagner

Sons David, left, and Jerry put in their appearances in 1929 and 1932.

Off on a family vacation—Jerry, Steve, David, Gladys, and Claude Ryan.

Ryan Aeronautical Library

most like his father. Meanwhile, on the other side of the country, Charles A. Lindbergh, Jr., made his debut, carrying a name known around the world.

Gladys had met Lindbergh only once, but much that she had heard about the famed flyer reminded her of the man she had married. Both cherished their privacy. Both were quiet, reserved. Both harbored a deep love of flying. And now, both had sons to carry on their work.

That was why the news of March 1, 1932, created for her a special kind of hell. That night twenty-month-old Charles A. Lindbergh, Jr., was kidnapped from the second-floor nursery of his parents' home in Hopewell, New Jersey. The kidnapper left a ransom note on the window sill demanding $50,000.

The news hit this nation like a thunderclap. In a time of great trials and tribulations, the people associated Lindbergh with victory, not defeat. The crime was a personal blow for millions of persons who had looked to people like Lindbergh for some sign of hope, some sort of reaffirmation of faith in the future.

A massive search spread out from the small New Jersey town where the Lindberghs had moved to raise their family. The search for the infant became a national obsession. But the desperate manhunt turned up nothing.

Finally, seventy-three days after little Charles had been kidnapped, a truck driver saw what appeared to be a shallow grave on the side of the road. The grave yielded the body of the Lindbergh baby, and a nation grieved.

On September 19, 1934, an obscure carpenter named Bruno Richard Hauptmann was arrested. He was convicted of murder in the first degree in February 1935, following a sensational trial which held the rapt attention of the world for nearly six weeks. After numerous attempts by his attorneys to save his life, Bruno Hauptmann died in the electric chair nearly four years after the kidnapping. Quietly, the Lindberghs moved across the Atlantic to restructure their lives in solitude.

"I was haunted by the whole thing," Gladys recalled. "They were very near the same age, Lindbergh's first child and our David. Night after night I checked David's room every few hours. It took a long time to get over the shock of that tragedy."

David lived to follow in the footsteps of his father—for awhile. Faced by the realities of the Korean conflict, Claude and David discussed what it would mean to both of them. David chose an Air Force career, and to prepare him with good basic flying training, Claude arranged for David to take instruction under Pete Larson, a former Ryan school instructor. David, too, soon acquired his father's love for flying.

In 1951, while the nation was at war, David joined the Air Force as an aviation cadet. He completed his training and was commissioned early in 1952 as a jet fighter pilot.

The next step would be Korea, and David began advanced training. On September 10, 1952, two days before he was to complete his training, David's F-86 Sabre jet failed to pull out of a low-level bombing run over rugged desert terrain near Las Vegas, Nevada. Lieutenant David Claude Ryan, twenty-two, died in the fiery crash on the desert floor.

Claude and Gladys, with their other two sons, Jerome and Stephen, had been vacationing in Europe and were on their way home aboard the liner Queen Elizabeth when word was flashed to them that David had died.

Like the Lindberghs, the Ryans had lost their firstborn.

U.S. Air Force

Lieut. David Claude Ryan, USAF.

It was a proud father who pinned military pilot's wings on his son David in 1951.

Ryan Aeronautical Library

Flight training at Dutch Flats, 1930.

CHAPTER SIXTEEN

School Days

THE STOCK MARKET CRASH in the autumn of 1929 plunged the United States, and thus the world, into an economic depression of staggering proportions. Now, many years after the world crumbled to its financial knees, the Great Depression is still vivid in the minds of those who lived through it and an enigma to those who came afterward.

Decades later, young people would be chastised by their elders because they had not lived through the great despair of the Depression, and thus could not appreciate the good life they had inherited. And for the young trying to understand the past, it became a blight in American history, transformed by the movies into something it never was and discussed by grandparents with a wave of the arms when words failed, as they always did.

But if the Depression was a mystery to many, it was a boon of sorts to others. Man is a strange creature, and it is an odd commentary on his nature that he has the capacity to make fun of his bleakest moments. Thus the Depression became a fertile field for comics, and it may well be that some young people have formed more of their impressions about the Depression by what they have heard from comedians than from their elders or their school books.

To the teenager of 1929, more inspired by the Lindbergh saga than concerned by economic anxieties which faced the older generation, a flying career was the strongest possible magnet. Parents of means who wanted

Ryan Flying School formally opened May 1, 1928, though Claude had been training pilots in San Diego since September 1922.

During days of Los Angeles–San Diego Air Line, pilot instruction was offered at both terminal airports.

to respond to their sons' ambitions found they could rationalize the decision of paying for flight training if the right school could be found. On this proposition Claude Ryan was able to capitalize and weave his way through the pitfalls of the Depression years.

Through hard, costly experience dating back to the American School of Aviation at Venice, Claude Ryan had learned the value of the competent instruction given at March Field as contrasted with the often-haphazard training then available at commercial schools. So, in formally opening the Ryan Flying School on May 1, 1928, after his return from Europe, Claude insisted on rigid, businesslike instruction methods. Not only did the Ryan School require more hours of flight training before graduation than did other schools, but it also provided more extensive instrument, night, and cross-country flight training.

Just prior to the Depression, the Department of Commerce adopted regulatory measures and began granting certificates of approval to qualified flying schools. At first, the department handed out only four certificates for the highest rating—transport pilot. One of these certificates went to the Ryan Flying School, which at that time operated under an agreement with Pacific Technical University allowing the latter to give ground school training.

The spark-plug at Pacific Technical was Earl D. Prudden, a real estate salesman and bachelor who had come from Detroit after his brother George started the Prudden–San Diego Airplane Company.

"He was a super-salesman if there ever was one," Claude recalled. "At my invitation Earl tried his hand one Sunday as a 'barker' at Ryan Airport selling sightseeing rides. He was so successful and such an outstanding personality in dealing with the public that we asked him in July, 1928, to join our organization full-time and be responsible for all sales activity.

"Whether in correspondence or in personal contact, Prudden was an irresistible charmer of parents whose sons had somehow gotten them to

170

Above: Claude presenting wings to Ryan flight students. Ground school was given at Pacific Technical University, below.

During the Depression, Ryan resumed his role as a flight instructor. With Claude and chief instructor S. E. (Robbie) Robbins at left is Earl Prudden. Below is the entire Ryan organization, 1930.

Earl DeWitt Prudden. He was everyone's friend.

Gladser-Mitchell

consider going to California to learn to fly. And when the student prospect arrived in San Diego, Prudden's 'den mother' concern for them was frequently the factor which closed the sale."

The scions of many a prominent family, both here and abroad, were among early Ryan students. The school had a peerless reputation for excellent, safe training practices. San Diego was a delightful place for year-around flying, and Claude Ryan had a name known in aviation circles throughout the world. Students came not only from every state, but from Europe, South Africa, China, and Latin America.

Once parents met or corresponded with Prudden and Ryan they felt comfortable that their sons—or daughters—would be in good hands. Like most parents, they wanted to satisfy their children's interest in a new venture—flying—but they wanted to be sure it was on a sound basis.

The embryo mechanic with little background or formal schooling from a small Midwestern town shared a common interest with the Eastern prep school graduate whose parents were often wealthy enough to buy Ryan out a hundred times over. In fact, some of the financing for expansion of Ryan activities came from parents who saw in Claude Ryan integrity, farsighted creativity, and keen business acumen. And he was an indefatigable worker. Self-made men found in Claude and Earl the very qualities from which their own success stemmed. There developed a rapport between students, parents, and the school which was refreshing and unique.

Together Ryan and Prudden formed an unbeatable flying school sales combination. Their advertising of San Diego's attractions during the winter months was particularly effective because it pointed out "the double advantages of Ryan tutorage and the shorter time required for training under the year-around blue skies of southern California."

1931 publicity picture featured vintage car, a poor-likeness plaster of paris statue of Lindbergh, and a Ryan Brougham sister ship of the *Spirit of St. Louis*.

Sensor Studio

Ryan Aeronautical Library

Ryan Airport at Dutch Flats became an international terminal in 1929 for early airlines operating to and from Latin America.

The company also offered charter flights and various other services, but as the Depression gained a foothold, the flying school remained the mainstay of the operation.

Fate, no doubt, played a significant role in that period of Ryan's life. He had built a substantial business, only to see it crumble at the hands of other men, and he knew it had crumbled because they had tried to do too much with too little. That memory was fresh when Ryan started again, and he moved cautiously, paying his way as he went along. Thus when the Crash hit, he was not overextended and he was able to maintain his balance.

Another reason behind Ryan's success—and perhaps more significant than any of the others—was the temper of the times. If he had been dealing in a commodity which depended upon the masses—such as selling used cars—he probably would have been wiped out along with thousands of others who were competing for the same scarce dollars. Many of those who made it during the Depression did so because they offered something that appealed to those who survived the great Crash, and they were not dependent upon trading with those who were hurt the most. Such was the case with Claude Ryan.

The nation cherished a fond memory of Charles Lindbergh's epic flight, and aviation offered an exciting avenue for the young man on the way up. Much of Ryan's student pilot clientele comprised well-to-do young men looking for an exciting avocation. That would change in time, but in the days of the Depression, it was often the dashing playboys, serious for the time being about aviation, who most helped to keep Ryan in the black.

Thus as the Depression continued to grind its way into American history, a closely knit but diverse group of students gathered at San Diego, where Ryan was again back in the teaching business. They didn't exactly come in droves, but they came often enough to keep the company solvent.

Ryan Airport at Dutch Flats became the center of commercial flying activity in the Southwest corner of the United States. In 1929 there were nearly 5,000 landings by trimotor transport planes at Ryan Airport. Maddux Airlines, with its Ford trimotors, was the largest operator, but

Trimotor Ford of Maddux Airlines appears to be taking off "under the direct supervision of T. Claude Ryan."

Ryan Aeronautical Library

173

Claude got double duty out of Great Lakes biplanes. He was both factory distributor and large user of them for pilot training.

Pickwick Airways, flying Bach airliners, and Western Air Express, with its Fokker F-10s, also used Ryan's airport, which had been officially designated as the port of entry from Mexico.

To avoid conflict with the original company, which was still doing business in San Diego, Claude changed the name of his operations to "T. C." Ryan Aeronautical Corporation, "T. C." Ryan Flying School, and "T. C." Ryan Flying Service.

"At Dutch Flats we had quite a variety of airplanes—eight different types of monoplanes and biplanes—which we featured as one of the advantages of our school," Claude recalls. "We had Wacos, a DH Moth, several Jennies, and some Standards, and, of course, my own M-2, but I wanted something better for training on which we could standardize. The Cirrus-powered Great Lakes, though a biplane, was more modern than what we then had. It was also very good for acrobatics, which we included in our training course because I had patterned the program pretty closely after the military Army Flying Cadet course.

"I went after and got the California distributorship for Great Lakes, so that we could market the planes as well as use them for student instruction."

Under the guidance of Earl Prudden, Ryan introduced a relatively new concept in marketing. The program offered a new Great Lakes plane, plus full training, including 200 hours of flying instruction, for the single price of $4,460. The plane itself sold for $3,185. Under the plan, the biplane belonged to the student. He took his own risks of damage and took care of his own maintenance.

The plan was advertised nationally and created great attention in aviation circles. The biplanes, built in Cleveland, were shipped to San Diego by the carload, six per car, and Ryan's operation claimed to be the only place in the world where airplanes were sold by the carload. But along about 1933 the Cleveland firm folded, another victim of the Depression.

174

Ryan Aeronautical Library

Breaking ground for Lindbergh Field terminal buildings, 1932. Framed by Claude's pick is Harbormaster Joe Brennan; to his left, former Ryan pilot Doug Kelley, Postmaster E. W. Dort, Earl Prudden, Department of Commerce's Jimmy Nall, banker Jack Hicklin, United Air Lines' Seely Hall, and Mayor Walter Austin with shovel.

In the flurry of interest following Lindbergh's flight, the voters of San Diego passed a bond issue to construct a new airport on the bay adjoining the fish cannery where the *Spirit of St. Louis* had been built. Work began in 1928 to fill the marshy area of the waterfront with material from dredging, but it was not until 1932 that enough of the tidelands had been filled in to make the field usable for airline operation.

The new airport was in a better location, closer to the city, and it was obvious to Claude that to stay in business he would have to be located at Lindbergh Field. Ticket offices for the airlines would be needed, and government agencies would have to have space at the terminal. The city budget could not provide funds, and since Ryan would need its own offices and hangar, Claude proposed to build the administration building and air terminal and rent space to others.

H. A. Erickson

Featuring Spanish architecture and tropical landscaping, Ryan facilities greatly enhanced San Diego's Lindbergh Field.

Six months after transatlantic flight, San Diego voters approved new Lindbergh Field airport which was dedicated in August 1928, above. 1931 photo,
below, shows Ryan locations: (1) waterfront airport, 1922; (2) Dutch Flats,
1923; (3) fish cannery factory, 1926; and (4) Lindbergh Field, 1932.

H. A. Erickson

By 1934 the Ryan air terminal and school buildings gave Lindbergh Field a modern, progressive look.

"In 1932," he said, "everybody was astounded that we had the audacity, in the depth of the Depression, to think about constructing new buildings at an airport. But I had never been through a depression before and, frankly, didn't know how one was supposed to act under these conditions. If we could get the money, and there was a need for the buildings, I thought we should go ahead and build them."

He went to several banks asking for a loan, but got the same answer every place he went. The bankers laughed. Nobody was anxious to loan money in those days, and they all offered the same advice: forget it.

Again Ryan turned to one of his more prosperous students, Warren Worcester. Worcester agreed to loan the money, at 7 percent interest. Ryan borrowed it, built the new administration building, and paid Worcester back within two years.

The actual cost of the construction was substantially lower than Ryan had expected. In those days, people who had a little money could make it go pretty far, since there were so many around who were on the brink of desperation. Companies offered to help in the project, just for the sake of the work itself, even if the profit was marginal. Materials were very inexpensive, since few people were selling anything, and the law of supply and demand worked in favor of those who were able to keep moving.

A Spanish-style administration building soon took shape, complete with a tiled roof, cement drives, and paved aprons. It was surrounded by date palms and tropical shrubbery. In those days, it was a showplace in southern California, and it represented a long, hard climb for a man who started his first business with an old piano box for an office.

On July 28, 1932, with 350 military planes flying overhead in a spectacular salute, the new buildings were dedicated. The honored guest who gave

Student pilot Jacqueline Cochran went on to set records as America's top woman flier.

H. A. Erickson

177

Don Phillips. His father proved
to be a wise investor.

the main address was an aviatrix named Amelia Earhart. For years that building housed many of San Diego's aviation agencies, and it stood as a monument to an extraordinary achievement during the height of the Depression. It served as San Diego's main air terminal for more than thirty-four years.

The Ryan School of Aeronautics, Ltd., was incorporated June 5, 1931. Claude received 3,150 shares for the $31,897 assets of his company. The first outside investor came in at this time with $18,000 of additional funds. He was Frank N. Phillips, father of Ryan student pilot Don Phillips, and head of the Washburn Wire Company of Phillipsdale, Rhode Island. On May 26, 1934, the corporation's name was changed to The Ryan Aeronautical Co., and on January 5, 1935, the Ryan School of Aeronautics was organized as a wholly owned subsidiary. The officers and directors of the parent company were T. Claude Ryan, president and treasurer; Earl D. Prudden, vice president; and E. A. Smith, secretary. "E. A." Smith was actually Miss Adelaide Smith, Claude's secretary, who had started in May 1928, but in those days it was not considered good business to reveal the key role of a woman in business. She was known as E. A. Smith for fifteen years, until she became Mrs. Earl D. Prudden in 1943.

Once training operations moved to the new Lindbergh Field location, school activities were expanded to include additional specialized training for mechanics. By 1936 new training planes were available, attracting even more flight students. Then as World War II approached, training was broadened again to include sheet-metal training for aircraft factory work and aeronautical engineering.

The success of the school and various other operations might have been enough satisfaction for most men, but Ryan grew restless again, as he had so often in the past and would so often in the future.

Board of Directors
RYAN SCHOOL OF AERONAUTICS
THE RYAN AERONAUTICAL CO.

T. C. Ryan   E. D. Prudden   E. A. Smith

178

The memory of the first flight in his original M-1 haunted him, and the thrill of the creative achievement whetted his appetite for more of the same. As the days of the Depression gradually passed, and the terrible oppression of that nightmare began to lift, Ryan's thoughts turned more and more to the development of another airplane.

Many years before, when he was struggling to learn the techniques of flying, he had made up his mind that airplanes should be designed only by master pilots. They were the only ones who really understood the language. A good engineer could run tests and offer suggestions, but only a man who had known the frequent exhilaration—and occasional terror—of flying was equipped to decide how a plane should be designed.

Once before, he had proved he could do it. And as the Depression finally drew toward an end, he was determined to see if he could do it again.

H. A. Erickson

CHAPTER SEVENTEEN

S-T, the Classic Airplane

IN EARLY SUMMER 1934, a sleek low-winged monoplane rose over San Diego on its first flight. The two-place craft, described by one reporter as a "silver bullet," was the prototype of one of the most popular small planes ever built—the Ryan S-T (sport trainer).

Thirty-five years later an aviation buff described in capsule form why the S-T was among the truly classic airplanes of all time. "Sleek and shining, like a model turned from solid silver," he said, "the first Ryan S-T caught the attention and affection of the flying world in 1934 and has held it ever since."

The S-T was born in the shadow of the Depression, a unique bird that signaled the approach of better days. The lively craft was far ahead of its day with an all-metal, streamlined fuselage, and it set a standard for sport planes that has rarely been equaled.

Indeed, the sister ship of the commercial S-T, the PT-16 primary trainer built for the military, was once criticized by a general who wondered if it was "too spirited" for novice pilots. He feared the high performance of the plane would help a lot of trainees get in trouble. But the PT-16s, the first monoplane trainers purchased by the United States military for primary training, and subsequent Ryan military trainers, proved their value during many, many years of service with the Army Air Corps, the Navy, and friendly foreign governments.

Those who flew the S-Ts remember them as a dream that put more

William Wagner

fun into flying than anything that had come along in years. One such man was J. G. "Tex" Rankin, who captured the International Acrobatic Championship in 1936 at the controls of his S-T.

Ryan built 1,500 planes in the ST-PT series, some of which are still flying more than three decades later. They were used as military trainers in Mexico, Honduras, and Guatemala before being purchased for military training in the United States. Others were sold to the military in China and the Netherlands East Indies, as well as many other countries.

The planes told a success story of the first magnitude. They also told of a basic change in the life of their creator, Claude Ryan. In the mid-1930s Ryan moved from the role of a pioneer pilot to that of an industrial leader soon to rise to significant stature. The new role was perhaps less romantic, less exciting, than the one enjoyed by the dashing young man in his flying machine. But it was a role which time and success thrust upon him; it was a product of changing times.

In the 1930s the United States emerged from a bitter depression, and the heroes of the day were the businessmen who were dedicated to business for the sake of business. They offered security for a troubled time, and the hope that the Great Depression would not return to haunt a nation that remembered, and trembled.

182

The world was changing, perhaps more profoundly than anyone realized in those days. In the years ahead, there would be others who, like Ryan, would set out with a vision and minimum financing and build their own companies with the sweat of their brows and the ingenuity of their souls. But they would come along less often.

None of that was apparent in the years before the birth of the S-T, when Ryan was running a laundry route in the Newport Beach area in the summer of 1922. He occasionally visited a flight strip near Santa Ana. One of the employees there was Millard C. Boyd, the young, slightly built, sandy-haired engineer whom Ryan had met in northern California while serving with the Forest Patrol. Boyd had taught himself to fly and had designed his own airplane. The two young men had much in common.

Eleven years later, Boyd and a fellow engineer, Will Vandermeer, showed up at Ryan's new operation on Lindbergh Field in San Diego and asked for a job. It was August, 1933, and they had just finished engineering a new plane for Kinner Airplane and Engine Company. Earlier Boyd had been with Zenith Aircraft in Santa Ana. Although Ryan desperately needed a full-time engineer to go ahead with his plans for the new low-wing sport trainer he envisioned, he doubted that the payroll could support even one engineer.

"Can you afford $200 a month?" Boyd asked.

"No," Ryan answered, reluctantly, as he mentally calculated the $400 monthly payroll for Millard and his Dutch friend, Vandermeer.

"But I mean for both of us."

The deal was too tempting. With the assistance of both engineers, the S-T could become a reality. But although the proposition was tremendous and appealing, $200 a month was a lot of money. Still, there was a way. . . .

During the depth of the Depression, as a personal venture, Claude had purchased a number of baseball game pinball machines, which were located in base exchanges, waiting rooms, and cafés in the San Diego area. It was only a fad, and in time the novelty would wear off, but the machines were then bringing in about $200 a month—just what Ryan needed to hire Boyd and Vandermeer.

So, with the income from the pinball machines, work finally got under way on the Ryan S-T, as Claude's own private risk venture. The plane was designed by Claude, with engineering detail and shop drawings by the two engineers.

Recalling his unfortunate experience with Bill Waterhouse and the plans for the M-1 in 1925, Claude didn't propose to find himself trapped a second time. The contract with Boyd spelled out in detail that "all of the drawings and designs are the sole property of Ryan; that they will not be used or sold by Boyd, or placed in the hands of any other party for building other airplanes."

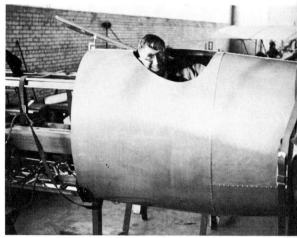

Millard Boyd was one chief engineer who was close to his work.

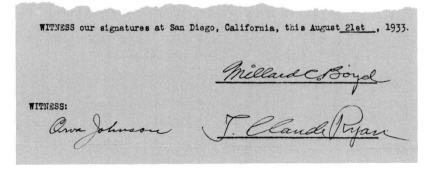

WITNESS our signatures at San Diego, California, this August _21st_ , 1933.

Millard C Boyd

WITNESS:

Orva Johnson   *T. Claude Ryan*

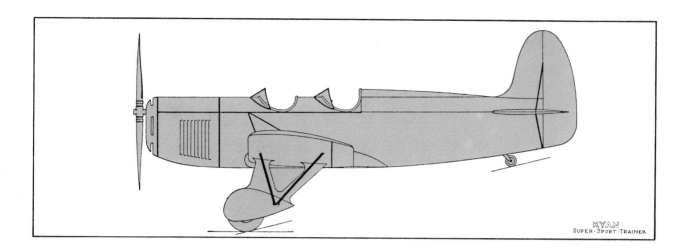

RYAN
SUPER·SPORT·TRAINER

The ceiling price for the engineering was set at $1,000, and the entire project, including building the prototype, flight testing, and government certification, was to be done in under four months.

The first drawings showed a rather angular, boxy fuselage with straight lines. Ryan revised the plan to give a far more graceful appearance to the plane's basic lines to make them compatible with the streamlined nose cowl covering the in-line engine. He also suggested a longer, narrower, more graceful wing.

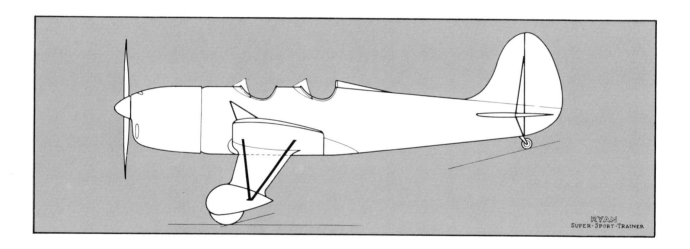

RYAN
SUPER·SPORT·TRAINER

Claude and Millard worked closely together, changing and refining details as they went along. With the constant polishing of the design features, the time schedule became unrealistic, and so Claude simply tore up the contract. But it was Ryan's concern for a beauty of line and perfection of detail which made the S-T one of the most sought after airplanes ever built.

Nine months after the first sketch was drawn, a sleek monoplane rolled out in front of the newly named Ryan Aeronautical Company. It was strangely reminiscent of the day the first M-1 rolled out, but things had indeed changed. This time, Ryan stood on the sidelines, holding the hands of his first two sons, David and Jerry, while another pilot climbed into the cockpit for the maiden flight.

Harry T. Bishop

Johnny Fornasero takes the S-T aloft on its first flight—June 8, 1934.

A small band of dedicated mechanics and students, who earned their flying time by working in off hours, handled the actual construction under Boyd's watchful eye. When special heat treatment of metal parts was required, Claude fell back on his contacts at North Island. Captain John H. Towers, the Navy's commanding officer at the base, saw to it that facilities were made available. Claude would take a part for the S-T, climb into an airplane, and make the three-minute flight across the bay. There the unit would be heat-treated; and, while it was still hot from the process, Claude would fly it back to his small plant on Lindbergh Field.

On June 8, 1934, the day of the first test, John B. Fornasero, chief instructor of the Ryan School, sat in the cockpit as the 95-hp Menasco B-4 Pirate engine whipped over. Fornasero made a few test runs down the field, and, finally, after what seemed like a laborious takeoff, the first S-T lifted into the sky. The bird made a few lazy turns and then returned after a flight of less than ten minutes.

Some who were on hand for the flight were quick to criticize the plane's performance, primarily because of the long run required for liftoff. But Ryan and his engineers soon discovered that the problem had been in the pitch of the propeller. A new prop was installed, and the plane performed brilliantly.

H. A. Erickson

The S-T team. From left, Johnny Fornasero, Claude Ryan, Millard Boyd, Will Vandermeer.

The shop crew. From left, Mel Thompson, Bert Matthews, Dan Burnett, Ed Morrow, Bob Kerlinger, Johnny Fornasero.

With its "N" license painted on the left wing, Claude proudly poses with the S-T prototype.

The S-T seemed like a winner from the start. But first it had to pass government engineering and flight checks. When it came time to submit blueprints, Will Vandermeer and Mel Thompson did the job at Will's house. They prepared the printing frame in the shade, carried it into the sunlight, counted to five, then retired to the bathroom to develop the prints in the bathtub. When Tina Vandermeer came home, she found dozens of blueprints flapping in the breeze on her clothesline.

Approved Type Certificate No. 541 was received in short order after Claude flew the first plane to Los Angeles for CAA tests. The prototype was put in service in the flight school to give it a thorough shakedown in hard daily service. But something happened just before Christmas which cast a shadow over the proceedings. One of the student pilots using the prototype for acrobatics over the bay went into a long spin and never came out. The death was Ryan's first to a student or passenger in twelve years of operation. Ryan waded out into the mud flats to help gather the pieces of the aircraft in hopes that the cause of the accident could be determined, but there were no clues to be found in the muddied waters of San Diego Bay.

One of the witnesses of the accident, Captain Towers of the Navy, reported that the student continued acrobatics so low he simply could not recover in time.

After careful consideration, Ryan decided to go ahead with the S-T, confident that the accident was not due to structural or design failure. Time proved him right. About this time San Diego got its second aircraft manufacturing company, when Major Reuben Fleet moved his Consolidated Aircraft Company from the rigorous climate of Buffalo, New York.

Consolidated Aircraft, far right, joined Ryan in 1934 as a major tenant on Lindbergh Field.

H. A. Erickson

The prototype S-T NC-14223 over Lindbergh Field with Johnny Fornasero at the controls.

Early in 1935, with additional financing obtained partially from stock sold to the father of another wealthy student, Johnny Funk, the first S-Ts went into production. The first buyer was from Seattle, and Claude duplicated his flight of nine years earlier in the first M-1 by delivering the S-T to the Northwest himself.

The planes were immensely popular because of their attractive looks and spirited performance. One contributing factor was Rankin, a sensational stunt pilot who flew his stock model S-T to the aerobatic championship after defeating several planes built specifically for the competition.

Rankin talked Ryan into letting him take an S-T on a barnstorming tour of the United States, drumming up business as he went along. As it turned out, he did a lot of fancy flying but not much selling. He just could not stay out of the cockpit long enough to talk business with the people who had watched, dumbfounded, as he put the plane through seemingly impossible maneuvers.

One Sunday morning, Ryan received a call at his home. Rankin was on the other end of the line.

"Claude, you'll never believe what happened to me," he said. "I was taking off to demonstrate the airplane at Detroit and believe this or not, the rudder fell off!

"Now, don't get excited, the airplane's okay. I didn't crack up. But you know something, that airplane you fellows designed is so stable and so controllable I didn't need a rudder. I flew it with the ailerons and elevator and made a perfect landing with no trouble at all."

Ryan's engineers discovered that the hinges which held the rudder on

Nine years after flying his first M-1 to Seattle, Claude Ryan was back there again—this time with the first S-T which he delivered to Leonard R. Peterson, left.

Ryan Aeronautical Library

187

Tex Rankin

were inadequate. They were replaced, somewhat to the disappointment of Rankin, who had become rather fond of the innovation and wanted to fly an S-T across the continent without a rudder.

The S-Ts were being sold almost as soon as they could be rolled off the production line. Some went to the Ryan School, some to other flying school operators, and many went to other pilots, both here and abroad, for their personal use. Most of them were sold singly, but in early 1936 Ryan landed what appeared to be his first major order. He received word through a stockbroker that a W. H. Irwin, an Atlanta capitalist, wanted to set up a distributorship in Georgia. Ryan had been cautioned not to be surprised if he found Mr. Irwin a rather strange fellow.

One day an old chap showed up at the plant. It was Mr. Irwin.

"I want to buy some of those airplanes," he said. He talked in terms of fifteen, which seemed like an astonishing number at the time.

"We will have to build them," Ryan said. "We don't have that many on hand. If you could give us a 'good faith' deposit to help us finance production. . . ."

"I'll pay for them when you're ready to deliver them," Irwin said. Then he reached inside his pocket and withdrew $25,000 worth of negotiable American Tel and Tel bonds and handed them to Ryan.

"Maybe you can borrow on these," the man said.

Ryan was flabbergasted. "Aren't you afraid to carry negotiable bonds

Backed by bonds and firepower, the first flight of fifteen S-Ts prepares to leave San Diego. From left are Ryan pilots Robert Pini, James Fornasero, and Cameron Rust. Atlanta capitalist W. H. Irwin and Claude Ryan at right.

around in your pocket?" he asked.

"I always keep a lot of negotiable stuff with me," Irwin answered. "I don't trust people much."

"But aren't you afraid you will get held up? Why do you trust us?"

Irwin slowly pulled back his coat and exposed the biggest six-gun Ryan had ever seen. Coldly, he looked straight into Ryan's eyes and said simply: "I killed a man once."

Ryan put the bonds in the safe and locked them up. He was afraid to borrow money on them out of fear that Irwin would insist on having them back on the spur of the moment—which is exactly what he did.

"I never did get myself involved with those bonds where I couldn't produce them," Ryan recalled years later, "because I remembered that six-shooter."

In time, the planes were delivered to Irwin, although Ryan had underestimated the cost and barely broke even on the deal.

Ryan School of Aeronautics' use of Ryan S-Ts helped to spread their popularity with private pilots and other flight-training schools. Student Peter Dana at right on cover of Ryan School brochure. Like many other Ryan secretaries, Orva Johnson, left, married a flight student.

Peter Dana and his record-setting plane, the third
S-T built.

Brazilian sportsman-pilot Amaral improvised hangar below for
his S-T when he flew into the interior on a hunting trip.

As the months rolled on, the reputation of the S-T grew sounder and more widespread, and it proved to be a bargain at $3,985. A larger, 125-hp engine became standard, and the improved performance of the S-T-A model attracted still more followers. Internationally known pilots and Hollywood luminaries interested in aviation dropped in to see, fly, and, with increasing frequency, buy the popular S-T. When the S-T-A Special version with supercharged 150-hp engine became available, the potential for military pilot training became even more apparent.

Claude and Earl Prudden revived their "airplane plus transport pilot course" package deal and found an additional ready market among the Ryan School flight students. One of these, Peter Dana, great-grandson of Richard Henry Dana, of *Two Years Before the Mast* fame, and of Henry Wadsworth Longfellow, gained fame for himself and for the new Ryan plane by setting transcontinental and Canada-to-Mexico records in his S-T.

By 1939, Ryan S-Ts were also being used in Australia, South Africa, Venezuela, Brazil, Bolivia, and Ecuador for civil or military flying.

Anesio Amaral, Jr., of São Paulo won the civil aviation cross-country

Girl flight students at Ryan School. From left,
Marjorie Towers (daughter of Navy Capt. John H.
Towers), Adelaide Smith, Mary Dalton, Ruth Clark,
Barbara Towne, and Barbara Kibbee.

Ryan School students and instructors ready to leave
on a cross-country training flight in the S-Ts.

cruise of the Aero Club of Brazil in his S-T for five successive years. In
1939, Lieut. James Harvey Gray flew an S-T across the Andes from
Santiago, Chile, to Mendoza, Argentina, at altitudes up to 17,000 feet,
the first time such a flight had been accomplished by a plane of that class.

The United States government, aware of growing tension throughout
the world, took steps to beef up the supply of pilots needed by the Army
Air Corps. In 1939, the Army invited manufacturers to compete for military
trainer aircraft contracts. Ryan was awarded one of three development
contracts out of a field of fifteen competitors for a military version of the
125-hp S-T.

The S-T was thus the first low-wing primary trainer to induce the Army
to break away from a thirty-year precedent of biplanes for initial instruction of aviation cadets.

Names make news. These sons of prominent families
were among Ryan School flight students in late
thirties. From left, Whitelaw Reid (New York
Herald-Tribune), Reid Woodward (Jello), Henry E.
Huntington, II (railroads), instructor Alex Hyde
(Mentholatum), and, in cockpit, John B. Knox
(gelatine). Thirty years later Knox owned and still
flew a mint-condition Ryan S-T.

191

William Wagner

S-Ts over Coronado with Pt. Loma and entrance to San Diego harbor
in background.

Ryan STM of Mexican Air Force over Popocatepetl.

The contract, specifically for the PT-16, sister ship of the commercial S-T, paved the way for the Army to adapt off-the-shelf commercial planes to military purposes, a move which was to have a profound effect in the years ahead as the United States once again braced for war.

The first of Ryan's military contracts had been with Mexico, for STM's powered with supercharged Menasco 150-hp engines suitable for Mexico City's airport at 7000-foot altitude.

A short time later, Honduras placed an order, and the three planes were flown to their destination. One of the pilots was a recent Ryan flight school graduate, William P. (Doc) Sloan. (Sloan's medical moniker dated from work in a service station where he occasionally prescribed axle grease for the relief of hemorrhoids.)

The Honduras delivery was followed by the largest prewar contracts with any Latin American government when Guatemala placed several orders with Ryan.

Meanwhile, the military situation in Asia worsened as the Japanese gained more control over China. In an effort to protect its territory, China ordered Ryan trainers to build up its pilot strength. The planes arrived in Burma late in 1940. They were transported to Rangoon, assembled by Chinese mechanics, and flown into the interior.

Other S-T military trainers—STM landplanes and STM-S2s equipped with floats—went to the Netherlands East Indies where they were used to train Dutch pilots who then returned to England to continue the fight against the Axis powers. From time to time, the training in Java was curtailed as Japanese planes made repeated raids on the base. When the action got too hot for training, the little planes were used to carry military supplies and medical equipment to outposts along the island coastline.

Against background of volcanoes, Guatemalan Air Force STMs come in for landing to join others on flight line.

The Japanese captured many of the planes and even used them to train their own army flyers. Finally the remaining planes were evacuated to Australia and used by the RAAF.

Back in the United States, the PT-16 and, later, the PT-20 had made a believer out of the Army. In September of 1940 the War Department

William Wagne

Given a day of piling cumulus clouds, the author and chief pilot Paul
Wilcox often teamed up to obtain dramatic flight photos of the S-Ts.

Movietone News

Deininghof Stelling, Soerabaja, N.E.I.

"The Ryan monoplanes in the Netherlands East Indies were primary, basic, advanced, and blind-flying trainers all wrapped up in one; and our students from Holland went directly from Ryan STM landplane and STM-S2 seaplane trainers to multiengined equipment."—John H. Russell, American instructor at Morokrembangan Naval Air Base, Soerabaja, Java, 1941. N.E.I. Army school was at Bandoeng.

Netherlands Information Bureau

Netherlands Information Bureau

Department of Air, Australian Commonwealth

Many N.E.I. STMs were evacuated to Australia and there flown by Royal Australian Air Force.

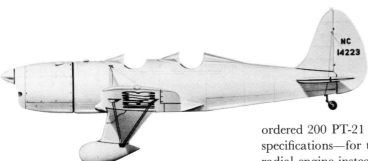

S-T

ordered 200 PT-21 primary trainers—updated versions, built to military specifications—for the Army. These were powered with a Kinner 132-hp radial engine instead of the earlier 125-hp in-line Menasco power plant. The War Department also ordered 100 NR-1s for the Navy, making a total of 300 planes. But even before production could start, the order was increased to 600 PT-22 "Recruit" trainers to be powered by 160-hp Kinner engines. A little over a year later the Army ordered an additional 450

PT-20

PT-22s. The "22" bore the official name "Recruit" but was more popularly known as the "Maytag Messerschmitt" since many a student pilot was washed out during his check ride with Ryan or Army flight instructors.

The man in charge of all Army aviation in those days was General Hap Arnold. Years earlier, Arnold had sold Ryan his first airplane, an old World War I surplus Jenny. But as World War II loomed over the horizon, it was Arnold who was buying planes from Ryan.

PT-20A

Despite the success story that it did, and still does, represent, the PT-22 with its exposed radial engine was no match in the affection of pilots for the beautifully streamlined and aerodynamically refined original S-T.

Although the classic S-T monoplanes were the biggest factor in Ryan production at that time, two other prewar Ryan designs—and one made early in World War II—made significant contributions to the state of the art.

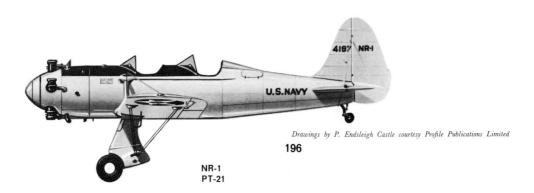

Drawings by P. Endsleigh Castle courtesy Profile Publications Limited

NR-1
PT-21

William Wagner

STM-S2

PT-21s off California coast.

Official U.S. Navy Photographs

Cadets at Naval Air Station, Jacksonville, Florida, received their primary training on Ryan NR-1s, Navy equivalent of the PT-21.

William Wagner

Claude found his new S-C sport cabin plane, above, useful for his own business travel.

With the success of the S-T apparent, Claude Ryan again looked a step beyond the open-cockpit model to a closed-cabin plane which could take even greater advantage of metal construction. Thus in 1937 the Ryan S-C sport cabin plane was introduced to the commercial market.

"She was a beautiful ship . . . and as easy to fly as she was beautiful. Those that are still flying look as modern and as at home today as they did thirty years ago." That is how one pilot wrote about the S-C in 1968.

To this can be added that the S-C was more than a trend-setter in its class; it was the first truly successful private plane to pioneer the all-metal, low-wing, enclosed-cabin concept.

"We planned the S-C from the beginning as a production job," Claude said recently. "We wanted to develop a type of construction so simple and so practical that it would lend itself to efficient manufacture in much larger quantities than had been customary in the past."

The S-C had everything going for it. When the war intervened, production facilities were switched to the military S-T trainers, but a few S-Cs served with the volunteer Civil Air Patrol on antisubmarine duty.

Then, in 1940, when military PT trainers were in full production, the Army Air Corps contracted with Ryan for a development quantity of short-range liaison observation planes designated YO-51 Dragonfly.

Three types in the Ryan product line: the S-T, the Brougham, and the S-C, the latter the Menasco-powered prototype.

H. A. Erickson

William Wagner

Its huge flaps extended, the YO-51 Dragonfly makes a short,
steep takeoff.

The Dragonfly on Army maneuvers at Fort Sill, Oklahoma.

Army Infantry School Photo

The tactical mission of the YO was to assist the artillery in locating military objectives and directing fire and to act as a liaison vehicle or "flying motorcycle" for infantry division commanders. The mission would clearly require new capabilities for short takeoff and steep landing with minimum ground roll.

Powered with 420-hp Wasp engine and supported by a 52-foot-span wing with leading edge slats and trailing edge flaps which increased the wing surface by 40 percent, the Dragonfly gave a sensational perform-

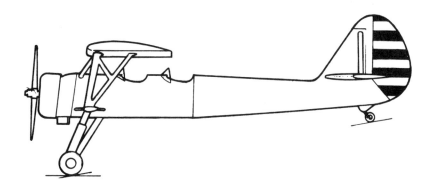

The newsreels take notice.
William Wagner

ance. It could take off and clear a 50-foot obstacle within 350 feet and maintain a minimum flight speed of 32 mph while holding a chosen altitude. It could make unbelievably quick takeoffs at seemingly vertical angles, and execute short, steep landings not possible with ordinary fixed-wing aircraft.

But Ryan was loaded with other military work, and the production contract for observation planes went to another company. After field tests with the three YO-51s at Fort Sill, Oklahoma, the Dragonflys disappeared from the military inventory.

202

The PT-25 plywood monoplane trainer.

Thomas T. Hixson

To safeguard so far as possible the supply of strategic metals needed elsewhere for war production, the Army asked Ryan in 1942 to develop an entirely new trainer. The result was the plastic-bonded plywood ST-4 model which received the military designation PT-25.

Aluminum alloys and other strategic metals were eliminated, with the exception of the engine cowling which represented less than 2 percent of the airframe weight. The lessons learned in years of service with other Ryan training planes used in commercial and military schools were incorporated in the flight, ground handling, and maintenance characteristics of the new PT-25.

Like the YO-51, the PT-25 was a good bird but did not reach the production stage. After the five service test planes were flown away from San Diego by the WASPs—Women Airforce Service Pilots—they were not used again.

Frank Martin

Old friends Charlie Lindbergh and Don Hall look over the PT-25 with foreman Dan Burnett, right.

Frank Martin

The PT-25 fleet, ready for delivery.

The classical PT-20, unequaled among military trainers for beauty of
line and flight performance.

PT-22s on the Army flight line at Hemet.

Thomas T. Hixson

CHAPTER EIGHTEEN

Fourteen Thousand Pilots

AFTER THE OMINOUS "MUNICH INCIDENT" OF 1938, most people in a position to know were convinced that the United States would soon be at war.

As military experts struggled to map out sound strategy for the difficult years that were bound to come, it became obvious that the approaching war would be different from those in the past. Perhaps most significant, it would be a war in which aerial capability would be the deciding factor in many campaigns, if not in the war itself. That left the United States with a major problem. Army flight training facilities at Randolph Field, Texas, had a maximum capability of 500 pilots a year, hardly enough to supply the starving demands for aviators in a time of war.

Within a few years, however, this nation was capable of training 100,000 Army pilots a year.

The inventive souls who made that happen were men like General Hap Arnold, who had climbed through the ranks to the Army's top echelon, and Claude Ryan, who answered Arnold's plea for help, repaying an old debt for his own superb Army pilot training.

Arnold, who had sold Ryan his first airplane, had watched as Ryan's flight school earned an international reputation for excellence. The crusty general decided that the solution to his problem rested in the hands of men like Ryan. Nine civilian flight schools, including the Ryan School of Aeronautics, answered Arnold's call for help, although there was no firm assurance in those days that his plan would be backed by the necessary

205

After refresher course, eight Ryan civilian instructors return from Army's Randolph Field. Left to right, Joe Duncan, chief pilot Paul Wilcox, Doc Sloan, Dick Huffman, Army Capt. Walter E. (Wee) Todd, Ben Hazelton, Pete Larson, Bill Evans, and Ben Johnson.

William Wagner

William Wagner
The first cadets arrive, fresh off the farm.

congressional allocations to pay the bills.

At Arnold's urgent plea, Ryan and Earl Prudden joined other commercial flying school operators in conferences at Washington. He didn't have the authority to pay them for the training of military cadets, Arnold explained, but the matter was critical. To build another Randolph Field capable of training 500 pilots annually was a five-year task. Something more practical had to be found, and right away. The immediate goal was 2,400 pilots a year, but it was later to be raised to 12,000, then to 30,000. In the end it went far higher.

On May 8, 1939, General Arnold announced the new training plan. Congress eventually authorized the program with just two votes to spare. Ryan and the other operators knew they had gambled, but they hadn't realized that the ice on which they were skating was quite that thin.

Back in San Diego the Ryan task force went to work with a vengeance. Construction of cadet barracks and additional technical training facilities was started, and auxiliary training fields were selected and prepared. Eight of the school's topflight instructors and commercial pilot graduates, led by chief instructor Paul "Pablo" Wilcox, were hustled off to Randolph Field for a cram course in military training methods. All passed the rigorous Army refresher course. Then seven more instructors were sent to Texas for indoctrination.

Shepherded by an Army officer, the first eight Ryan instructors flew into San Diego on June 17, 1939, with their Army PT-13 biplane trainers. Nine days earlier the Army had announced it would buy modern new Ryan S-T low-wing trainers for its expanded program. Then, on July 1, the initial class of thirty-five aviation cadets reported to Army Capt. John C. Horton and Lieut. Lloyd P. Hopwood, and began flight training. It had been less than eight weeks since the plan was announced. Such was the pace of the emergency.

New classes arrived each six weeks for the three-month training program, which included 65 hours of flight time and 225 hours of technical instruction. In a few months the classes of incoming cadets were increased to sixty-five student pilots, and then to ninety-five.

In the beginning, only the old Army Stearman biplanes were used to train the students, but when the first Ryan PT-16 military trainers rolled off the line, they were put into service with the second class of cadets to train at Ryan. Other contract schools and two more Ryan schools also used later military versions of the S-Ts.

From the start, the Ryan program was conducted with efficiency and competence, and graduates of the course made their mark in advanced training and later in combat. Just two weeks after the first cadet took off on a training flight, Brig. Gen. Barton K. Yount, with an inspection team, was on hand to check progress. Yount, who had been the commanding officer at March Field when Claude was a cadet, was there in his role as assistant chief of the Army Air Corps in charge of training.

While training schedules moved along at a fast clip, problems soon developed with the PTs. Hour after hour of intensive student flying proved too much for the Menasco engines, which had been adequate in commercial programs. The decision was reached to substitute Kinner radial engines for the Menasco in-line power plants, but that required Army approval, and that required time, of which there was precious little.

As luck would have it, General Arnold was passing through San Diego at the time. Ryan buttonholed him, but the general was on such a tight schedule he did not have time to discuss the problem. So, at Arnold's suggestion Ryan and Lieut. "Hoppy" Hopwood hopped aboard the general's C-47 and explained it while they were flying to Tulare, California.

Before the plane touched down, Ryan had won his point. Arnold had Brig. Gen. K. B. Wolfe, the West Coast procurement officer traveling with him, send a message to Washington approving the change, short-circuiting all the red tape.

Unfortunately, Army procurement officers in Washington later refused to pay the cost of the engine change. Ryan, faced with the impossible task of paying the bill himself, sent an associate, Frank Seifert, one of the Army pioneers at Rockwell Field, to the nation's capital to work out the problem, but he was promptly escorted out of the procurement office.

Desperate, Ryan flew to Washington. He walked into Arnold's office and explained the problem.

"Well, Ryan, you better explain it to the procurement office," Arnold said.

"But I've just come from there, and they won't listen," Ryan lamented.

"Go back and see them again."

Ryan walked back down the hall to the procurement office. As he walked in, the officer in charge hung up the phone.

"How much did you say it would cost?" he asked sheepishly.

Ryan told him, and the crisis quickly ended.

Ryan returned to San Diego, where life seemed basic compared to the bureaucratic jungle of Washington.

At the end of a typical flying day, when instructors gathered to hangar-fly, it was not the routine successes but the tall tales of hairy flights with inept cadets which were told and retold. Today they are legends, and there are a million of them.

Some of the cadets had never been near a plane, and while most had a genuine yearning to fly, they were not all equal in aptitude. That became

William Wagner

World War I ambulance driver Earl Prudden stands at attention as instructor Pete Larson gets going over from General Yount.

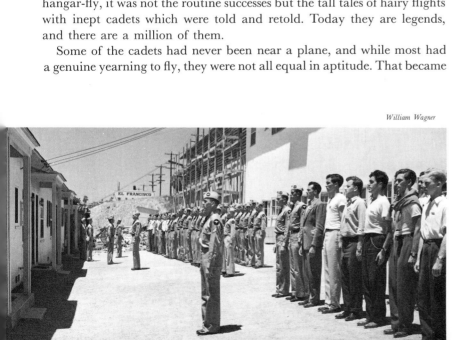

William Wagner

Cadets not yet outfitted in uniforms arrived while barracks were still under construction.

PT-20As on the flight line at Lindbergh Field.

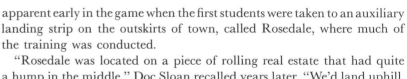

Oops! (It's a PT-16.)

Walt Balch gives a cadet the true word about engines.

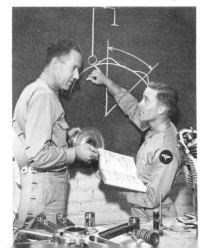

apparent early in the game when the first students were taken to an auxiliary landing strip on the outskirts of town, called Rosedale, where much of the training was conducted.

"Rosedale was located on a piece of rolling real estate that had quite a hump in the middle," Doc Sloan recalled years later. "We'd land uphill, bounce over the crest, and brake to a rolling stop in the downhill side. Watching a solo student land from the head of the runway was always an experience. The Stearman biplanes weren't quite as suspenseful as the Ryan PTs because when a student groundlooped on the downhill side with the biplanes we could watch the upper wing rotating. In the Ryans we could only watch the cloud of dust and wonder what in hell was happening."

It was a trying time for both the instructors and students. One of the instructors, Clarence Prescott, was working with a youth one afternoon who just couldn't hold level turns in the traffic pattern. After three trips around the field with the student making hair-raising climbing turns, Clarence's patience wore thin.

"There's nothing like a hard rap in the belly to get a student's undivided attention, and this could be accomplished by pushing the stick forward and then yanking it back," Sloan recalled. "Watching his student very carefully in the rear-view mirror, Clarence suffered through the second climbing turn at 400 feet and then whapped the stick forward, diving the plane.

"The student had forgotten to fasten his seat belt, and he popped out of the cockpit like a pea from a pod, still in a sitting position with his hands where they should have been on the stick and throttle, but actually about 5 feet above the airplane. Fortunately, the student popped his chute in time, and it blossomed just before he hit the ground. No injuries, but we all learned a lesson."

One of the more unpleasant tasks for the instructors was watching hopeful students wash out of the training program. Most of the kids wanted to be pilots more than they wanted to eat, but some of them just didn't have it.

"When I had advanced to the omnipotent position of squadron commander, it was my unpleasant chore to have the final ride with each failing student before recommending him for the elimination ride with the Air Corps check pilot," Sloan reminisced. "Often, the student's knowledge that he was up for washout made his poor flying even worse. On many occasions we would bend over backwards to salvage any student who had a glimmer of potential, but some of them were extremely tense and apprehensive.

"I think the worse example I flew with was a kid who hung onto the stick like his life depended on it, and as if the rudder pedals were practically set in concrete," Sloan said.

Somehow, Sloan managed to wrestle the controls away from the terrified student and land the plane. He was making notations on his grading slip when the student climbed out of the cockpit, glassy-eyed. Instead of staying on the catwalk next to the fuselage, the cadet walked straight out on the wing. As he was taking his third step, his leg broke through the fabric covering the wing and the youth was trapped.

"He didn't panic," Sloan said. "He calmly reached over and pulled the ripcord on his parachute, spilling beautiful white silk all over the parking apron. He was one student I didn't recheck."

Not all the laughs were on the students, however. Instructor Ned Chase was up with a fledgling pilot one afternoon when the engine in their Stearman quit. Chase landed the biplane in the mesquite bushes, but it flipped over on its back and rested several feet above the ground on top of the bushes.

"Don't panic," Chase warned his student, hanging upside down in his cockpit. "Don't loosen your safety belt until you have put your goggles behind your helmet. Brace yourself carefully against the sides of the fuselage, ease your belt open slowly, and swing down feet first."

The student did as instructed and called back all clear to Chase, who immediately popped his belt and fell 8 feet straight down on his head, smashing his goggles and cutting his forehead with the broken lenses.

Instructor Ben Johnson and cadets.

"Ned Chase . . . fell 8 feet straight down on his head."

Things got done in the flying cadet program because Ryan and Army heads worked with a common goal. These are the men who accomplished miracles. From left, Paul Wilcox, director of flying; Claude Ryan; Army Capt. John C. Horton and Lieut. Lloyd P. Hopwood; Earl Prudden, and Walter K. Balch, director of technical training and maintenance.

William Wagner

Cadets and planes line up in a "V for Victory" salute as the pilot training program swings into full operation. Below, a formal review at Lindbergh Field with new Ryan Aeronautical Company factory in right background.

William Wagner

And so it went, day in and day out, as Ryan's instructors at San Diego made Army flyboys out of their cadets. In the first ten months, 10,000 flying hours and 1,000,000 miles of training were logged without a serious accident. The Army was so pleased with the success of the school that before a year was out Ryan was asked to expand its facilities and begin training more students in another area.

William Wagner

Ryan School facility at Hemet, a wartime miracle of getting impossible jobs done.

Army Capt. Lloyd P. Hopwood, who had helped set up the program in San Diego, worked with Ryan on the selection of a new site. They found an ideal location in the Hemet Valley not far from March Field in Riverside County, north of San Diego. Residents of that area, concerned over the prospects of war, went before the County Board of Supervisors and persuaded the board to purchase 320 acres near the city of Hemet and make the land available to Ryan at a nominal rental.

The area was considered ideal, with excellent weather and good terrain. The valley was remote from heavy airlanes, and thus the students would not be bothered by other traffic. However, there was no airport.

"It was a pretty daring plan," Hopwood remembered years later after serving as the head of all Air Force personnel and retiring as a major general. "We needed the facility, but there was no assurance we could get the money to do the things we needed to do. And the pressure for more pilots was so great that every day we lost was critical. So we went ahead and did the things we needed to do, and then asked ourselves later if it was possible."

Joining Hopwood from the Ryan side in getting the new facility going were Wilcox, director of flying and later to be general manager; Colin A. Stillwagen, the wiry controller who made up in sheer bombast what he lacked in avoirdupois; and, of course, Prudden and Ryan.

"The site had a flourishing little farm on it," Hopwood recalled. "Houses had to be moved, barns knocked down, trees uprooted and removed, and the ground prepared for landing mats and the ramp. Actual construction took only thirty-seven days from the time it was begun until the first cadets were stationed at Hemet.

"Three million square feet of the field were oiled. The hangars were in use three weeks after construction began, and the barracks and mess hall served the first cadets eighteen days after work started."

Stillwagen—demonical ramrod.

The Hemet spread was so vast that Earl Prudden and resident manager Doug Maw took to horseback for inspection tours.

211

William Wagner

Army cadet barracks, Hemet Training Detachment.

Water was in such short supply that it had to be trucked to the area to meet the enormous construction demands. But in spite of these problems, training started at Hemet on September 9, 1940. Within a month, another construction program was launched to expand the school to handle 600 cadets.

When this still bigger push came and Ryan was asked to accomplish superhuman tasks, there was no one to say it couldn't be done.

Classes got bigger, planes got fewer, courses got shorter—but still the Ryan team met each challenge as it came. Lights burned late as ground school instructors labored to help some discouraged cadet. The ground school men took their motto, "If the student hasn't learned, the instructor hasn't taught," seriously.

Maintenance supervisors invented ways to service planes faster and wound up with a production-line maintenance system that was the marvel of the Army. Flight instructors devised new tricks of scheduling, takeoff, and parking which boosted flight hours per plane from the old average of $4\frac{1}{2}$ per day to $7\frac{1}{2}$. And they sweated it out in the air with every last cadet until they hung up an all-time record of 98.5 percent graduations from the biggest class that ever hit Hemet.

Again and again Hemet ran either first or second among all West Coast schools in percentage of graduations—because Ryanites seemed obsessed with the idea of doing more than they had to.

More than they had to. Maybe that was the key to the whole spirit of Ryan.

And there were, of course, many proud moments for the cadets. Take, for example, those later serving under Lieut. Col. James H. Doolittle, of whom Sir Winston Churchill in later years observed that "never was anyone more inappropriately named."

The humiliation of Pearl Harbor left the American people stunned and infuriated. They got their first taste of revenge on April 18, 1942, when Jimmie Doolittle led a flight of B-25s off the aircraft carrier Hornet, which, in the first attack on the Japanese homeland, bombed Tokyo. In the cockpits of four B-25s were Travis Hoover, Rodney Wilder, Kenneth Reddy, and Lucian Youngblood—all graduates of the first Army cadet classes at San Diego.

William Wagner

Travis Hoover.

William Wagner

On first bombing raid over Japan were Cadet Captain Lucian Youngblood, second from left, and Cadet Lieutenant Rodney Wilder, far right, of Class '41-E.

It took a hundred civilian flight instructors to "keep 'em flying" at Hemet.

Cadets' sloppy flying occasionally received unwanted publicity.

Within five years, the barrier of the speed of sound, always considered impenetrable, was broken when a Ryan graduate, Capt. Charles E. Yeager, flew his X-1 rocket plane past mach 1. Meanwhile, instructors had the satisfaction, as news reports came in from combat areas, of being able to identify cadet after cadet who had distinguished himself.

As the requirement for pilots burgeoned, additional schools were added to the original nine. Two old friends were among the new contractors— J. Lloyd O'Donnell, known from numerous escapades in the early twenties, and Tex Rankin, whose full name, known only to a few intimates, was John Gilbert Rankin.

Old-time publicist Tom Mathews, too, had a hand in the wartime training program, putting in 1,100 hours as a flight instructor in PT-22s at King City, California. In typical Mathews style, he soloed all his students in less than the required eight hours dual instruction.

"My thinking on this was very simple," Mathews said. "An instructor was safer on the ground if he could keep the maniac cadets upstairs."

Ryan PT-22s on the flight line at Hemet.

Auxiliary training field, Hemet Valley.

William Wagner

The Tucson team. From left, Earl Prudden; Robert J. Kerlinger, Ryan's director of flying; the Army's Major Don Haarman; Claude Ryan, and Hal Neff, Ryan resident manager.

William Wagner

Thomas T. Hixson

Pre-Women's Lib wartime maintenance crew.

The Hemet facility became the mainstay of Ryan's cadet training program, although training continued at San Diego until 1942, when that area was classified by the military as a combat zone. Ryan was requested to move the school inland, which led to the establishment of a third facility for 500 cadets near Tucson, Arizona, on June 15, 1942.

The site was barren, and with the war in full swing every second counted in preparing the area for the new school. The facilities were built during the hottest summer on record in that part of the Arizona desert. Everything had to be done from scratch, and under great pressure, but six weeks after the first lumber arrived, planes were operating from the field.

The cadets who began their training in San Diego completed their primary flight training in Arizona. Planes, personnel, and equipment were transported 400 miles over a single weekend without the loss of a day's flying time. Dozens of low-wing Ryan PT-22 planes were flown to Tucson, even though hangars and service facilities were not yet completed.

By the time the war ended, some 250,000 cadets had been trained in primary schools and 193,131 had graduated from advanced training. By contrast, between World Wars I and II, the Air Corps trained only 3,577 pilots. Ryan's schools furnished the Army Air Corps with 14,000 pilots before they closed in December 1944. At the peak of activity, in the fall of 1943, more than 1,200 cadets were in training at Ryan schools at the same time.

And there were other statistics which spoke volumes:

Of all the Army officers lost in combat, the Air Corps lost nearly twice as many as the ground forces, 23,879 and 12,773, respectively.

Of the 34,578 Army officers missing in action, 28,746 were from the Air Corps.

"We don't like to use these figures, but they show that the product of

PT-22 over Ryan Field, Tucson, Arizona.

Thomas T. Hixson

As training neared end at Tucson, two Ryan corporate directors merged. Adelaide Smith, long Claude's secretary, became Mrs. Earl D. Prudden.

the pilot training program was a pretty dedicated officer," Maj. Gen. Hopwood recalled.

The statistics, of course, told only part of the story. The nature of World War II proved that Hap Arnold and those who had shared his convictions were right. The airplane emerged as the most effective tool in the entire military arsenal. To combat troops on the ground, the arrival of "friendly aircraft" usually meant hell for the enemy and relief for the "dogfaces" and "grunts" for whom the term "war" has a special meaning. And to those behind the scenes, who shouldered the oppressing responsibility for planning strategies which meant that some men would live and others would die, the airplane meant their vision could be extended across the lines of enemy fire, making their decisions far more intelligible, if not easier. And in the end, it was the airplane that delivered the terror of nuclear war to the heart of the Japanese mainland, bringing an end to an era of profound madness.

The men who flew those missions were of an uncommon breed. They played hard and they died hard, and when the final chapters of World War II were written, they were among the principal authors of victory. They paid a terrible price to help the world regain its sanity.

For Claude Ryan and the operators of sixty other contract schools, the end of the war brought a quiet peace. Their nation had called. And they had been ready.

Two years after V-J Day, President Harry S. Truman awarded the civilian Certificate of Merit to Claude Ryan for his wartime contribution.

Ryan training complex on the desert at Tucson.

On behalf of President Truman, Assistant Air Force Secretary Eugene M. Zuckert presents Presidential Certificate of Merit to T. Claude Ryan. Responding, Claude said, "I am proud to receive this award through the Air Force in which, as an Aviation Cadet 28 years ago, I also received my first sound aeronautical training."

American flag at Tucson parade ground still flying proudly in a desert sand storm, Army Air Corps pilot training came to an end on December 28, 1944.

Vertijet vertical takeoff at the Pentagon.

CHAPTER NINETEEN

The Business Matures

ALMOST ANY MAN WHO HAS BUILT A COMPANY with pennies from his pocket and the sweat from his brow tends to think of that company as an extension of his own personality: a living part of himself rather than a separate, inorganic entity. And there is strong justification for that belief. Just about any company represents an embodiment of the wisdom and the foibles of the man who put it together and the people who make it work.

But as the company grows, there comes a time when it supersedes the founder and becomes something unto itself. It becomes bigger than the man who created it. As new people with new ideas join the operation, it loses some of its basic traits, but in many cases is able to retain its fundamental personality.

Ryan Aeronautical Company passed its adolescent stage and moved toward maturity in the days when this nation was struggling to meet the challenge of a coming war. In 1939 business volume exceeded $1 million for the first time. Six years later, wartime production caused the annual volume to soar to over $55 million, with 8,500 employees on the payroll.

A principal source of revenue early in World War II resulted from a relatively new venture for Ryan. During the *Spirit of St. Louis* days, one of the workers had been a metalsmith by the name of Fred Rohr. He was a genius at focusing his efforts on challenging production targets. As a result, he could tackle a single project—such as the manufacture of airframe and engine components—and do it better than almost anyone else.

219

Fred Rohr and a Ryan piston-engine exhaust system.

World War II production chief Gen. William S. Knudsen confers at new Ryan plant with Claude Ryan, Gen. Hap Arnold, and Major E. R. McReynolds, resident Air Corps inspector.

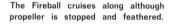

The Fireball cruises along although propeller is stopped and feathered.

Using techniques developed by Rohr during his early San Diego days and later with Boeing, Ryan entered the subcontracting line with great success. The company gained a major part of the industry's business for exhaust collector systems for piston-powered military aircraft. The company also produced wing panels for the B-24 bomber, gun turrets for PBY flying boats, and control surfaces for various aircraft. Later, stainless steel parts for jet engines and jet engine afterburners were added to the product line. For years, subcontract manufacturing brought in most of the revenue. Recognizing the potential, Rohr left Ryan in 1940 to form his own company which rose to be the largest subcontracting firm in the aircraft industry.

By late 1942, with production virtually completed on PT military trainers, it was clear that the company would need some new prime contract work to stay in business. Claude visited Wright Field, but officers there could offer no hope of additional Army contracts.

In Washington, Ryan called on an old friend, Adm. John H. Towers, newly named Chief of the Navy Bureau of Aeronautics. How could Ryan now contribute to war production needs? The timing was right, for Towers knew the Navy needed a second source to produce the Curtiss-developed SOC Seagull.

Ryan was given the job of building the SOR-1 version of the ship- or land-based observation plane. The company plunged into the new task but within a year the air war dictated changes in tactical requirements, and the project was not carried through by the Navy. Instead, Ryan and his top engineer, Ben T. Salmon, were called to Washington, where they obtained a new top-secret assignment.

The first American jet engines had just been built. They were still a military secret, but Salmon had an idea for a new airplane configuration. When he and Claude returned, they carried a contract to develop the Navy's first jet fighter, the Ryan Fireball.

The need for the Fireball grew out of the dangerous situation faced by Navy pilots in the Pacific. Japanese pilots were equipped with planes that could outclimb and outmaneuver U. S. Navy aircraft, giving enemy flyers a deadly edge in the critical air war. Ryan was given the challenge of

220

FR-1 Fireball production line.

building a plane which would not only outperform the Japanese planes, but operate from the smallest aircraft carriers as well.

Pure jets, then in their infancy, could not operate from carriers, even large ones, because of their slow takeoff acceleration. Prop planes, though capable of operating from the carriers, were no match for the Japanese fighters. The solution to that dilemma was brilliantly simple—a fighter which used a propeller in the nose and a jet in the tail—two birds in one.

The result of that concept was the birth of the jet-pushed, propeller-pulled Fireball, a unique plane in many ways. It could fly on either its jet engine alone or the conventional power plant alone, or both. It combined the advantages of jet propulsion for efficient high altitude and high-speed operation, and the conventional piston engine for the short takeoff and long cruising range necessary for aircraft-carrier operations.

In the Fireball's nose was a nine-cylinder Wright Cyclone reciprocating engine of 1,350 hp. In the fuselage, aft of the pilot, was the newly developed General Electric I-16 turbojet with 1,600 pounds static thrust.

The combination gave the Navy an aircraft capable of engaging the enemy at any altitude from sea level to the substratosphere. The high rate of sustained climb made the Fireball more independent of altitude than any other aircraft of that period. High-speed maneuverability gave the Fireball the shortest turning radius at comparable speed of any combat aircraft of that time.

The XFR-1 came out of the factory in June, 1944, for its first flights, and by October the test program was well along. Then tragedy struck,

Captain John H. Towers while commanding officer of North Island, 1934–36. Jack Towers was Naval Aviator No. 3.

Posing for the traditional photo after first flight of the Fireball. From left, Earl Prudden, Claude Ryan, designer Ben Salmon, test pilot Bob Kerlinger, and Lieut. Comdr. R. O. Deitzer.

Fighter pilots of VF-66 flying their Fireballs on jet power only.

Thomas T. Hixson

After V-J Day, Fireballs were publicly shown for first time by
Johnny Gray and his VF-66 squadron.

Fireballs during service trials. They were first jets aboard carriers and
first carrier planes with tricycle gear.

U.S. Navy Photo

Great Fireball pilots—squadron leader Johnny Gray, above; test pilot Al Conover, below.

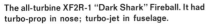
Thomas T. Hixson

when Robert Kerlinger, the popular chief test pilot, lost his life in an accident to which there were no witnesses. Despite the tragic loss, the test program pressed ahead.

Early flight testing was carried out with maximum secrecy in San Diego. Jet engines were more than a novelty: no one had ever *seen* a plane equipped with both a jet and a propeller engine. Many strange stories were generated by the new planes.

A favorite yarn, improved in the telling, concerns a twin-engined P-38 fighter, its pilot just back from overseas combat duty. With typical Air Force pride, the pilot buzzed the new Navy fighter, feathered a propeller, and did a series of single-engine barrel-rolls around the strange aircraft. Imagine the bewilderment of the P-38 pilot when the Fireball's propeller also stopped, but the plane went on to execute a series of no-engine barrel-rolls, powered only by the jet engine "hidden" in the fuselage!

Ryan received a production order for 100 FR-1 Fireballs on December 2, 1943. Later, 600 additional FR-1s were scheduled.

In an effort to get the new planes into combat at the earliest date, the Navy formed a special fighter squadron under Lieut. Comdr. John F. Gray, a hard-hitting ace with a total of twenty-four enemy aircraft destroyed. The squadron, designated VF-66, included five aces on its roster. The first Fireballs joined the squadron in March, 1945, and went aboard the USS Ranger for preliminary carrier-qualification trials.

Meanwhile, the Japanese were taking a terrific pounding by bombers in the Pacific. It all ended on August 15, 1945, with V-J Day. The Fireballs never had their day in court. Carrier-qualified and ready to go, their sailing date, set earlier, was two weeks after V-J Day!

But six weeks later the Fireballs made public demonstrations the likes of which had seldom been seen. At Anacostia, new Ryan chief test pilot Al Conover put on one of the greatest solo performances in the recollection of seasoned observers at Washington. The same day at San Diego, Johnny Gray and his group, in full squadron strength, showed the remarkable capability of the composite-powered FR-1s.

In October, 1945, VF-66 was decommissioned. The planes were transferred to squadron VF-41, and during the following two years Fireballs operated from a total of five aircraft carriers. On June 21, 1947, the Fireballs put to sea aboard the USS Rendova for the last time. The saga of the Fireball and its all turbine-powered XF2R-1 Dark Shark successor came to an end.

The all-turbine XF2R-1 "Dark Shark" Fireball. It had turbo-prop in nose; turbo-jet in fuselage.

Thomas T. Hixson

The end of the war brought problems which Ryan had never had to face in the past. At its peak, the company's annual volume had climbed to over $55 million, but following the war it dropped to $8 million. Employment had reached an all-time high of 8,500 during the war, but with the loss of contracts Ryan was forced to reduce that figure to 1,200.

With termination of military pilot training contracts in 1944, Ryan sought other areas where he could ensure his school's financial stability, but he was not always successful. The Ryan School of Aeronautics asked for airline passenger and freight routes to Hawaii and various local feeder pickup lines throughout California, but was turned down.

In a search for postwar diversification, the Ryan factory decided to manufacture metal burial caskets. But since Ryan had relatively little experience in marketing consumer products and because aircraft manufacturing methods resulted in high costs, the activity was short-lived. There were a few jokesters around the Ryan plant, however, who took it upon themselves to guarantee immortality for the ill-fated venture into the burial casket business. One popular slogan was "For Flyin' or Dyin', See Ryan." Airplanes on the production line became known, of course, as coffins with wings, while the metal caskets were known as coffins without wings.

In 1947, because of declining business volume and its unsuccessful casket venture, the company reported its only operating loss in all its years in business.

Elsewhere in the aviation industry, other manufacturers were having similar problems. In Los Angeles, J. H. (Dutch) Kindelberger of North American was building a private plane for business use in anticipation of a post-war boom in flying. It was based on design features of the famed P-51 Mustang fighter. The four-place, low-wing, all-metal Navion was a financial disaster for North American. Production and marketing costs were high, and the company knew little about the private airplane business. The plane sold for about $6,000, but it cost three times that to build. The story is told that a friend once called Dutch and asked to buy a Navion "at cost." Dutch was only too glad to comply.

Meanwhile, Ryan hit upon the Navion as a good chance for getting back into the private airplane market he knew so well, and he had soon worked out acquisition of design and manufacturing rights for the plane.

Donald B. Doerr

Ryan Navion helped demonstrate versatile utility of business/executive planes.

In Korea, Generals Douglas MacArthur, center, and Matthew B. Ridgway, left, used Army L-17 Navion as "flying staff car."

The 1949 personal-business Ryan Navion and the Army's L-17B liaison plane.

Donald B. Doerr

Again, a plane of his own. Claude Ryan at the controls, with son Jerry, right.

Donald B. Doerr

"Look! No hands!"

Chris Wren

Army plane on an aircraft carrier? True enough. An L-17 Navion on the USS "Leyte."

U.S. Navy Photo

The details of that financial transaction have never been disclosed, except to a few close associates, but the popular story had it that for the Navion Ryan traded Dutch his crack Fireball test pilot, Al Conover, who took over a top testing job at North American.

Ryan's first move was to establish himself with purchasers of North American Navions in hopes that he could shape up the plane's somewhat tarnished image. An owner questionnaire helped the company focus on areas which needed improving—and there were many—while preserving those which the owners found desirable. Mostly, the owners liked the planes because they were big, rugged, fast, safe, and easy to fly. On this catch-all listing of virtues, Ryan went after the private plane market on behalf of the new Ryan Navion.

Once again Claude could climb into a plane and, at the controls, personally evaluate the design improvements being made by the engineers.

The first Ryan-built Navion was delivered in October, 1947, and from then until May, 1951, when production ended, more than 1,200 Ryan Navions were delivered to customers in the United States, exported to many foreign countries, and provided to the United States military for a variety of liaison missions.

Oil companies, farmers, contractors, manufacturers, doctors—a wide cross section of users—proved that the Ryan Navion had the utility which gave executive planes an accepted role in the expanding transportation system. In 1950, Navion sales soared to new heights, and a banner year was certain for 1951. But once again, war interposed its own will over Claude Ryan. The United States was at war—this time in Korea—and Ryan was again asked to devote his factory to the national effort by expanding production of fuselage sections of Boeing KC-97 aerial tankers used for midair refueling.

It was a heartbreaking decision for Ryan, who felt a responsibility to answer his country's needs. He had hoped to stay in the private aircraft business, but he suspended the program in 1951. Meanwhile the company had also been manufacturing Ryan L-17 Navions for the military. They were widely used in Korea, but after that war ended, the story of the Navion at Ryan closed.

226

If stopping the Navion was a disappointment to Claude, the death of their eldest son, Lieut. David Claude Ryan, was a great personal tragedy. Then, two years later, almost on his fifty-seventh birthday, Claude was shelved for a period by a heart attack.

One reason the Navion never went back into production was the emergence of a new project which has proved to be Ryan's most important continuing military program. Pilotless aircraft were a real novelty in 1948 when Ryan was declared the winner of a design competition to build an experimental jet-powered target airplane to be used for air-to-air and ground-to-air training. The unusual plane was designed to simulate the performance and maneuvers of jet fighters and thus provide a realistic flying bull's-eye for the training of air and ground crews.

Production on the Firebee target drones got underway on a volume basis in 1952. Over the years, the role of the Firebee has so expanded that today Ryan holds worldwide leadership in the field of pilotless aircraft. In recent years the company has also been producing a supersonic target drone, the Firebee II.

In other areas, the company turned much of its attention during the Korean war period to the manufacture of major airframe and engine components—fuselage sections, gun turrets, external fuel tanks, and control surfaces—for other aircraft manufacturers.

The company also branched out into the area of electronics for aerospace applications. The first such project involved the Ryan Firebird, the first Air Force air-to-air research missile. Missiles which could be launched from fighter aircraft were under development when Ryan entered the field, but there was a great need for a new electronic seeker, which would make it possible for the missile to find and track its target.

Using radar studies it had done earlier, the company developed a guidance system using continuous-wave radar propagation and the Doppler shift. The system was founded upon the principle that a radar beam reflected back to the missile from the moving target will indicate velocity and course of the target relative to the missile. In like manner, a beam projected from an airplane to earth can provide velocity data for navigation.

An understanding and application of this concept permitted Ryan to embark on a lengthy role in aerospace electronics which led to the development of a wide variety of aircraft navigation and positioning equipment, including helicopter hovering devices, altimeters, and remote sensors.

U.S. Air Force

Firebee test at desert base in New Mexico. From left, Ryan's Mickey McDaniel, Bruce Smith and Claude Ryan.

Gun camera catches XAAM-A-1 Firebird missile at moment of launch from F-82 Twin Mustang fighter.

U.S. Air Force

Perhaps the culminating achievement in this area came with the first soft landings on the moon. The radar landing system which guided the Surveyor unmanned spacecraft to the lunar surface was built by Ryan Electronics.

And the landing system which permitted Apollo astronaut Neil A. Armstrong in July, 1969, to guide his lunar module spaceship *Eagle* to the Sea of Tranquility and man's first landing on the moon was built by Ryan, thus giving Ryan a significant role in man's two greatest aeronautical feats—Charles Lindbergh's crossing of the Atlantic and Neil Armstrong's first step on the moon.

Concurrently with its work in target drones and electronics, Ryan was involved in a wide range of historic projects, with special emphasis on vertical takeoff and landing (VTOL) aircraft.

Thomas T. Hixson

. . . it would be possible . . . to take off straight up.

Pete Girard in the saddle, flying the vertical beast in the backyard.

Donald B. Doerr

When test pilots were flying the famed Fireball fighter, it became increasingly apparent that the day was not far distant when the thrust available from the expanding potential of the jet engine would exceed the weight of the aircraft in which the turbine was installed. With this capability, if proper control systems could be developed, it would be possible for the first time for an airplane to take off straight up.

In 1947, the Navy awarded Ryan a contract to explore the feasibility of reaction controls for jet aircraft. Three years later a Ryan vertical test rig lifted itself off the ground for the first time, its jet engine and reaction controls handled by remote control from a pilot on the ground. By 1953, results of the Navy-sponsored work were so encouraging that the Air Force awarded Ryan a contract to design and build two manned vertical-takeoff jet research planes.

Soon thereafter the world's first piloted hovering jet flight was made by Ryan's chief engineering test pilot, Peter F. Girard, in "the beast in the backyard"—a tethered vertical test vehicle equipped with temporary controls and a "saddle" for the pilot.

Two years later the first Ryan X-13 Vertijet flew in conventional configuration with a normal landing gear at Edwards Air Force Base in the California desert. On April 11, 1957, the Vertijet demonstrated for the first time the full cycle of VTOL operation when Girard, lifting the plane clear of its ground service trailer, climbed vertically and then made a transition to conventional horizontal flight. Later he converted the plane back to a nose-up hovering position and made a vertical landing by hooking onto the ground service trailer.

228

Photo opposite: Donald B. Doerr

Duplicating the acceptance flight of the first military airplane, the X-13 Vertijet, right, lands vertically at the very steps of the Pentagon. In photo above, Katharine Wright, the inventors' sister, watches preparations on the Wright Flyer for its final test.

Ryan's X-13 test director W. T. Immenschuh and test pilot Pete Girard with project officer Col. Walter Maiersperger.

The chief scientist of the Air Force called it "truly a historical flight of great significance." Claude Ryan, too, always considered the X-13 one of the company's greatest achievements. It had made the world's first vertical-takeoff jet flight.

Then on July 30, 1957, the Air Force project officer, Col. Walter P. Maiersperger, arranged one of the great spectaculars of all time. With Girard at the controls, the X-13 took off vertically almost at the front door of the Pentagon. After flying the exact route to Alexandria and back followed forty-eight years earlier by Orville Wright and Lieut. Benjamin D. Foulois in the final acceptance flight of the first military airplane, the Vertijet nosed up to a vertical hover, and then gently backed down over the Potomac lagoon to a hook-on landing at the River Entrance.

A further development for the Army, in 1956, was the VZ-3RY Vertiplane, a Ryan aircraft of conventional configuration that utilized the deflected slipstream principle for short takeoffs and landings. In a manner quite similar to that employed in the YO-51 Dragonfly of 1940, the Vertiplane achieved near-vertical takeoff and hovering by deflecting the propeller slipstream with huge wing flaps.

With all its "garbage" extended, including huge flaps to deflect the slipstream, the VZ-3RY Vertiplane was no beauty queen, yet was an effective V/STOL research plane.

U.S. Navy

Propellers acting as rotor blades, the triservice, tricompany tilt-wing V/STOL transport comes aboard an aircraft carrier.

In 1962, Ryan joined with two other aerospace companies in the development of the XC-142A triservice transport, which employed the tilt-wing principle to achieve vertical- and short-takeoff flight characteristics.

Meanwhile, Ryan engineers since 1955 had been working on the Vertifan concept for the Army based on the use of jet-turbine-driven fans submerged within the wings of the aircraft to achieve vertical flight. The system employs standard jet engines, mounted in the fuselage, for conventional jet flight. For vertical flight, the jet exhaust is diverted to drive large fans in the wings and nose. By this unique concept, vertical thrust of up to three times that of the engines is provided, permitting the plane to take off straight up.

The XV-5A Vertifan performed a demanding series of tests from 1964 through 1966. Not only was the validity of the lift-fan concept confirmed, but basic design information was obtained for adapting the Vertifan concept to many future applications. The aircraft was turned over to NASA for further research work after completion of tests by Ryan and the Army.

The Vertifan and other VTOL concepts were killed by indifference. Ryan had made significant technical breakthroughs—more than any other company—but there was not sufficient interest on the part of either the military or the air transportation industry to fund the application of VTOL technology to production aircraft.

Richard A. Stauss

The two XV-5A Vertifans at Edwards Air Force Base. Note fan in nose as well as wings.

Richard A. Stauss

Ron Garrison

Original test pilots on XV-5A Vertifan were Val Schaeffer, left, and Lou Everett, right. Everett had previously been Ryan test pilot on VZ-3RY Vertiplane and XV-8A Fleep. Photo left demonstrates vertical lifting capability of Vertijet for rescue operations. Pilot Bill Anderson joined test group when later XV-5B version, with landing gear further outboard, was tested for NASA, below.

Charles Schneider

First vertical takeoff and hover.

Ryan produced not only jet engine pods for the DC-8 transport, right, but also the pylons by which they were suspended from the wing.

These projects occupied Ryan's creative talent, but they did not account for the bulk of the company's work. About 70 percent of Ryan's business during the 1950s consisted of serving as a subcontractor for other companies: fuselage sections for the Boeing Airplane Company's KC-97 and KC-135; jet power packages for the Douglas DC-8 transport; and high-temperature jet engine parts.

By 1960 Ryan was again looking at the perplexing problem of how to achieve diversification. One solution was to acquire or start new companies to operate in specialized fields. Such an acquisition was Aerolab Development Company of Pasadena, which specialized in the design and production of high-altitude sounding rockets and space probes. Ryan also established two new subsidiaries, Ryan Transdata and Ryan Communications, but they and Aerolab were discontinued in 1961 when they failed to be self-supporting.

Meanwhile, Ryan electronic navigation systems had caught on strongly, and in 1961 they accounted for 50 percent of business volume. Production of electronic equipment was shifted to a newly acquired plant at Torrance, a suburb of Los Angeles.

Pioneer aviation industrialists Donald W. Douglas, left, and T. Claude Ryan on roll-out of first DC-8 jetliner in 1959.

Donald B. Doerr

Donald B. Doerr

Manufacture of precision jet engine components, left, extended over a period of more than 15 years. In photo above Claude Ryan is seen with jet engine afterburner and new Firebee target drone, right.

For Boeing Airplane Company, Ryan produced huge fuselage sections for aerial refueling tankers—nearly one thousand each for the KC-97 and KC-135 models.

Donald B. Doerr

Astronaut Neil A. Armstrong, right, first man on the Moon, inspects Ryan's lunar module landing radar with company founder.

1969 "Tranquility Base here. The Eagle has landed."—Astronaut Neil Armstrong from the Moon.

1927 "Lindbergh landed Le Bourget at 10:21."—U.S. State Department dispatch from Paris.

In both journeys, Ryan played a key role as it had in many other historic events in the forty-two years which separated these great aerospace achievements.

For the Apollo 11 mission, Ryan Electronic and Space Systems designed and built the lunar landing radar used in final phases of descent to the Moon's surface. Similar Ryan radar systems were used earlier for five soft lunar landings of unmanned Surveyor spacecraft.

July 20, 1969—Moonprints of Neil Armstrong and Edwin Aldrin create the first man-made disturbances of the lunar surface.

236

U.S. Navy Photo

Ryan electronic specialists were early developers of Doppler velocity sensors used for aircraft and helicopter navigation which enable pilot, right, to achieve absolute hover needed in anti-submarine warfare. Panel at bottom of page shows production and testing of electronic systems.

Richard A. Stauss

Both: NASA

At Surveyor 6 control center, Pasadena, are JPL's Dr. William Pickering, Caltech President Dr. Lee DuBridge and Claude Ryan. Apollo 12 astronauts Pete Conrad and Alan Bean photograph Surveyor 3 against Lunar Module background, right. Both landed using Ryan descent radars.

Ron Garrison   *Stephen M. Ryan*

Thomas T. Hixson

George C. Woodard. Money manager, 1942-1959.

Over the years, Ryan Aeronautical Company grew steadily and soundly into one of the nation's leading corporations in the field of aviation. The change in terms of hardware and plant facilities was obvious, but there were other changes as well. The company had shifted from one man's dream to the lifework of many.

With the success of the S-T assured, Ryan in 1936 sought out the firm of G. Brashears and Company of Los Angeles, which was then underwriting the first stock issued by Lockheed and other new aviation enterprises. Ryan recognized the need for public financing, and George C. Woodard, treasurer and director of Brashears, took the project under his direction. In 1942, Woodard became a director of Ryan and moved to San Diego to take up new duties as the company's executive vice president. Just as Earl Prudden had backstopped Claude Ryan for many years, Woodard took over as the key number two man.

Both Ryan and Woodard believed the best fiscal policy was to "plow back" most of the earnings for use in expanding the business rather than paying out profits in cash dividends. There were those who disagreed. Vance Breese, the M-1 demonstration pilot who had served Ryan well in the past, and several stockbrokers failed in an effort to win election to the board of directors in 1943. Ryan, Prudden, and Woodard were reelected by a margin of four to one. The following year the board was increased to five members with the addition of C. Arnholt Smith, a San Diego banker, and Frank N. Phillips, father of student pilot Don Phillips, who was one of the first investors in the young Ryan company.

After twenty-seven years service, Prudden retired in 1955 because of ill health and passed away three years later.

In 1955, when the notice of the annual meeting of stockholders was issued, a somewhat mysterious name, Emtor, Inc., turned up for the first

Ryan Aeronautical Company, foreground, on San Diego's close-in Lindbergh Field.

Donald B. Doerr

Richard A. Stauss

During the decade of the sixties, a period which brought the company to financial maturity, Robert C. Jackson, right, shared with founder Claude Ryan, leadership of Ryan Aeronautical Company management.

time. As it turned out, Emtor was a Los Angeles-based holding company into which a number of investors, gathered together by George C. Knox, a brilliant investment counsel, had lumped their Ryan shares. This gave them 20 percent of the company's stock as compared to Claude Ryan's holding of 12 percent. Naturally, Emtor became a major factor in company operations from that time on.

One of the main investors in Emtor was Los Angeles business executive Robert C. Jackson, a fellow student of Knox's at Harvard Graduate School, who in 1957 became a member of Ryan's board of directors. Two years later, when Woodard's health began to fail, Jackson moved to San Diego and replaced him as executive vice president. With a fine record as banker, certified public accountant, World War II Army finance officer and business manager already behind him, Jackson moved up to the Ryan presidency in 1961.

When diversification by acquiring and forming subsidiaries proved unproductive, the company sought an investment in an already-established concern—preferably one in a strong financial position but lacking top-notch, aggressive management and tight fiscal control.

The 1961 Ryan annual report indicated that an investment was being made "in a marketable security." Month after month investments continued to be made in Continental Motors Corporation of Detroit. By October 1965, Ryan was the majority owner of Continental, holding just over 50 percent of the stock.

In addition to its long-established target drone and electronic systems production and VTOL research, Ryan continued to make strides in such fields as flexible wing vehicles, like the XV-8A Fleep, and solar panels for spacecraft, along with many other areas involving advanced technology.

In 1965, the citizens of San Diego paused to take stock of community leadership and named Claude "Mr. San Diego" for the coming year.

NASA

Mariner solar panels.

XV-8A Fleep.

Richard A. Stauss

239

Robert Stewart

Claude Ryan as "Mr. San Diego," 1966, is eulogized by his predecessor, contractor Morley Golden. At left, Gladys Ryan; at right, John Quimby, Grant Club president.

The toastmaster for the occasion included these remarks in his speech:

The quiet-mannered, good-natured pioneer flier, who used to barnstorm in rickety planes out of a makeshift flying field, can today survey three large San Diego plants which produce some $50 million worth of products annually.

Because of one man's vision more than 40 years ago, his company has pumped more than a third of a billion dollars in payrolls through San Diego's economic veins in the past ten years alone.

Claude Ryan has always been a practical down-to-earth engineer. His interest as a designer and engineer is as sharp as ever. Many of the ideas for Ryan aircraft both now and in the past have come from Claude.

Two score of Claude's oldest and closest friends gathered to honor him on his seventieth birthday with presentation of symbolic sculptured glass sail. From left, veteran contractor Roscoe E. Hazard, banker and Ryan director C. Arnholt Smith, and Joe Brennan who helped start Ryan on his aviation career in San Diego.

Stephen M. Ryan

And this technical interest goes beyond aviation. An avid sailor, Claude joined with marine architect Skip Calkins in the design and development of that rarity, a fine sailing sloop with auxiliary power. Anyone who has ever sailed in the Sabrina knows what great result can come from painstaking care and personal interest.

240

Matt Giacalone

For the Paris Air Show 1967, where United States participation featured the "Spirit of St. Louis II" duplicate of Lindbergh's Ryan monoplane, a souvenir medallion was struck and the first one presented to President Johnson by T. Claude Ryan and Robert C. Jackson, company president.

Accepting the Horatio Alger Award of the American Schools and Colleges Association, New York, May, 1958.

Claude and his father, William Marion Ryan, who saw to it that his son's early aviation ambitions were realized.

Dedication of the Ryan Library at the California Western Campus of United States International University, San Diego. In front row are Stephen, Jerry, Gladys, and Claude Ryan. At microphone, Dr. William C. Rust, university president.

Supersonic Firebee II flies at Mach 1.5 at 60,000-foot altitude.

Recovered by parachute after each flight, this Navy Firebee has already flown thirty-six missions.

Richard A. Stauss

Most widely used jet target drones in the world, more than 4500 Firebee systems have been built by Ryan. Remotely controlled, Firebees are used primarily as realistic "flying bull's-eyes" which simulate enemy jet aircraft to challenge the missile-firing skills of jet pilots and ground crews. In both subsonic and supersonic versions, Firebees are also adaptable to a wide variety of other unmanned missions. Four BQM-34A subsonic Firebees are ready for launch from a Lockheed DC-130, above.

Pre-launch check.

Richard A. Stauss

Ed Wojciechowski

Richard A. Stauss

Ground launch.

Parachute recovery.

Helicopter retrieval.

Low-level dash as an "enemy" target.

U.S. Navy photo

U.S. Air Force

Firebee—favorite jet "bull's-eye" of fighter pilots at weapons meets for two decades.

U.S. Air Force

Firebee ground launch.

Much had happened over the past few decades, and another era of Claude Ryan's life was drawing to a close. Attracted by Ryan's financial and technical success, and a business volume which had grown to $430 million in 1968, the company became a prime target for acquisition. In response to a $128 million offer from Teledyne, Inc., of Los Angeles for all Ryan shares, Claude and Bob Jackson, along with other directors and the Emtor group, tendered their stock.

While walking back to his office one day soon after consummation of the sale, Ryan's thoughts drifted back over the past, and he began to chuckle.

"What's wrong?" asked a longtime associate who was walking beside him.

"I was just thinking," Ryan said. "This all seems so familiar. A long time ago I went through this same thing, and then Charles Lindbergh came along and I missed the greatest opportunity in aviation history. I hope it doesn't happen again."

By February, 1969, Ryan Aeronautical Company was a wholly owned subsidiary of Teledyne. Jackson moved up to Chairman of the Board at Ryan and was named a director of Teledyne. Claude continued as a Ryan director, but not as an operating executive. Dynamic, public-spirited Frank Gard Jameson was advanced to the Teledyne Ryan Aeronautical presidency.

Stephen M. Ry

Aboard USS Chicago, Frank Gard Jameson, Teledyne Ryan Aeronautical president, right, presents Firebee "kill" plaque to Vice Admiral Bernard F. Roeder.

But was it all over? Did a legal transaction and a transfer of ownership mean that the emptiness which must have haunted Ryan in those first few days was justified? Perhaps not.

During his many, many years of business, Ryan always put one thing above all others—dedication. He remained devoted to aviation and to the people who worked with him, a devotion which "change of ownership" could not nullify.

Shortly before the company was sold to·Teledyne, Doc Sloan,who had been with Ryan for most of his adult life, suffered a severe heart attack while working at the San Diego plant. He was rushed to a hospital for emergency care. While recovering, he sketched a few lines to be read during a reunion of Ryan School students and employees from days gone by. Something of the bond which existed within the corps of long-time Ryanites came through strong and clear:

"Having a heart attack is like losing your only engine at 500 feet over the lava beds—and this is the day you left your chute home to be packed—it is truly hard on the pucker string.

"They hauled me off in grand style in the meat wagon with the sirens and horns and all the noise you can imagine—and it could have been minutes—or days—or hours—I don't really know—but when that elephant finally stepped off my chest, there I was in this beautiful big air-conditioned hangar—spotless as Gene Bovet's kitchen at Hemet and filled with the most marvelous airplanes. Johnny Fornasero takes me over to this immaculate P-51 and sez, 'We've been saving this one for you, Doc!'"

David Koser

Doc Sloan. The elephant finally stepped off his chest.

"I just wish you could have seen them all with me—every last one of those marvelous old moldy, wonderful, lovable Ryanites who have gone West. Bill Evans wondered what had kept me so long in getting there; Ben Johnson asked if it had been a smooooth trip; Pete Larson kept saying, 'Yoost a minute, don't talk so fast'; and Earl Prudden cut off an argument with St. Peter about enrollment fees long enough to come over and give me a ten-minute indoctrination into the advanced version of the new school.

"Eventually, all of you people here tonight will know the joy and glory of the moments I spent with that immortal group. Yet—somehow—I wasn't completely free to join them. I seemed to feel the tiny pressure of a very small hand in mine. The tiny fingers were just the size of my tiniest granddaughter, and they kept pulling and holding ever so slightly to keep my soul and my mind and my body on this side of the known sky even as I looked into the doors of that marvelous hangar.

"I don't know when the powers of renewed life began to build into an awareness of being. I was completely out of touch with the world from a standpoint of voice, touch, or feel. And call it what you will—love—prayer—man's unguarded and unknown love for his fellow man—the unspoken compassion that must exist in each of us—these things began to build a physical strength in my body and my mind.

"And I began to feel a little uncomfortable in the cockpit of that beeeeeautiful P-51. Dammit!

"We had a pretty good argument going as to whether I'd stay or go. But since Claude Ryan was in Europe and Earl wouldn't gamble with St. Pete, J. C. tossed the coin. Darned if it didn't come up tails and I'm back here."

Hundreds, perhaps thousands, built their lives around Claude Ryan and the groups he put together. His contributions went far beyond mere technical accomplishments in aircraft design and business expansion.

With his ownership interest in the company out of the way, and affairs arranged through Ryson Corporation, the Ryan family business, Ryan began to feel the old creative urge gnawing at his soul again. Steve, the youngest Ryan son, encouraged by his father, was pursuing his own career in photography and the arts. Jerry, the oldest, left the Ryan Company after fifteen years to join his father in new ventures.

Away from prying eyes, Claude and Jerry and a few engineers of long association, including X-13 Vertijet test pilot Peter F. Girard, are working quietly on their own on new concepts for aircraft. Somehow, Claude reasoned, there must be a way in this age of ever-increasing technical complexity to return to basic concepts and put the fun back in personal flying. It is almost—but not quite—a repetition of the birth of the M-1 mail plane and the graceful S-T sport trainer.

Many years earlier, when aviation was in its infancy, Claude Ryan started with nothing but a few dollars in his pockets, a piano box for an office, and a passion to fly. That passion, coupled with sound judgment and an unyielding sense of responsibility, made him an extremely successful man. His decisions profoundly influenced the course of aviation and the lives of many hundreds of people.

But in 1969, when he stepped down from the company he had founded so long ago, he became a young man again—a young man with an undiminished passion to create and to fly.

At seventy-three, it's back to the drawing board for T. Claude Ryan, whose interest in new aircraft concepts has never diminished. Engineer and test pilot Pete Girard listens to the boss' latest ideas.

Robert Weissinger

Name Index

Acosta, Bert, 127
Aiken, Ed T., 41–43
Aldrin, Edwin, 236
Alexander, J. B., 59, 62, 68, 89, 93, 96, 102, 103, 115, 163
Allen, Mrs. Agnes, 97
Allen, George, 54, 59, 63, 68, 71, 75, 76, 96–98
Amaral, Anesio, Jr., 190
Amundsen, Roald, 96
Anderson, Bill, 232
Anderson, Capt. E. Robert, x
Armstrong, Neil A., 137, 228, 236
Arnold, Gen. Henry H. (Hap), vii, ix, 28, 32–35, 45, 52, 196, 205–207, 216, 220
Austin, Mayor Walter, 175
Ayars, Fred, 151

Bacon, Mayor John L., 71
Bailey, Bill, 18
Balch, Walter K., 208, 209
Ball, Phil DeC., 145
Barrows, Joe, 62, 76, 77, 103, 104
Beachey, Lincoln, 152
Bean, Alan, 237
Bell, Lawrence (Larry), 13
Bellanca, Giuseppe M., 96
Benton, Lt. John, 25
Bertaud, Lloyd, 132, 133
Best, Lloyd M., 145
Bixby, Harold M., 116, 146
Bleriot, Louis, 4, 135
Bodie, Bill, 109
Booth, Larry, x
Borthwick, Anderson, 111
Borthwick, Mrs. Georgia Mathias, 109–111, 115, 131, 140, 142, 154
Bovet, Jean, 245
Bowen, Gladys (see Ryan, Mrs. Gladys Bowen)
Bowers, Peter M., x
Bowlus, C. D., 110
Bowlus, Mrs. Inez, 47
Bowlus, William Hawley:
    learning to fly, 16–19
    joining Claude Ryan, 46, 47
    rebuilding planes for airline, 51, 55, 59, 68, 70, 110
    building the M-1, 82–87, 96
    building the *Bluebird*, 105, 106
    building Lindbergh's plane, 119, 122, 128–131
    after Lindbergh's flight, 137, 140, 145, 148, 152–155
    rejoining Claude Ryan, 165

Bowman, C. R. (Dick), 59, 96–98, 109, 151
Boyd, Gordy, 110
Boyd, Millard C., 32, 183–185
Brashears, G., 238
Breder, Sam C., 153
Breese, Vance, 102, 103, 238
Brennan, J. W. (Joe), ix, 34, 114, 175, 240
Brodsky, Benjamin, 68
Bronte, Emory B., 98
Brooks, George, x
Burnett, Daniel B., Jr., x, 46, 59, 68, 110, 120, 124, 127, 130, 131, 186, 203
Byrd, Comdr. Richard E. (Rear Adm.), 118, 125, 127, 132, 133

Calkins, Wendell H. (Skip), 240
Carranza, Capt. Emilio, 142, 143
Cassagneres, Everett, x
Chamberlin, Clarence D., 127, 132
Chase, Ned, 209
Chester, Art, 89
Christofferson, Silas, 7, 8, 91
Churchill, Sir Winston, 212
Clark, Ruth, 190
Cochran, Jacqueline, 177
Coli, Lt. François, 125, 131, 132
Comstock, C. N., 92–95
Coney, Lt. W. D., 66
Conover, Al, 224, 226
Conrad, Pete, 237
Cordry, Peter, 4
Corrigan, Douglas, 59, 128–131
Cotton, Henry Hamilton, 71
Crawford, Walt, 124, 131
Crosson, Joe, 147
Crosson, Marvel, 147
Curtiss, Glenn H., 4, 11, 158

Dalton, Mary, 190
Dana, Peter, 189, 190
Dana, Richard Henry, 190
Davis, David R., 65–68
Davis, Lt. Comdr. Noel, 125, 127
Day, Buford, 7
Deitzer, Lt. Comdr. R. O., 221
DeWitt, Peggy, 129, 131
Doolittle, Lt. Col. James H. (Lt. Gen.), 212
Dooman, Dr. David, 133
Dort, E. W., 175
Douglas, Donald W., 13, 27, 87, 88, 234
    the *Cloudster* airliner, 65–73
DuBridge, Dr. Lee, 237
Duncan, Joe, 206

Eaker, Lt. Gen. Ira C., ix, x
Earhart, Amelia, 178
Edwards, A. J., 106, 115, 119, 122, 123,
    131–134, 138–141, 145, 152–154, 163
Erickson, Maj. H. A. (Jimmie), x
Evans, C. W. (Bill), 206, 245
Everett, Lou, 232

Fisk, Edwin M., 16, 19
Fitzgerald, F. Scott, 148
Fleet, Maj. Reuben H., 79, 80, 150, 186
Fokker, Anthony H. G., 67
Fonck, René, 118, 127, 133
Ford, Henry, 82
Fornasero, James, 188
Fornasero, John B., 185–187, 245
Foss, Maj. Joe (Brig. Gen.), 138
Foulois, Lt. Benjamin D. (Maj. Gen.), 230
Frank, Dr. Hans, 164
Funk, Johnny, 187

Girard, Peter F., 228, 230, 246
Golden, Morley, 240
Gorst, Vern C., 91–98, 103
Gray, Lt. James Harvey, 191
Gray, Lt. Comdr. John F., 223, 224
Gray, O. L., 125, 154
Guggenheim, Harry F., 133
Gun, Charlie, 16

Haarman, Maj. Don, 215
Habuto, Fumio, 143
Hall, Donald A.:
  joining Ryan Airlines, 114, 115
  building Lindbergh's plane, 119–135
  after Lindbergh's flight, 137, 138, 148–155,
    203
Hall, Mrs. Elizabeth Walker, 150, 151
Hall, Seely V., 175
Hammond, George, 132
Hanson, Ole, 71
Harrigan, J. J. (Red), 71, 75–78, 110, 121,
    131, 132, 149, 153, 154
Hart, Jess, 38
Hatfield, David, x
Hauptmann, Bruno Richard, 167
Hawks, Frank M., 115, 140, 141
Hazard, Roscoe E., 240
Hazelton, Ben, 206
Hearst, William Randolph, 4
Hennessey, James R., 33, 41
Henry, Bill, 66
Herrick, Myron G., 135
Hicklin, Jack, 175
Hoff, Joseph, 16
Hoover, Travis (Col.), 212
Hopwood, Lt. Lloyd P. (Maj. Gen.), 206–
    211, 216
Horton, Capt. John C. (Brig. Gen.), 206,
    209
Huffman, Dick, 206
Hunold, Henry, 151
Huntington, Henry E., II, 191
Hyde, Alex, 191

Immenschuh, W. T., 230
Irwin, W. H., 188, 189

Jackson, Robert C., 239, 241, 244
Jameson, Frank Gard, 244
Jensen, Martin, 48, 59, 62, 142
Johnson, Ben, 206, 209, 245
Johnson, Pres. Lyndon B., 241
Johnson, Orva, 189

Kelley, Doug, 76, 106, 175
Kelly, Lt. Oakley G., 67, 95
Kerlinger, Robert J., 186, 215, 221, 224
Kibbee, Barbara, 190
Kindelberger, J. H. (Dutch), 225, 226
Kinney, Thornton, 68
Kirk, Preston, 44
Knight, Harry F., 116, 146
Knox, George C., 239
Knox, John B., 191
Knudsen, Gen. William S., 220

Lanphier, Maj. Thomas (Col.), 153
Larson, Pete, 167, 206, 207, 245
Lawrance, Charles L., 133
Lawson, Lee, 44
Lesh, Olga (see Mathews, Mrs. Olga Lesh)
Levine, Charles, 127, 133
Lindbergh, Mrs. Anne, 152
Lindbergh, Charles A.:
  building his plane, 115–131
  flight, San Diego–New York–Paris, 132–
    135
  after the flight, 137–155, 159–162, 167–
    169, 172–178, 203
Lindbergh, Charles A., Jr., 167
Lindbergh, Mrs. Evangeline, 127
Locke, Walter O., x, 106, 119, 122, 131,
    153, 154
Lockheed, Allan, 88
Longfellow, Henry Wadsworth, 190

MacArthur, Gen. Douglas, 225
McDaniel, Mickey, 227
McKee, Ray, 8, 9
McNeel, O. R., 59, 128–132, 151
McPherson, Aimee Semple, 105
McPherson, O. R., 153
Macready, Lt. John A., 67
McReynolds, Maj. E. R., 220
Magula, Fred, 124, 154
Mahoney, B. Franklin:
  partnership in Ryan Airlines, 57–69, 71
  the beer run, 73–76
  development of M-1, 80–84, 88, 89
  airmail planes, 92, 98, 99
  parting of the partners, 109–115
  building Lindbergh's plane, 119–135
  after Lindbergh's flight, 137–155, 160–166
Mahoney, Mrs. Helen Post, 57, 109
Mahoney, Mrs. Jennie, 57, 59, 145
Mahoney, Mrs. Tommy, 147
Maiersperger, Col. Walter P., 230
Mankey, W. A. (Art), 87, 88, 114, 147, 149
Martin, Glenn L., 8, 9, 13, 65, 67
Mathews, Mrs. Olga Lesh, 62
Mathews, Thomas P., x, 53, 54, 58, 61–64,
    74–77, 83, 84, 96, 101–104, 106, 115,
    128, 142, 144–149, 213
Mathias, Georgia (see Borthwick, Mrs.
    Georgia Mathias)
Matthews, Bert, 186
Mattingly, Joseph, 15, 17

248

Maw, R. Douglas, 211
Meierhofer, Swede, 19
Miller, Max, 76, 161
Mirow, William, 99
Mitchell, Gen. William (Billy), 23, 65, 112
Monteith, Boyd (Monte), 52, 59
Morgan, Lt. John, 28
Morrison, Shirley, 128, 130
Morrow, Ed, x, 68, 114, 126, 129, 130, 186
Mumford, Frank, 16

Nall, Jimmy, 175
Neff, Hal, 215
Neher, Eddie, 98
Nixon, Pres. Richard M., 71
Northrop, John K., 87–89, 95, 105, 149
Nungesser, Capt. Charles, 125, 131, 132

O'Brien, J. J., 95
O'Donnell, Mrs. Gladys, 49
O'Donnell, J. Lloyd, 47–49, 54, 213
Orteig, Raymond, 118, 135

Parker, Merle, 44
Patterson, Howard, 16
Patterson, William A., 98
Pepperdine, George, 31
Perkins, Glen, 157–159
Perkins, Lois, 158
Peterson, Leonard R., 187
Phillips, Don, 178, 238
Phillips, Frank N., 178, 238
Pickering, Dr. William, 237
Pini, Robert, 188
Pitts, Lt. (Big), 27
Pitts, Lt. Y. A. (Little), 27
Post, Helen (see Mahoney, Mrs. Helen Post)
Prescott, Clarence, 208
Prudden, Mrs. Adelaide Smith, 178, 190, 216
Prudden, Earl D., 170–178, 190, 206–211, 215, 216, 221, 238, 245
Prudden, George H., 152, 153, 162, 170

Quimby, John, 240

Randolph, A. C., 124, 127, 131
Rankin, J. G. (Tex), 182, 187, 188, 213
Reddy, Kenneth, 212
Reed, O. E., 7
Reid, Whitelaw, 191
Reynolds, Vera, 60
Ridgway, Gen. Matthew B., 225
Robbins, S. E. (Robbie), 171
Roberts, Clete, 88
Robinson, Richard T., 115, 145
Robischon, E. W., x
Rocheville, Charles, 162
Rodgers, Calbraith P., 3–6, 9, 26, 68
Roeder, Vice Adm. Bernard F., 244
Rohr, Fred H., 124, 131, 153, 219, 220
Royer, Lloyd, 82
Russell, John H., 195
Rust, Cameron, 188
Rust, Dr. William C., 241
Rutledge, Jim, 98
Ryan, Lt. David Claude, 166, 167, 184, 227

Ryan, Mrs. Gladys Bowen, 158–167, 240, 241
Ryan, Mrs. Ida Ziegler, 3, 7–10, 14
Ryan, Jerome Donald, 166, 167, 184, 226, 241, 246
Ryan, Kathryn, 3, 51, 69
Ryan, Louise, 3, 51, 69, 163
Ryan, Stephen Michael, 166, 167, 241, 246
Ryan, T. Claude (refer to Contents and Index of Ryan Planes)
Ryan, William Marion, ix, 3, 6–10, 14, 21, 241

Salmon, Ben T., 220, 221
Samuels, Frank E., 119
Saunders, Russ, 157, 158
Schaeffer, Val, 232
Schnitzler, John, 105
Schoenhair, Lee, 96, 104
Schwab, Mrs. Ruth, 7
Seifert, Col. Frank, 207
Shramm, Lt. Ned, 102
Sloan, William P. (Doc), 193, 206–209, 245
Smith, Bruce, 227
Smith, C. Arnholt, 238, 240
Smith, E. A. (see Prudden, Mrs. Adelaide Smith)
Smith, Ernest L., 98
Smith, Lt. Lowell, 86, 87
Springer, Eric, 13, 27, 66–69
Stillwagen, Colin A., 211
Stout, William B., 102, 162

Tallman, Frank, 150
Thompson, Mel, 186
Timm, Wally, 15
Tindale, Bert, 128
Todd, Capt. Walter E. (Lt. Gen.), 206
Towers, Capt. John H. (Adm.), ix, 185, 186, 190, 220, 221
Towers, Marjorie, 190
Towne, Barbara, 190
Truman, Pres. Harry S., 215, 217

van der Linde, H. J., x, 47, 59, 68, 71, 74, 78, 83, 89, 105, 110, 121, 126, 130–135, 153, 154, 161
Vandermeer, Mrs. Tina, 186
Vandermeer, Will, 183–186
Van Dusen, C. A., 13
Vignola, Robert, 60
Virden, Ralph, 98

Walker, Elizabeth (see Hall, Mrs. Elizabeth Walker)
Wanamaker, Rodman, 125
Waterhouse, William J., 82–89, 101, 151, 183
Waterman, Waldo, 15
Wheisel, Sgt. Hal, 29, 30
Widmer, Charles, 59–62, 96, 98, 110, 119
Wilcox, Paul, 194, 206, 209, 211
Wilder, Rodney, 212
Wiley, Frank W., x, 52, 59–62, 74–77, 104, 105, 126
Wilson, Al, 14, 17–20
Wilson, Herb, 16

249

Wolfe, Brig. Gen. K. B., 207
Woodard, George C., 238, 239
Woodward, Reid, 191
Wooster, Lt. Stanton, 127
Worcester, Warren B., 177
Wright Brothers, 4, 10, 230
Wright, Katharine, 230
Wright, Orville, 4, 10, 230

Wright, Wilbur, 4, 10

Yeager, Capt. Charles E. (Brig. Gen.), 213
Youngblood, Lucian (Col.), 212
Yount, Maj. Barton K. (Lt. Gen.), 27, 28, 207

Zuckert, Eugene M., 217

Index of Ryan Planes

(by year of introduction)

1924 Ryan Standard:
  use on airline, 51–64, 82–85
  use on beer run, 73–77

1925 *Cloudster:*
  at March Field, 27
  use on airline, 65–72, 82–85
  use on beer run, 73–78

1926 Ryan M-1/M-2:
  building the M-1, 79–89, 110–113, 141, 151
  use by airmail lines, 91–99
  promoting M-1 sales, 101–107
  relationship to Lindbergh's plane, 115, 120–124, 128, 130, 132
  Claude Ryan's own M-2, 158, 161, 163, 174

1926 Ryan *Bluebird,* 105–109, 115, 124, 159

1927 Ryan NYP (*Spirit of St. Louis*):
  building the *Spirit,* 117–135
  after the Paris flight, 137–155
  Spirit II, 139, 241

1927–1929 Broughams:
  Ryan B-1, 114, 115, 120, 123, 140–146
  Lindbergh's B-1X, 145, 146
  Ryan B-2, 141
  Mahoney-Ryan B-3, 146
  Mahoney-Ryan B-5, 146
  Ryan Aircraft B-7, 147

1928 Ryan Mechanics' *Lone Eagle,* 151

1930 Ryan Aircraft C-1 Foursome, 147

1934–1943 Ryan ST/PT Series:
  1934 S-T, 181–200, 206
  1938 STM, 193–195
  1939 PT-16, 181, 193, 206–208
  1940 PT-20, 193, 196, 204, 208, 210
  1941 STM-S2, 193, 195, 197
  1941 PT-21 and NR-1, 196–199, 210
  1942 PT-22 Recruit, 196, 205, 213–216
  1943 Ryan PT-25 (ST-4), 203

1938 Ryan S-C, 200

1940 Ryan YO-51 Dragonfly, 200–203, 230

1942 SOR-1, 220

1945 Ryan FR-1 Fireball, 220–224, 228

1946 Ryan XF2R-1 *Dark Shark* Fireball, 224

1948 Ryan Navion and L-17, 225–227

1949 Ryan XAAM-A-1 Firebird, 227

1951 Ryan Firebee I Target, 227, 235, 242–244

1957 Ryan X-13 Vertijet, 219, 228–230

1959 Ryan VZ-3RY Vertiplane, 230, 232

1963 Ryan XV-8A Fleep, 232, 239

1964 Ryan XV-5A Vertifan, 231–233

1967 Supersonic Ryan Firebee II, 227, 242, 243

Index of Other Aircraft and Spacecraft

Apollo/Lunar Module Spacecraft, 228, 236, 237

Bach Airliner, 174
Bellanca transatlantic plane, 119, 127, 133
Bleriot monoplane, 4
Boeing KC-97, 226, 234, 235
Boeing KC-135, 234, 235
Boeing Model C seaplane, 48, 49
Bowlus Albatross sailplane, 152

Consolidated B-24, 220
Consolidated PBY, 220
Curtiss F flying boat, 45
Curtiss JN Jenny, 1, 2, 10, 12, 14, 18, 23–27, 33–44, 47–51, 54–57, 62, 63, 85, 88, 174, 196
Curtiss seaplane, 4
Curtiss SOC Seagull, 220

de Havilland DH-4, 10, 28–32, 66, 79, 80, 87, 95
DH Moth, 174
Douglas C-47, 207
Douglas *Cloudster,* 27
Douglas DC-8, 234

Fokker *America* trimotor, 118, 127
Fokker F-10, 174
Fokker T-2, 67
Fokker *Universal,* 123
Ford trimotor, 173

Great Lakes biplane, 174, 175

Hall X-1, 148, 149

Keystone Pathfinder, 125, 127

Lockheed DC-130, 243
Lockheed P-38, 224

Mariner spacecraft, 239
Martin MB-1 bomber, 13

Norge Dirigible, 96
North American B-25, 212
North American F-82 Twin Mustang, 227
North American Navion, 225, 226
North American P-51 Mustang, 225, 245

Prudden trimotor, 162

SE-5, 28, 45
Sikorsky transatlantic plane, 118
Spad, 28
Standard J-1, 51, 52
Stearman PT-13, 206–209
Surveyor spacecraft, 228, 236, 237

Thomas-Morse Scout, 47, 60, 85, 110

Vought-Hiller-Ryan XC-142, 231

Waco biplane, 162, 174
Waterhouse Cruizair, 89, 151
Waterman MonoEagle, 15
Wright Flyer, 230
Wright Model EX, 4–6

Yackey monoplane, 89

Zenith Albatross, 162

FLY WITH ME
TAKE A
Real Trip Thru The Clouds
RYAN, The Aviator is in Your City